RECOGNIZING OURSELVES

RECOGNIZING OURSELVES

*Ceremonies of
Lesbian and Gay Commitment*

ELLEN LEWIN

COLUMBIA UNIVERSITY PRESS

NEW YORK

Columbia University Press
Publishers Since 1893
New York   Chichester, West Sussex
Copyright © 1998 by Columbia University Press
All rights reserved
Library of Congress Cataloging-in-Publication Data
Lewin, Ellen.
    Recognizing ourselves : ceremonies of lesbian and gay commitment /
Ellen Lewin.
        p.   cm.—(Between men—between women)
    Includes bibliographical references and index.
    ISBN 0-231-10392-1 (alk. paper) — ISBN 0-231-10393-X (pbk.)
    1. Gay couples—United States. 2. Same-sex marriage—United
States. 3. Marriage customs and rites—United States.   I. Title.
II. Series.
HQ76.3.U5L49   1998
306.84'8—dc21   97-45672

∞

Casebound editions of Columbia University Press books are printed on
    permanent and durable acid-free paper.
Printed in the United States of America
c 10 9 8 7 6 5 4 3 2 1
p 10 9 8 7 6 5 4 3 2 1

The five lines of poetry in chapter 5 are from "Unending Love," in *Rabindranath Tagore:
    Selected Poems*, trans. William Radice (New York and London: Penguin Books, 1985), 49;
    copyright © 1985 by William Radice. Reproduced by permission of Penguin Books, Ltd.
Photograph on page 29 © 1998 Michael Loeb.
Photograph on page 47 courtesy of Danny Moreno and F. Ross Woodall.
Photograph on page 87 © 1998 Julie Nestingen.
Photograph on page 123 courtesy of Scott Anderson and Ali Ishtiaq.
Photograph on page 159 © 1998 Jere Visalli, Jere Visalli Photography.
Photograph on page 193 courtesy of Bert Bloom and Gwynn Goodner.

BETWEEN MEN ~ BETWEEN WOMEN

Lesbian and Gay Studies
Lillian Faderman and Larry Gross, Editors

Between Men ~ Between Women is a forum for current lesbian and gay scholarship in the humanities and social sciences. The series includes both books that rest within specific traditional disciplines and are substantially about gay men, bisexuals, or lesbians and books that are interdisciplinary in ways that reveal new insights into gay, bisexual, or lesbian experience, transform traditional disciplinary methods in consequence of the perspectives that experience provides, or begin to establish lesbian and gay studies as a freestanding inquiry. Established to contribute to an increased understanding of lesbians, bisexuals, and gay men, the series also aims to provide through that understanding a wider comprehension of culture in general.

In memory of my mother,
Fannie Slotkin Lewin,
and
for Liz,
who taught me about marriage

CONTENTS

ACKNOWLEDGMENTS

In many ways, the process of working on this book has been the most exciting venture of my professional life. I encountered so much en thusiasm from virtually everyone I told about the research that my usual neurotic process of doubt and anxiety could hardly establish itself before it was demolished by waves of excitement. If I ever had even slight questions about the centrality of the cultural creations we call "commitment ceremonies," "holy unions," or "weddings" to the unfolding panorama of gay and lesbian life, the responses people had to my project made clear that I had chosen a topic that was endlessly fascinating not only to gay men and women but to virtually everyone else. I don't think I encountered a single person who lacked a definite opinion on the issue or who was unwilling to engage in debate and discussion about it.

Whether people approved, disapproved, or merely wondered why same-sex weddings seemed to be becoming ubiquitous, they made it clear that the issues raised were important and anything but fleeting. Almost everyone—gay or straight—to whom I mentioned the study had a story to tell: a wedding they had attended, an article they'd seen in the newspaper, a theory about what it all meant. I got so many volunteers, referrals, suggestions, and ideas that I could never follow them all up; as the deadline for completing this book loomed closer, I had to resolve myself to accepting limitations on a project that seemed naturally to have none.

The need to finally stop looking for new couples to interview and ceremonies to attend has meant that there are gaps and lacunae in this work. At the same time that I found that there are patterns in the way gay men and lesbians construct and construe their commitment ceremonies, I also found seemingly endless variations. Each ritual event, then, was both uniquely creative and resonant of other events. This means, on the one hand, that I can stand behind the interpretations in this book and feel fairly certain that my research has captured some fundamental truths about these evolving cultural forms. But, on the other hand, I cannot claim to represent the full range of creative possibilities and symbolic maneuvers that gay men and lesbians employ in constructing commitment ceremonies, be they religious or secular, "traditional," or innovative.

With that caveat in place, I'd like to thank the many people whose contributions to this book or personal support of me during the process of creating it made its emergence possible. First, of course, the couples whom I interviewed and whose ceremonies I attended were enormously generous both with their time and with access to a very intimate part of their lives. They were thoughtful and self-reflective about their experiences; their interpretations of the rituals they had staged informed the evolution of my analysis throughout. Most of these people, who I hesitate to characterize as "informants" in the way anthropologists most often do, were willing and even eager to be identified by name in the text. In most cases, however, my concern that their privacy (or that of other persons mentioned in their narratives) be preserved and my commitment to distinguish the anthropological work I intended to produce from a work of history overcame their openness, and except for instances when individuals are public figures or have a historical role in the process I describe, I decided to follow anthropological custom by using pseudonyms when telling their stories.

A one-year fellowship I received in 1994 from the National Endowment for the Humanities provided crucial financial support during the research. I was also aided by a Visiting Professorship at the University of Cincinnati and by a travel grant from the Marilyn Yalom Fund at the Institute for Research on Women and Gender, Stanford University. Being an affiliated scholar at the Institute put me in the excellent company of a congenial group of feminist colleagues while I was working on this book and also provided access to Stanford University libraries.

As the idea for the book began to take shape, the enthusiasm of my editor at Columbia University Press, Ann Miller, was enormously encouraging. During its preparation, I presented preliminary findings in papers at the annual meetings of the American Ethnological Society (in Los Angeles) and the American Anthropological Association (in Atlanta and in Washington, D.C.), the Sixth North American Conference on Lesbian,

Gay, and Bisexual Studies (in Iowa City, IA), the Fourth Annual Lavender Languages Conference at American University (Washington, D.C.), and at "Relatively Speaking," a conference sponsored by the Center for Lesbian and Gay Studies (CLAGS) of the City University of New York. I also developed many of the materials that appear in this volume in lectures at the University of Chicago, the University of California, Santa Cruz and Los Angeles, San Diego State University, the New School for Social Research, the University of Arizona, the University of Iowa, and the University of Akron. Comments from the audiences at these presentations and discussions that followed were often very thought-provoking and helped me to come to an understanding of the best approach to take to the material I was gathering.

I owe a special debt of gratitude to Rabbi Yoel Kahn, formerly of Congregation Sha'ar Zahav in San Francisco. Rabbi Kahn has devoted a great deal of thought to the theological and specifically Jewish issues involved in same-sex weddings and is responsible for a manual that considerably simplifies the process of creating ceremonies for Jewish couples; he is also the author of a number of scholarly articles on the topic. He has been the most influential single voice in Reform Jewish circles on questions having to do with the integration of lesbian and gay Jews and specifically with respect to debates over the place of same-sex marriage in Jewish tradition. He also officiated at my own wedding, changing my mind forever about the value of ritual.

A number of clergy and religious scholars were supportive of the research and helped orient me to religious traditions of which I had little knowledge at the outset. Some of these consultants did not want to be personally identified, and I thank them for their contributions. I also want to thank the Reverends Ann Keeler Evans, Ruth Frost, Jeff Johnson, Peter Koopman, Jim Mitulski, Jean Richardson, Janie Adams Spahr, Weston Stevens, and Sharna Sutherin for their valiant efforts to educate me in the mysteries of Christian theology and politics as they intersect with questions of gay and lesbian marriage. Any confusion I betray in these areas is entirely due to my naïveté about all things Christian. The late Kevin Calegari kept me spellbound for hours as he expounded on the theological complexities that arise when homosexuality and Roman Catholicism meet. I regret so much that I couldn't share the results of this project with him.

Other people with extensive knowledge of particular issues relevant to gay/lesbian unions were also very helpful. I want especially to thank

Becky Butler, the editor of *Ceremonies of the Heart,* for her input. Judy Dlugacz of Olivia Records and Travel introduced me to the world of pleasure-cruise commitment ceremonies, which I was unable, regrettably, to incorporate into my fieldwork.

I benefited a great deal from conversations and correspondence with attorneys and activists involved in various aspects of the same-sex marriage/domestic partnership debates. Particular thanks go to Evan Wolfson and Amanda Craig, both of the Lambda Legal Defense and Education Fund, Larry Brinkin of the San Francisco Human Rights Commission, and San Francisco Supervisor Tom Ammiano. I apologize for any errors produced by my faulty interpretation of legal issues they so painstakingly explained to me.

Many colleagues and friends have been supportive throughout the research and writing processes, keeping isolation at bay and helping me to maintain a sense of professional connection despite not having a permanent academic job until the book was already in press. Rayna Rapp and Kath Weston, who carefully assessed the manuscript for Columbia University Press, helped me to hone the argument more finely; at the same time, their enthusiasm for the emerging text assured me that I was on the right track. Carole Browner, Christopher Carrington, Soo-Young Chin, Jane Garrity, Lisa Handwerker, reneé hoogland, Bill Leap, Carol McClain, Sabina Magliocco, Esther Newton, Larry Rudiger, and Helene Wenzel patiently read partial and complete drafts of the manuscript as I produced them and made astute comments on various aspects of the analysis. Bill Leap's and Esther Newton's readings were particularly vital as I tried to extend my understanding of the complexities of gay men's culture. Their comprehensive understanding of the constantly changing landscape that is gay and lesbian anthropology kept the project in focus. Jared Braiterman, Dennis DeBiase, Ann Merrill, Virginia Olesen, and Helene Wenzel helped sharpen some points as I developed them for lectures I gave on this material. Thanks are also due to Deb Amory, Lawrence Cohen, Sage Foster, Larry Rudiger, and Gayle Rubin for insights into some unfamiliar cultural practices.

Liz Goodman, as always, was the first and last reader of every word, combining a unique appreciation for evocative ethnographic writing and a meticulous eye for minuscule errors with her roles as spouse, best friend, and co-mother of our cats. Wanda, Annabel, Boris, and Sadie helped to create an environment suitable for serious thought even though my activities usually mystified them. I hope they approve of the result.

Getting married was never something I thought I would do. Despite having grown up during the profoundly conventional years of the 1950s and early 1960s, I can't recall any time in my youth when I wanted to get married. When I was twenty-three my then boyfriend suggested that, having lived together for a year or so, the next step would be to get married; without really thinking about it, I said yes, but then went into the bathroom and threw up. At the time, I had been involved in the fledgling women's liberation movement for about two weeks, and I had yet systematically to consider the ramifications of feminism for either my sexual orientation or my attitudes toward family and marriage. But my body responded for me in a way I couldn't ignore, and I didn't get married.

Over the years that followed, though I entered into two serious and fairly long-term lesbian relationships, the possibility that we should solemnize our unions with some sort of ceremony never came up. Although gay and lesbian "weddings" occasionally made an appearance in gossip or in the popular press during the 1970s and 1980s, such occasions struck me more as quirky curiosities than something that might one day have meaning in my own life. Like many other lesbians and gay men who developed a sense of political entitlement in the wake of Stonewall[1] and under the influence of Second Wave feminism, I gloried in the ways that my "lifestyle" differed from that of the mainstream. From my point of view, and that of most of my friends, women's and gay liberation was, at least in part, about freeing ourselves from the negative messages and assaults on self-esteem generated by attempts to "measure up" in the eyes of straight society. This not only meant choosing persons as our sexual partners deemed inappropriate by most other people, but questioning—indeed assaulting—the standards for sexual conduct that institutionalized heterosexuality had erected.

Among the prime targets of these critiques of patriarchy and heterosexism were monogamy (serial or otherwise), childbearing, conventional gender expectations vis-à-vis education, work, sports, clothing, fashion, and, of course, marriage. Some of the early targets of feminist street theater, in fact, were bridal fairs and other commercial events that marketed products related to marriage; along with beauty pageants and Playboy clubs, such events were regarded as significant contributors to the ongoing oppression of women because they reinforced our relegation to decorative and socially devalued roles.[2] It was clear to me and other radical feminists during this time that marriage was an institution that not only regularized and enforced what Adrienne Rich called "compulsory heterosexuality,"[3] but that it might be considered the linchpin of the entire system of gender inequality.[4]

So it was with some amazement that, in early 1992, I found myself planning a commitment ceremony with my partner, Liz Goodman. Though our relationship was only a bit over a year old and we had both been in other serious relationships, something about our connection felt deeper and more permanent. Still, it was hard for us to explain, to ourselves or to others, why we wanted to have a ceremony. Looking back on the decision, it seems that we longed to share our discovery of one another with the world, or some little piece of it; we wanted to make the fact of our relationship public and official, even though there seemed to be nothing that required us to do so.

I come from a secular Jewish family that for generations has shunned both religion in all guises and any sort of behavior that could be construed as "making a spectacle of oneself," an attitude that in my parents' generation relegated family weddings to City Hall and scheduled them to coincide with the newlywed couples' lunch hours. In my own generation, some of my cousins had, in fact, put on real weddings which older family members had attended, albeit grudgingly. Despite these defections from tradition, then, the family ethos still conveyed to me that it was better not to stage such an event, that people who registered for wedding gifts were gauche and materialistic, and that such items as engagement rings constituted vulgar display. As a lesbian who had no expectation of getting married, I found that my ability to perform according to family standards was, paradoxically, enhanced. These lessons, along with my long-standing and vaguely anarchistic opposition to conventional expectations that everyone should marry, made me uncomfortable about doing anything that might seem to be a bid for attention (not to mention gifts) or that might be interpreted as conveying a message of "couple-chauvinism."

Liz's family had a more conventional style of celebrating life-cycle rituals than mine did. Following expectations for upper-middle-class, mainline Christian, and socially prominent families in a large southern city, her sister's wedding a few years earlier had been a large and formal affair featured on a two-page spread in the local newspaper. In Liz's family, wedding presents were customarily put on display at the bride's home, bridal dresses were ordered from Neiman-Marcus, and the round of cocktail parties, receptions, and dinners surrounding weddings frequently took weeks to be completed. But Liz's family had indicated that they would not attend our ceremony. Though they expressed their general good wishes by sending us some modest but elegant gifts, their response to our invitation made clear that the event simply made them uncomfortable. This wasn't a "real" wedding in their eyes, and thus didn't call for a family presence.

During the early days of our relationship, Liz and I had joined Congregation Sha'ar Zahav, a predominantly lesbian and gay Reform temple close to our home in San Francisco. Liz found Judaism compelling—she eventually decided to undergo conversion—and as our discussions about the commitment ceremony evolved, we were both drawn to the idea of having it at the synagogue. We planned the specific features of the ceremony during a series of meetings with our rabbi, Yoel Kahn, who presented us with a range of options he had assembled based both on Jewish traditions and on particular rituals other lesbian and gay couples had devised—sort of a menu approach—from which we selected specific ritual elements and found opportunities to insert personal touches. The ceremony generally followed Jewish custom though we omitted circling each other at the beginning. Historically, this ritual feature had involved the bride walking around the groom seven times, symbolizing, it seemed to us, his supremacy in the marriage and her subservience to him. Revising the circling to make it equal and reciprocal (that is, with each partner circling the other an equal number of times, as is now the custom in many heterosexual Jewish weddings) was an option that some other couples had selected, though it didn't seem to us that any revision could cleanse this particular custom of its patriarchal underpinnings.[5]

We incorporated several friends and one relative from my side of the family into the ceremony. (Predictably, perhaps, the reaction of some of my relatives to the news was to ask why we were getting married in a synagogue—not why I was celebrating my relationship with another woman.) A close friend, an operatically trained baritone, came from the East Coast to serve as cantor. Another close friend lit the candles; four others held the *chuppah* (canopy) aloft; an additional seven read English translations of the Seven Blessings (the first and seventh were also chanted by our cantor in Hebrew). Our vows closely followed the wording of our marriage contract, the *ketubah*.[6]

While we conformed to my family tradition by organizing a ceremony marked by extreme simplicity, some accouterments were absent more because we forgot to arrange for them (e.g., flowers in the synagogue and programs) or couldn't afford them (e.g., professional photographer, wedding rings, and custom-calligraphed *ketubah*—ours was instead produced on the synagogue's laser printer) than because we were philosophically opposed to them. After the ceremony, we held a reception at our home, and largely because our caterer (also a friend) was experienced with such occasions, the event took on the contours of a wedding. The tiny sandwiches and roasted miniature vegetables he prepared were exquisitely arranged on a table decorated with white flowers; champagne and cake were served, and our friends raised their glasses to toast our future life together.

In looking back on this event from my current perspective (that is, from the point of view of someone who has since interviewed some sixty lesbian and gay couples about their commitment ceremonies, who has attended about ten such ceremonies, and who has viewed over twenty videotapes of lesbian/gay weddings), I am amazed by how minimal my expectations for my own wedding were. As a lesbian, I never seriously entertained the notion that my friends or relatives from out of town would travel to San Francisco to attend (with two exceptions they didn't), and did not invite a number of relatives who I later learned would have been delighted to be included. I never expected that anyone would buy us gifts (though we received many, including four sets of wind chimes, which can be what happens if you don't register). In short, I was terribly nervous about claiming any privilege or attention and not sure at all that anyone would view our ceremony as either legitimate or worthy of support.[7]

The event itself proved to be far more powerful than I could have anticipated. There was something about the exposure of a public ceremony that seemed to seal our intent to make the relationship permanent; indeed, after the wedding something *felt* different, though I wasn't quite sure what. Many of the guests later reported being enormously moved, though even their most intense reactions paled beside Liz's flood of tears during the ritual itself. In short, our ceremony turned out to have the classic attributes—socially standardized, dramatic action wrapped in a web of symbolism that links the present, past, and future, and that generates powerful emotional reactions among participants—that have long made ritual a key area of concern for anthropologists.[8]

My experience with my own commitment ceremony was the direct inspiration for this book. It led me to move as far from the age-old dictum of anthropology, the field in which I was trained, to study the remote, the foreign, the exotic as I could, beginning three years of research on lesbian and gay commitment rituals in 1993 and continuing to interview couples and to attend ceremonies until I finished writing in 1996. The project benefited, as I will discuss later in more detail, not only from my personal "feel" for the subject matter and my access to the population in question, but from the generosity of many people who were willing and even eager to share their experiences with me and in the process to join me in pondering the political and spiritual meanings of lesbian and gay weddings.

As an "insider" par excellence, I am acutely aware that I cannot claim neutrality on the symbolic significance of lesbian and gay weddings or on the related issue of legalizing same-sex marriage.[9] I have tried earnestly to avoid the pitfalls of cheerleading or polemics, but the astute reader will no doubt detect my enthusiasm for and engagement with the phenomena I report on in these pages. I still believe that married life is not for everyone and that all kinds of living arrangements deserve respect. But the stories couples told me added to the feelings produced by my own ceremony, convincing me that the normalization of gay relationships effected through wedding rituals cannot help but have a profound impact on the ways lesbians and gays view ourselves and on the views others adopt toward us. I would not go as far as Andrew Sullivan has in arguing that lesbian/gay marriage is *the* political issue on which all other elements of our liberation will rise or fall, but I do now think that particularly the ritual dimensions of marriage ceremonies have the ability to transform identity and to shape action. Lesbian and gay weddings involve multiple levels of communication between and across lines of sexual orientation; they allow, or even demand, that images of lesbian and

gay lives be wrenched from the cliches of "lifestyle" that generally sur-
round them and be propounded instead with even more complexity
than the participants may anticipate. Gay and lesbian weddings, as we
shall see below, have the ability to encapsulate many different expressive
dimensions of ritual, to be both models *of* and models *for*, as anthropologist Clifford Geertz would have it,[10] while also facilitating performance
of both resistance and conformity, intertwined and indissoluble. These
rituals may be seen from this point of view as classic examples of the
overlapping and indeterminate nature of ritual as both cultural performance and tool of socialization.

Recognizing Ourselves

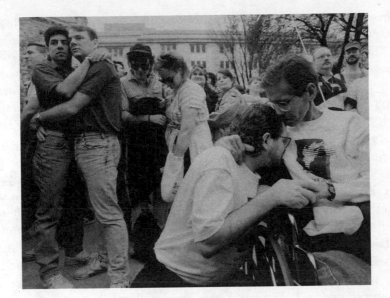

1

EQUAL RITES

As we emerged from the subway near the Internal Revenue Service headquarters, it was clear that my partner Liz and I were part of a large mass of people all going to the same event. It was Saturday, April 24, 1993, the day before the national March on Washington for Lesbian, Gay, and Bi Equal Rights and Liberation, and "the Wedding" was one of many related activities taking place throughout the march weekend. Organized by Metropolitan Community Church (MCC) founder Troy Perry,[1] the Wedding was advertised as an event that would combine a marriage ritual with a protest against the continuing lack of legal recognition for lesbian and gay marriage. Its location, in front of IRS headquarters (which was, of course, closed on Saturday), emphasized the injustice done by a system that uses marriage to confer innumerable

"The Wedding," Washington, D.C., April 24, 1993
(Photo by Wilfredo Lee courtesy the Associated Press)

financial and civil advantages on heterosexual couples, but denies these advantages to lesbian and gay couples who cannot legally wed.

Liz and I had traveled to Washington both to join friends and colleagues participating in the march the following day[2] and to launch my research on lesbian and gay weddings by observing the biggest lesbian and gay wedding of them all. Our own ceremony was behind us, so we felt that we could stand back, as it were, from the proceedings to try to get a sense of what sorts of people were participating and how their participation might be understood.

Nearing the area where the Wedding was scheduled to occur, we began to see more and more couples and groups arriving, some dressed in clothing that reflected the special purpose of the day—tuxedos, white veils, matching kente-cloth ensembles, coordinated black leather outfits—and others clad in the standard T-shirts, jeans, tennis shoes, and baseball caps that are virtually uniforms for demonstrations and marches. Vendors hawked buttons, miniature rainbow flags, bumper stickers, commemorative T-shirts, and refreshments. People seemed festive and exuberant, greeting each other with nods and smiles, inspecting each other's accouterments as these confirmed the spirit of the event.

The outfits people were wearing reflected the varied moods of the crowd. Some of those not wearing markedly symbolic clothing looked around as though checking out a new kind of gay occasion; they watched those arriving in costumes with the same appreciation and amusement usually reserved for drag performances or the sidelines of Gay Pride parades. Particular approval seemed to be reserved for outfits that were especially campy or incongruous: the two lesbians wearing T-shirts, jeans, and white bridal veils; the Jewish couple walking under a *chuppah* (canopy) borne by their attendants; a scattering of couples clad in black leather with dog-collars, leashes, and other S/M paraphernalia; but most common of all, male couples wearing every imaginable variety of formal wear.

This would be the second such demonstration held in Washington, the first having been organized at the 1987 march. Since the early 1970s, the MCC had been performing lesbian and gay weddings as part of the regular services provided at its churches around the country, and while some other denominations, not predominantly gay/lesbian, had also extended themselves in this direction more recently, MCC could claim leadership in solemnizing same-sex unions.[3] Over the years since MCC had begun performing commitment ceremonies, or "holy unions" as they called them in the early years, gay and lesbian weddings had become ever more visible, and some couples even began to raise the question of access to legal marriage. While not a prominent demand in the early days of the gay rights movement, by 1993 marriage was moving toward becoming a core dimension of the intensifying gay and lesbian civil rights agenda. Predictions that spring were that same-sex marriage would soon be made legal in Hawaii, and debates over marriage as a civil rights goal had begun to figure prominently in both the gay and mainstream press.

Marriage in Context: The Shape of the Lesbian and Gay Rights Movement

Obtaining recognition for lesbian and gay unions is only one of a series of intensely contested issues that have arisen since the U.S. gay and lesbian rights movement rose to prominence in the heated political climate of the 1970s. As historians of gay civil rights and queer politics have shown, early activism focused more on trying to wrench some modicum of tolerance from the mainstream than on dreaming of achieving legitimacy for forbidden relationships. The early homophile movement that preceded the advent of gay rights organizing (the latter usually dated from the historic 1969 rioting at New York's Stonewall Inn)[4] hoped to defuse hatred of homosexuality and to unravel such malignant myths about homosexuals as those that imagine them preying on children. Activists from the 1950s and 1960s argued that homosexuality was not necessarily a form of mental illness and certainly not antisocial or criminal behavior; to demonstrate that lesbians and gay men were upright citizens who deserved respect, activists dressed neatly and conventionally in public and tried to downplay images that disrupted "normal" gender expectations.[5] A key piece of research from this period, still cited by many psychologists, is Evelyn Hooker's work regarding the "normal" homosexual man. Using a nonclinical population of gay men and comparing their scores on various psychological measures with those of comparable heterosexual men, Hooker was able to demonstrate that there was no particular psychological profile that could be used to distinguish or identify the gay men. While this sort of research would go on to be the basis for a large body of comparative study, its impact on the popular imagination over the long run probably has more to do with its insistence that gay people could be ordinary than with its scientific significance.[6]

The appropriation of wedding rituals and marriage imagery by lesbians and gay men was not totally unknown in the pre-Stonewall period.[7]

John Boswell's *Same-Sex Unions in Premodern Europe* argues that such ceremonies have a very ancient lineage in Christian history and that they may, in fact, precede the development of a notion of heterosexual marriage as demanding sacred sanction.[8] Though Boswell's assertions raise significant questions about the extent to which "homosexual" may be a concept that is applicable to the social life of antiquity, many advocates for gay marriage see them as a religious justification and some couples have adopted liturgical materials from these ceremonies for use in their own weddings.

Jonathan Katz's *Gay American History* documents a number of cases from various historical periods, including a number of instances in which cross-dressing women so successfully passed as men that they were able to marry other women without detection.[9] A particularly celebrated case of this type, only discovered in 1989, involved a jazz musician named Billy Tipton, prominent in the 1940s and 1950s. Billy married Kathleen Flaherty in the late 1950s, and together they raised several adopted children. In 1989, after refusing medical attention, Tipton died of a bleeding ulcer and was only at that point discovered to be biologically "female."[10]

In *Gay New York* George Chauncey documents use of the term "husband" to describe masculine men who preferred "fairies" as partners in New York during the 1920s and 1930s; the use of this term is linked with a wider terminology that stressed gender differences between "fairies" or effeminate homosexual men and the "real men" who sought them out as sexual partners. Chauncey also reports the use of kinship and marriage terminology by gay men in the same period to evoke their relationships with other gay men and play off the ironic convergences between gay life and the "natural" categories of heterosexual family. Thus, calling someone "sister" marked that person as an inappropriate sexual partner, removed from the pool of possible liaisons by injunctions against "incest." With similar logic, couples who believed their relationships were marked by a division of labor reminiscent of heterosexual marriages might call each other "husbands" and "wives."[11]

A number of accounts of lesbian life in Depression-era Harlem describe weddings of butch/femme couples in elaborate ceremonies that included attendants and bridesmaids. Real marriage licenses were sometimes obtained, Lillian Faderman reports, either by masculinizing one partner's first name or by having a male surrogate apply for the license. The lesbian blues singer Gladys Bentley, a "bulldagger" who wore a tuxedo and top hat when she performed and was famous not only for cross-dressing but for the sexually suggestive lyrics of her songs, lived openly with a white lover whom she later married in a well-publicized ceremony.[12]

The tradition of solemnizing gay unions through wedding rituals has continued into the present, not only in large metropolitan areas that are reputed to be more accepting of gay people but in rural areas and small towns throughout the United States.[13] Neil Miller's accounts of such ceremonies in *In Search of Gay America* point to their diversity and geographical distribution. Miller's description of a gay male couple who live in a small town in Oklahoma, for example, emphasizes the similarities between their daily routine (which revolves around "work, the TV ... and church" and that of their neighbors. To punctuate this point, Miller explains that, "like most of their neighbors, Gene and Larry were married, joined in 'holy union' by the minister of a gay church in Oklahoma City." In other examples, Miller describes a lesbian couple in Bismarck, North Dakota, married in a Unitarian-Universalist ceremony and a gay male couple in Rapid City, also united in the Unitarian-Universalist church.[14] Some of the couples whose stories he presents are gay activists who view their unions at least partly in a political light; others seem resolutely mainstream, with marriage just one of the ways they seek to fit in with their neighbors.

Miller speculates that commitment ceremonies and weddings may be more common in smaller communities and rural areas because of the increased pressure to conform, but he also describes weddings in the highly politicized San Francisco gay/lesbian community. In one of these cases, the two women decided to marry "because they wanted to have children." Although one of the women initially resisted the idea, based on what she called "the women's studies point of view" which takes marriage to be a heterosexual institution with little to recommend it, her partner eventually convinced her "that marriage simply represented an expression of love and commitment that was neither intrinsically heterosexual or homosexual." The two women became "engaged" about six months prior to the wedding date they selected—the day before the annual Gay Freedom Day Parade. They both wore full-length white gowns to the ceremony in Golden Gate Park, which was followed by a reception in a Thai restaurant. Many decorative and ceremonial details were chosen to represent their two ethnic heritages—Filipino and Hawaiian—in addition to their gender.[15]

In another San Francisco example Miller relates, a Jewish lesbian couple whose wedding was scheduled to take place a few days later were called up to the pulpit during Friday night services Miller attended at a predominantly gay synagogue. Lifting his prayer shawl over the couple, the rabbi blessed them and the congregation sang a traditional song of congratulations while pelting the couple with candies. Himself of Jewish background, Miller is astonished by this ritual, called an *aufruf*, reporting afterwards that he "needed to sit alone for a moment and sort things out." He expected to find abundant references to the AIDS epidemic in the service. "But here also were love stories, marriage and babies, gold paper cranes and chocolate candy kisses. It wasn't just a question of life going on in the midst of crisis. There was more to it. I felt as if I was witnessing the formation of a new culture—one of gay and lesbian families, gay marriages, gay religious schools, of ancient traditions merging with a long-stigmatized sexual identity."[16]

Other popular accounts of gay and lesbian lives also make note of wedding and commitment ceremonies, pointing out important class variables in the style couples choose for celebrating their unions. In Martha Barron Barrett's *Invisible Lives*, for example, we read about a working-class couple clad in matching white tails and turquoise bow ties celebrating their church wedding in a Castro district lesbian bar. One woman at the bar proudly proclaims that she caught the bouquet while other bar patrons not part of the wedding party continue to order drinks and play pool.[17]

Recent advice manuals and books on how to strengthen relationships regularly include examples of couples who have cemented their bonds with a commitment ritual. Merilee Clunis and G. Dorsey Green, for example, make a point of how diverse such couples may be: "While some lesbian couples . . . feel a part of the lesbian community, other couples are isolated from the lesbian community and identify themselves as belonging to other communities." In this latter category, they place women who live in small towns and rural areas for whom the experience of seeing "others like us" requires a long excursion to a major city. In *The Two of Us*, Larry Uhrig, until his death an MCC minister in Washington, D.C., focuses on helping couples design their ceremonies and leads them through the complications of making the contractual arrangements that stand in for the legal rights automatically accorded heterosexual married couples.[18]

These examples reveal the strong hold that marital and kinship imagery has had for gays and lesbians even during periods of intense oppression and secrecy. Even when full-blown or public ceremonies might not have been attempted, gays and lesbians sometimes have staged private commitment rituals, exchanging rings and vows with some of the accouterments of traditional wedding rituals: champagne, special food and clothing, a particularly romantic setting, or a site that has sentimental importance for the couple, such as the place they met or the location of their first date. Another ritual element of such occasions might be embodied in the date selected, often a major anniversary such as the fifth or the tenth, or an association with a straight wedding. One San Francisco man now in his early seventies told me how he and his long-term lover silently exchanged vows many years ago while attending the heterosexual wedding of a relative. As the couple spoke their vows, the two men mouthed the same words, nodding to each other from across the room as one of them stood in the wedding party and the other sat in the congregation. They "felt married" and were moved by the romantic atmosphere of the straight wedding, knowing, of course, that their relationship would never be recognized by their families.

Early Legal Efforts

As far back as the early 1970s, gays and lesbians have challenged the legal restriction of marriage to men and women, though none of these earlier efforts received serious judicial attention. While the constitutional arguments raised in these cases have varied, the responses to them have ranged from bafflement to outrage as judges cited presumably commonplace understandings that marriage is "naturally" the union of a man and a woman, and therefore cannot be entered into by members of the same sex.

In 1970 the Reverend Troy Perry performed what was described by the *Advocate* as "the first marriage in the nation designed to legally bind two persons of the same sex," presiding over a ceremony between Neva Joy Heckman and Judith Ann Belew. Reverend Perry issued a church marriage certificate under a California law exempting common-law couples from obtaining marriage licenses. When the law in question was found to specify "man and wife," however, the union was found to be invalid.[19]

In a 1971 case, for example, in which a comparison with the successful 1967 constitutional challenge (*Loving v. Virginia*) to earlier restrictions on racially mixed marriages was cited by the plaintiffs, the Minnesota Supreme Court drew "a clear distinction between a marital restriction based *merely* upon race and one based upon the *fundamental* difference in sex."[20] In similar fashion, the Kentucky Court of Appeals in 1973 called upon "nature" to justify its rejection of a constitutional claim to the right to marry for same-sex couples using the following language:

[A]ppellants are prevented from marrying, not by the statutes of Kentucky or the refusal of the County Clerk of Jefferson County to issue them a license, but rather by their own incapability of entering into a marriage as that term is defined. A license to enter into a status or a relationship [that] the parties are incapable of achieving is a nullity.[21]

Here the court's opinion rests on the implicit assumption that marriage is actualized through a sexual act that demands particular (presumably "opposite") anatomical attributes in each of the parties, attributes that make procreation a possible outcome. Most notably, the court sees no need to specify the source of the "definition" it cites; the notion that marriage is simply a state that is defined by generally agreed upon characteristics prevents the court from seriously engaging with the issue of gender.

Other examples of efforts by same-sex couples to legally marry are scattered throughout recent legal literature. In 1975 the district attorney in Boulder, Colorado, ruled that no laws bar same-sex marriages; based on that ruling the county clerk of Boulder issued six marriage licenses to same-sex couples. After a month, the state attorney general ruled that such marriages were illegal and ordered the clerk to stop issuing the licenses. In 1976 two Chicago women were arrested four times for staging sit-ins at City Hall, finally being sentenced to one year in state prison for demanding a marriage license.[22]

The current serious discussion over the legalization of same-sex marriage, in contrast, reflects a cultural climate vastly different from that of just ten or twenty years ago. As other gay/lesbian issues have achieved prominence, and perhaps particularly as the AIDS epidemic has brought many Americans face-to-face with the gay community and gay individuals for perhaps the first time, legalization of marriage has emerged as the surprise demand of the 1990s, generated not by a top-down stratagem but rather by a grass-roots mandate. Unlike the issue of gays and lesbians in the military, chosen by gay activists in the Democratic Party as a problem that could effectively dramatize the predicament of patriotic gay citizens, marriage has simply appeared as something that gays and lesbians—at least some of us—want.

In 1990 Craig Dean and Patrick Gill sued the government of Washington, D.C., for refusing them a marriage license. They argued that the District's marriage law does not specify gender and that its human rights law, which prohibits discrimination on the basis of sex or sexual orientation, should permit them equal access to the rights of married couples.

In response to their suit the Superior Court of the District of Columbia took refuge in quotations from Genesis, Deuteronomy, Matthew, and Ephesians, arguing that the "societal recognition that it takes a man and a woman to form a marital relationship is older than Christianity itself." In 1995 the District Court of Appeals upheld that decision, interpreting the marriage law to exclude same-sex couples and claiming that the District's human rights law permitted discrimination in the right to marry.[23]

While Dean and Gill worked closely with legal counsel from the beginning of their case, some other cases may develop without the same sort of support by gay civil rights attorneys. On May 18, 1995, two men, Toshav Greene and Phillip Storrs, applied for a marriage license in Ithaca, New York. Greene and Storrs explained their desire to marry, rather than to file for the domestic partnership status available in Ithaca, as stemming from their belief in marriage and family. "Marriage is the basic social unit in society," Greene is quoted as saying. "We're not doing anything bizarre or unusual," he added. "We're living life the way that we were brought up: You date somebody; you get engaged; you get married. And then you establish a family."

Although the city clerk initially kept the license from being issued, the couple pointed out that no explicit legal prohibition of same-sex marriage existed. This led the case to be considered both by the city attorney and by Ithaca's mayor, Benjamin Nichols, whose initial response was supportive. The mayor, a seventy-four-year-old veteran of the civil rights movement, said, "If they really want to go ahead with it, my position is that they should be granted a license."[24]

The couple's request generated a furor not only among antigay conservatives but among gay rights advocates working on the then pending Hawaii same-sex marriage case. Concerned that a challenge to the marriage laws in New York (or any other state) would sabotage the effort in Hawaii by creating an unfavorable precedent, lawyers from the Lambda Legal Defense and Education Fund and the Empire State Pride Agenda urged the couple to withdraw their request. The city eventually acceded to official pressure from the state and the strategic concerns raised by gay rights activists, explaining that a legal memorandum issued by the State Health Department, which oversees marriage licenses, had stated unambiguously that "city clerks should not issue a marriage license to persons of the same sex." One newspaper account explained, "Dick Dadey, executive director of the Pride Agenda, a statewide political group [in New York], said that, had the license been issued in Ithaca, 'we would have won a small yet historic battle, but we would have been faced with losing a larger war in recognizing our families, had the state seen fit to take action against Mayor Nichols' decision.' "[25]

In the context of these demands for public recognition and in view of wide resistance to the legalization of gay marriage, some gay activists have championed domestic partnership status as a sort of compromise position. Domestic partnership offers limited legal protections to lesbian and gay couples without seeking outright to legalize their unions; registration as domestic partners is not in most cases limited to gay couples, but is also offered in some jurisdictions to straight couples who do not wish to marry but want some sort of official recognition of their situations.[26]

The earliest domestic partnership statute was passed in Berkeley, California, in 1984, offering health and other benefits to both same-sex and opposite-sex couples who were city employees. In 1985 the newly incorporated city of West Hollywood, California, home to a large and politically active gay population, followed suit, though its ordinance offered no real benefits beyond symbolic registration. Since that time a growing number of municipalities around the country have established various sorts of domestic partner registration mechanisms, some of which confer some level of benefits on city or other employees and others of which are more clearly symbolic, offering the couple little more than a certificate that attests to their registration. The specific requirements for registration vary from city to city but generally include some evidence of joint residence and economic interdependency, as well as a declaration that neither party has such a relationship with anyone else. Dissolution of domestic partnership can generally be accomplished by filing a notice with the agency that registered the partnership.

The benefits offered to domestic partners—bereavement and sick leave for city employees when a partner dies or is ill, tenancy succession, and health insurance for partners of city workers—in no way alter provisions of the state and federal governments that limit benefits in areas such as inheritance rights, taxes, and immigration status to "legally married" husbands and wives.[27] In 1995 San Francisco voters expanded domestic partner benefits to include pension rights for surviving partners, and in 1996 the city's Board of Supervisors voted to offer an optional "wedding ceremony," formally similar to the civil ceremony provided heterosexual couples, though not in any sense legally binding.[28] Unlike marriage, however, there is no implication in domestic partnership statutes that anything beyond the immediate relationship is involved; that is, there is no agreement to divide property acquired during the partnership, nor any expectation that either party will help support the other for any length of time after the relationship ends.[29]

These statutes are mirrored in the world of employee benefits by a growing movement of employers who offer identical or roughly comparable health and other benefits to the domestic partners of employees, thereby attempting to equalize compensation levels for gay and straight workers. While in some cases domestic partner registration is required for employees to avail themselves of such benefits, the measure of "commitment" is by no means uniform or universally agreed upon. Employers offering such benefits include many public and private colleges and universities as well as a variety of corporate entities, particularly in the entertainment and high-tech fields.[30] Many employers restrict these benefits to same-sex couples, arguing that opposite-sex couples have the option of legal marriage and shouldn't need to avail themselves of these compensatory programs.

These policies are controversial, to say the least. For example, in December 1992 suburban Williamson County, north of Austin, Texas, refused to approve a tax abatement plan that would have brought a huge Apple Computer facility to the area. Although the project would have created more than 1,500 high-wage jobs and brought some $300 million into the local economy in the next several years, the county commissioners cited Apple's domestic partner benefits policy as one that would undermine traditional family values. One commissioner voiced the fear that voting yes on Apple would mean being identified as "the man who brought homosexuality to Williamson County." Other speakers at an emotional hearing cited hostility to "same-sex lovers and live-in lovers" coming into their community. After a week of pressure from Governor Ann Richards, the commissioners relented, restructuring (but not reducing the value of) the package offered to Apple so that it would not appear that the county was offering the company a tax abatement. The commissioners could then claim that the new agreement did not use "taxpayer dollars to subsidize, and therefore tacitly endorse" the company's domestic partner policy.[31]

The Hawaii Case

The most dramatic development in the ongoing public debate over whether to recognize gay and lesbian relationships is the Hawaii same-sex marriage case. In 1991, Honolulu attorney Daniel R. Foley brought suit against the state on behalf of two gay male and one lesbian couple who had been refused marriage licenses. Now known as *Baehr v. Miike* (formerly *Baehr v. Lewin*), the case asserts that denial of the right to marry to same-sex couples violates the state's constitutional guarantee of equal gender rights. After a lower court ruled against the plaintiffs, the case moved to the State Supreme Court, where a 1993 ruling remanded the case to the lower court to determine whether such discrimination is "permissible" because it is supported by a "compelling" state interest.[32] Because of Hawaii's Equal Rights Amendment, gender discrimination is subject to "strict scrutiny," and the court expressed doubts that the restriction could be legally supported.

Those arguing in favor of same-sex marriage have compared the policy of restriction with the antimiscegenation laws that were once pervasive in the United States but which were finally struck down in *Loving v. Virginia* in 1967. From this perspective, the logic that once dictated the criminalization of marriage between persons of different races was based on assumptions about "nature," although it illustrated the ability of the state to define not only the boundaries of marriage but the parameters of "nature" itself. As race was once construed, sex (or gender) was then, as it is now, understood as a fixed biological category.

At the same time, however, as civil rights attorney Nan Hunter has pointed out, definitions of race and sex have proved to be far more flexible than their rigid institutionalization at any particular time would indicate. Her historical survey of marriage laws reveals not only that race is no longer considered a legitimate basis for restricting marriage, but that courts no longer enforce the authority of the man and the dependence of the woman—once a key assumption of the law—in defining the legal requirements for marriage. In other words, changing mores are reflected in the laws that define and buttress marriage just as they are in other cultural domains.[33]

Others involved in the debate also have pointed out that legal precedents do not support limiting marriage to having procreation as its purpose; couples who are unable to bear children are allowed to marry and infertility cannot be used as grounds for divorce. Even couples who cannot have sexual relations at all—as when one of the partners is incarcerated or severely disabled—have the legal right to marry, which courts have long interpreted as having both spiritual and cultural significance beyond the level of sexuality or procreation. Since it is unlikely that the state will be able to develop a convincing justification for restricting marriage to opposite-sex couples, most legal analysts, as of this writing, predict the eventual legalization of same-sex marriage in Hawaii.[34]

The likelihood that the Hawaii case will legalize same-sex marriage has inspired a vigorous reaction around the country, as states rush to pass legislation aimed at invalidating such marriages. Commenting on the veritable avalanche of such preventive legislation, Lambda attorney and cocounsel in *Baehr v. Miike* Evan Wolfson said, "The backlash has started before we have lashed." Laws invalidating same-sex marriages have been passed or debated in many states, often unleashing acrimonious legislative battles that have polarized communities.[35] In Hawaii, state legislators anticipating a State Supreme Court decision favorable to same-sex marriages have considered a number of strategies in order to forestall its implementation. Among these have been proposals to create a gender-neutral domestic partnership arrangement which could offer an alternative to marriage and attempts to amend the Hawaii state constitution to invalidate same-sex marriages.[36]

Probably the most intense national controversy unfolded in 1996 with Congress's passage of the controversially named Defense of Marriage Act (DOMA), which authorized states to refuse to recognize same-sex marriages performed in other states. President Clinton's widely criticized midnight signing of the bill only intensified election-year accusations that he was trying to appeal to more conservative voters while still attempting to represent his policies as moderate and tolerant. Since same-sex marriage was still not legal in any state, however, passage of the bill represented little more than an opportunity for politicians to carve out positions on the issue rather than being an actual threat to gay civil rights efforts. Ironically, while this bill passed by a wide margin, legislation that some of its opponents had introduced at the same time that would have banned workplace discrimination based on sexual orientation lost by only one vote. The national debate over same-sex marriage made the lives of ordinary gay and lesbian people visible to an unprecedented degree, adding to some of the gains that were the ironic result of the earlier debacle over gays in the military.[37]

Debate on the Issue

As these legal cases unwind in the courts and legislatures, images of marriage and commitment between people of the same sex have become common both in gay and lesbian cultural venues and in the mainstream media. Debates about the wisdom of instituting legal same-sex marriage are virtually constant on the op-ed pages of newspapers around the country, and letters to the editor taking one or another position appear almost daily. As the resolution of the Hawaii case nears, predictions about its national impact proliferate; news of decisions on the partial or complete legalization of same-sex marriage in other countries—the Netherlands provides one recent example of a country considering such a measure—also stimulates speculation and debate about the wisdom of such policies and their likely effects on the future of the American family, the AIDS epidemic, the national health care debate, and a host of other issues. The response has been varied, representing everything from alarm to applause, as the question intersects with diverse philosophies and interests.[38]

Interestingly, not all lesbians and gays see same-sex marriage as a welcome development. Over the past few years, the legalization of gay/lesbian marriage has emerged as a key point that arguably distinguishes the politics of accommodation from the politics of resistance. The question of whether gays and lesbians should embrace or repudiate difference has been raised with regularity, from the very start of the gay liberation movement.[39] Lesbian activist Urvashi Vaid characterizes this opposition as the central strain in queer politics, tracing virtually every strategic misstep to a dispute grounded in the resistance-accommodation dichotomy, while more conservative gay authors like Andrew Sullivan and Bruce Bawer focus on the legitimation of marriage as a key index of progress toward general acceptance.[40]

At the same time, then, that *queerness*, a term that roughly designates a resolutely oppositional stance vis-à-vis the normalization of homosexuality, has become a central theme in recent gay/lesbian cultural formations as well as in a variety of political sites,[41] other tendencies seem to also be taking hold among people who identify (or find themselves identified) as lesbian or gay. These moves might be described in terms of powerful images of nostalgia that largely shape their formal attributes, or might otherwise be characterized in terms of the sense of entitlement revealed in the claims they make. I include under this rubric a range of civil rights issues, from inclusion of lesbians and gays in the military to the insistence of lesbian and gay conservatives that they be acknowledged as part of the gender-variant rainbow, to the growing presence of gays and lesbians in mainstream politics, to the demand by lesbians and gay men that they be able to marry.

Most noteworthy in all these discussions is the apparent disappearance of the closet as a viable option even among those gay figures most unwilling to challenge the wider social order. This means that even self-styled gay conservatives want their relationships recognized as equal in importance to those of heterosexuals, and while they reject the notion that homosexuality challenges traditional social norms, they refuse to hide their partners or try to pass as heterosexual. Conservative gay writer Bruce Bawer, for example, argues that discrimination against homosexuals is most marked when a couple decides to live together and that the choice to form a joint household is thereby a courageous stand against bigotry. "When two straight people decide to marry, everyone celebrates their commitment," he explains. "When two gay people decide to move in together, they commit themselves to insult and discrimination and attack. . . . Living alone, most gay people can conceal their sexuality; living together, a gay couple advertise theirs every time they step out of the house together. Is it any wonder, then, that so many gay men have historically been promiscuous, shunning long-term relationships in favor of one-night stands?" He elaborates on this topic bitterly, citing incident after incident in which his publicly committed relationship and those of his friends are slighted by presumably well-meaning heterosexuals. "I have longtime professional associates who routinely ask other men 'How's the wife?' but to whom it never occurs to ask me 'How's Chris?' Recently, when a gay friend of mine was singled out to work on a holiday, he had to call off plans with his companion. But a co-worker explained: 'It's only fair. We all have families to go home to.' "[42]

Bawer reserves his angriest words for his description of a heterosexual wedding he and his partner attended together. Though they knew the couple very well, and indeed had introduced them, they were the only invited couple not called for formal portraits by the wedding photographer. But even worse, in the ceremony itself, though the two men walked in the procession and stood together at the altar near the bride and groom, the ceremony read by the judge, and written in consultation with the bride, contained a statement that "marriage between a man and a woman . . . was 'the only valid foundation for an enduring home.'" Bawer and his partner felt both betrayed and patronized. "If she had appreciated and valued my relationship with Chris for what it was, those words would have jumped off the page the moment she saw them. But they didn't; and this suggested to Chris and me that, in her view, our relationship *wasn't* comparable to her marriage. . . . To both of us, our omission from the 'couples' pictures and the callous wording of their

marriage ceremony . . . drew an unmistakable line of demarcation between their relationship and ours."[43]

At the same time that individual gay writers speak persuasively of the
emotional costs of trying to establish equality in a society that, by val-
orizing heterosexual marriage, effectively erases the existence of committed gay and lesbian relationships, civil rights activists have argued the
issue in both moral and strategic terms. The most explicit and polarized
statement of opposing views in the debate over marriage that has erupt-
ed in gay political circles appeared in a pair of articles by two attorneys
affiliated with the gay public-interest law firm, the Lambda Legal Defense
and Education Fund, originally published in a 1989 issue of *Out/Look*.
The lead articles in a section labeled "Strategy" were headlined, "Gay
Marriage: A Must or a Bust?" Speaking on the pro side, Tom Stoddard de-
velops the idea that gays and lesbians should fight for the right to marry
not because this should be the goal of all gays, but because they should
have the same rights as other members of the society. Marriage, he notes,
confers more than superficial advantages on those who enter into it; beyond representing recognition of the legitimacy of a relationship, it offers many layers of economic benefits that gay citizens are denied. This
means, most simply, that lesbians and gay men are paid substantially less
than their heterosexual colleagues if the benefits that accrue to spouses
and children are considered an element of compensation. It also means
that gay spouses are vulnerable to legal challenges from biological families from which heterosexual partners are virtually immune. While Stoddard acknowledges that "marriage may be unattractive and even oppres-
sive as it is currently structured and practiced," he argues that "enlarging
the concept to embrace same-sex couples would necessarily transform it
into something new."[44]

The opposing piece, by Paula Ettelbrick, questions the wisdom of pursuing gay and lesbian marriage as a civil rights issue. Ettelbrick reviews
the long historical connection between marriage and patriarchy, asserting that marriage is an institution grounded in inequality that should be
interrogated rather than sought after. Beginning with an emphasis on the
broader inequalities that give marital benefits their significance, she argues that if the United States offered its citizens a national health care
system, for example, gaining health insurance through one's spouse
would no longer serve as a reason to marry. Probably more crucial to her
opposition, however, is her position that gays and lesbians are not in fact
similar to heterosexuals in all but civil rights, but that they are "funda-

mentally different." Her argument rests on the notion that difference, not assimilation, lies at the foundation of gay liberation and that for that reason, "marriage runs contrary to two of the primary goals of the lesbian and gay movement: the affirmation of gay identity and culture; and the validation of many forms of relationships. . . . Being queer," Ettelbrick continues, "is more than setting up house, sleeping with a person of the same gender, and seeking state approval for doing so. It is an identity, a culture with many variations." Drawing on a broader feminist analysis of the family, Ettelbrick claims that gay marriage will not challenge existing privileges for the few or affect the "systematic abuses" of society.[45]

Nancy Polikoff continues this discussion, recalling feminist critiques of the family and questioning the need to parody this most unappealing of patriarchal institutions. Her critique of William Eskridge's review of historical and cross-cultural precedents for same-sex marriage argues that "an effort to legalize lesbian and gay marriage would make public critique of the institution of marriage impossible. . . . Marriage would be touted as the solution to [gay couples'] problems; the limitations of marriage, and of a social system valuing one form of human relationship above all others, would be downplayed."[46] Polikoff ties her argument to a similar point about the struggle to allow gays and lesbians to openly serve in the military; their presence may bring certain benefits, but it cannot be expected to transform the nature of military institutions. Marriage, she asserts, is a social form historically based in gender inequality; seeking access to its privileges can only be expected to broaden its damaging effects.

But proponents of gay and lesbian marriage argue instead that to make a claim like Polikoff's is to essentialize marriage as thoroughly as marriage statutes have historically essentialized gender. Like gender, Nan Hunter explains, marriage is a social construction that has no natural existence outside of U.S. legal regulations; it is ancient but its form has changed throughout history and it ought not to be confused with "coupling," which implies no societal legitimation. Hunter thus supports efforts to legalize same-sex marriage, arguing that it "would radically denaturalize the social construction of male/female differentness." Rather than favoring the wealthy, as Ettelbrick asserts, Hunter points out that marriage offers the least expensive mechanism for allocating property, functioning as it does to automatically arrange matters between partners that otherwise would require a variety of legal devices, such as wills, powers of attorney, and other costly (and sometimes ineffective) agreements.[47] Hunter insists that lesbian and gay activists acknowledge that *family* is a complex term that must be understood in all its multiple and situated meanings before an assault is mounted against it; in couching her argument in this nuanced understanding, Hunter echoes the views of those who have attested to the enduring and multifaceted meanings of *family* for many gay and lesbian people, particularly for those with roots in communities of color.[48]

Taking a different approach, political philosopher Morris Kaplan has looked at same-sex marriage as a type of civil disobedience, one that has the potential to transform public understandings of basic institutions. "One of the merits of focusing on queer families," Kaplan notes, "is its small-scale and associational character," a shift in political emphasis which he sees as encouraging the questioning of taken-for-granted assumptions about the family. "The proliferation of queer couples and families may help to redefine the social and legal conditions available to sustain intimate and domestic relationships more generally," Kaplan continues, arguing that lesbian and gay marriage would lead to a challenge to the moral consensus that enforces compulsory heterosexuality; the resulting rethinking of the meaning of rights of privacy would contribute, in his view, to a larger "democratic contestation of the organization of personal life."[49]

Lambda attorney Evan Wolfson, a member of the legal team arguing the Hawaii case, denies the argument posed by a number of gay marriage critics that seeking marriage rights for gays and lesbians will obliterate struggles to broaden notions of family and commitment, including efforts to regularize and expand domestic partnership arrangements. But he also observes that "domestic partnership fails to resonate with the emotional, declarative, and often religious power most people feel inheres in marriage."[50] Same-sex couples, he points out, feel entitled to more than a limited package of benefits, and indeed, reducing their desire for legal marriage to those (admittedly important) advantages misses the essence of what the struggle for marriage is all about.

While activist attorneys like Nan Hunter and Evan Wolfson advocate gay marriage as a fundamental challenge to the status quo, author Andrew Sullivan presents a drastically different rationale. After finding fault with a range of positions on gay rights from the most radical to the most conservative, Sullivan espouses "equal access to civil marriage" as "the centerpiece" of the new politics he hopes to see emerge from the gay and lesbian community. Because marriage is a bond that demonstrates fundamental similarities between heterosexuals and homosexuals, legal gay marriage "could bring the essence of gay life—a gay couple—into the heart of the traditional family in a way the family can most understand and the gay offspring can most easily acknowledge. It could do more to heal the gay-straight rift than any amount of gay rights legislation." Beyond this, gay marriage would have positive effects on gay children imagining their futures, countering the fear and shame that lack of such legitimacy fosters. Sullivan argues that "gay marriage is not a radical step; it is a profoundly humanizing, traditionalizing step. . . . It is ultimately the only reform that truly matters."[51] Rather than being a political move, marriage can be, Sullivan claims, a route to the "prepolitical" level of social life that is prior to the state.

Debates about the legalization of gay and lesbian marriage are nothing if not passionate. Both adherents and detractors see the emergent battle over the issue as key to shaping the welfare of future generations of gays and lesbians; they situate it squarely within the broader division between the politics of difference and assimilation, or between radical and conservative strategies in the gay rights movement. Not unlike a comparable debate in feminism, both subversive and accommodationist rationales can be generated for virtually any position in the spectrum.[52] Adherents of marriage may claim that it will revolutionize gay-straight relations because of its fundamental acceptability, or they may maintain that marriage will undermine traditional constructions of gender and thereby make acceptability a moot point. In like fashion, gay opponents declare marriage to be so conventional that it can only create changes that would intensify current sources of inequality, while conservative heterosexuals perceive the demand for access to marriage as a direct assault on core cultural and religious values. Evan Wolfson sums up these apparent contradictions by declaring that "the brilliance of our movement's taking on marriage is that marriage is, at once and truly, both conservative *and* transformative, easily understood in basic human terms of equality and respect, and liberating in its individual and social potential."[53]

Popular Reflections

These legal, political, and cultural maneuvers have paralleled a virtual explosion of attention to the subject in the media of popular culture, as an almost dizzying array of representations of gay and lesbian marriage and wedding ceremonies appeared in the early and mid-1990s, most of which have drawn on rather sympathetic portrayals of the couples involved. On television, such shows as *Roseanne, Friends,* and *Northern Exposure* have devoted episodes to gay weddings, lampooning straight attitudes but treating the weddings themselves as unremarkable. The 1994 British film *Four Weddings and a Funeral* presents a gay male relationship which ends in the death of one of the partners. Although it takes this death to bring the relationship fully into the open, it is nonetheless offered as the epitome of true love, particularly in the wrenching funeral scene when the two men's love is contrasted with the foolish shenanigans of the straight couples in the film. The upbeat ending of the film, in which all the characters, including the survivor of the gay relationship, end up blissfully coupled, slyly alludes to a future wedding between two men, sandwiching it quickly between images of heterosexual unions.

The June 13, 1994, cover of the *New Yorker* magazine featured a drawing titled "June Grooms," which pictured two men in formal attire standing behind a wedding cake topped with tiny figures in their image. A 1994 documentary film about a lesbian wedding, *Chicks in White Satin*, was nominated for an Academy Award, and the 1996 Sundance Film Festival featured another film on the same theme, *Late Bloomers*. Newspapers from all parts of the country and mass circulation magazines including *People, Newsweek,* and *Harper's* have run features on gay and lesbian weddings and domestic life, sometimes focusing on celebrities who have come out. In some cases, media treatments of weddings, families, or romance in general include lesbian and gay weddings in their roster of "alternatives" or as examples of "diversity." For example, the *San Francisco Examiner* for Sunday, February 11, 1996, ran a Valentine's Day series of short narratives titled "First Person: Romance" which focused on the place each person presented in the series identified as the most romantic location in the city. Along with stories from an ethnically varied group of heterosexuals from around the Bay Area about where they had met their partner, or where they were when their spouse proposed, was the story of one gay couple's romance. Leroy Thomas, an African-American man, recalls his first date with his "soul mate," Dwight Shealey, at the Cliff House, a San Francisco landmark overlooking the Pacific Ocean. "We sat and talked about our dreams. We're both Christian, we like to travel, we like antiques, we wanted a monogamous relationship. We're both HIV positive." The autobiographical sketch noted that the two men had recently held a commitment ceremony and just bought a home together.[54]

In San Francisco and other cities with large and visible gay populations, local merchants regularly target advertisements to the gay community for wedding-related and household goods and services, including everything from flowers to catering. Further seeking to increase their
share of the gay-wedding market, bridal gift registries at department and
specialty stores in many cities have deleted gender-specific language
from their registration systems, exchanging the traditional categories of
"bride and groom" for "registrant and co-registrant" or other efforts at
gender-neutral terminology. Not wanting to miss the boat, in 1994
HarperCollins brought out a sophisticated manual, *The Essential Guide
to Lesbian and Gay Weddings*, leading couples through virtually every decision they might have to make in planning a commitment ceremony.[55]
Gay and lesbian weddings, both in the context of the demand for legal
marriage and as independent events, have become visible as never before,
even as this visibility implies a commodification that approaches that
long typical of heterosexual weddings.

Lesbian and gay popular culture has also become flooded with wedding images and stories about long-term romance. In San Francisco a
large hardware store in the Castro district typically uses a same-sex wedding theme to decorate their June display windows. The windows feature
mannequins representing two brides and two grooms, with attractively
arranged housewares (suitable as wedding gifts) arrayed around them.
Also in the Castro, a gay-oriented gift shop called Husbands is decorated with candid photos of both male and female couples from all over the
world who have visited the store. Each photo is inscribed with the couple's name, where they are from, and how long they've been together.
The store's owners, who take particular pride in having a gay-owned
community business and in being actively involved with neighborhood
issues such as AIDS and crime prevention, pointed out two of their favorite photos when I visited the store: a mixed race gay-male couple
from New York with two children and two elderly men from North Carolina who have been together for sixty years. They explained that they
chose the name for the store because "husband" means to them more
than "boyfriend" or "lover," and because they feel that it is a concept that
crosses national boundaries.

Along these same lines, many gay and lesbian publications have taken
to running inspirational stories of romances that work and couples who
have stayed together for many years. These stories tend to focus on how
couples survive the many challenges they perceive to such longevity, the

host of forces that are arrayed to undermine and damage their love and trust. In a typical example, *San Francisco Frontiers*, an advertiser-supported free magazine, featured Del Martin and Phyllis Lyon on the cover of their February 1, 1996, Valentine's Day issue. Martin and Lyon, virtually a San Francisco institution, have been lovers for forty-three years. They are two of the founders of Daughters of Bilitis (the first national lesbian rights organization, begun in 1955 as a secret society), the authors of *Lesbian/Woman*, an influential feminist book published in the 1970s, and perennial activists on the local scene. Their story, which recounted how they met and why they think their relationship has been so resilient, joined those of five other couples in the cover article, "Love That Lasts: Six Couples, with More Than 130 Years of Togetherness, Talk about Life, Love, and the Long Haul." Along with Martin and Lyon, the article profiled two other female and three male couples, all at least somewhat prominent in local political or business circles. "Cliché be damned," the article leads off, "there's no denying that the love that dare not speak its name occasionally learns to speak the beloved's until the end of time."[56]

Following the article, a three-page album of twenty pictures submitted in response to the magazine's request for "photographs celebrating their love" further expands on the romantic theme of the issue. The photos include both male and female couples, two (of women) also including children (and in one case a dog) and five (of men) featuring leather paraphernalia and erotic poses. A prominent full-page display at the beginning of the issue advertises Bonds Limited, a gay/lesbian matchmaking service. "Bonds Limited," the ad reads, "uses a highly confidential, safe, and comfortable process to bring together loving, stable, carefully screened, same-gender partners committed to long-term, monogamous relationships." Framing the text are four photographs of paired, clearly same-sex (two male, two female) hands, all sporting wedding bands. In two of the pictures (one male and one female), a child's presence is also evoked, in one case by a tiny foot and in the other by a pair of small hands holding the two adult hands.

These popular concerns with enduring relationships are also reflected in an ever-growing catalogue of self-help, advice, and didactic literature about relationships and family issues, supplemented by a plethora of inspirational tales published by and about "exemplary" couples. Rod and Bob Jackson-Paris's 1994 volume, *Straight from the Heart: A Love Story*, for instance, takes the reader from the body builders' first meeting, their courtship and romance, through to their wedding ceremony, giving hints on how the couple manage the stresses and strains of a committed union.[57] Advice books with titles like *The Lesbian Couples Guide: Finding the Right Woman and Creating a Life Together*, *Lesbian Couples: Creating Healthy Relationships for the 1990s*, *Permanent Partners*, *Staying Power: Long-Term Lesbian Couples*, *Gay Relationships*, *Intimacy Between Men*, *Gay Men's Guide*, and even *Unbroken Ties: Lesbian Ex-Lovers* regularly turn up in bookstores that cater to gay and lesbian patrons. At the same time, many publications aimed at lesbian and gay readers have problematized the question of same-sex marriage, subjecting the issue to analysis and criticism from all directions. Letters to the editor, opinion pieces, and feature articles debating the pros and cons of marriage appear regularly in such national magazines as *The Advocate* and *Out* as well as in regional publications from around the country.

In 1993, Theatre Rhinoceros, a gay repertory company in San Francisco, staged *Jumping the Broom*, a series of vignettes on the marriage and domestic partnership question. After the final performance, a real couple, two gay men from the East Bay suburbs, came up on stage and held a wedding ceremony. Though they brought several friends with them to serve as witnesses and attendants, the audience attending the play constituted a congregation that provided a community context for the ritual (see chapter 3).

Also in 1993, the San Francisco Metropolitan Community Church put on a fund-raiser for the church called "Bob and Jerry Get Married," advertised as "just your average wedding." Tickets, sold at locations around the city, resembled formal engraved invitations. During the weeks before and after the show, the church hosted a "wedding faire" in which both gay community and mainstream businesses advertised their wedding and marriage-related wares, including hotels and churches suitable for ceremonies and receptions, tuxedo rentals, florists, bakeries, caterers, and financial planners. Ads for these same businesses also appeared in the program for the show. This "faire" was widely publicized in the community as "America's First Lesbian/Gay Wedding Faire," most notably with a giant elevated billboard at the central intersection of Castro and Market.

Other lesbian and gay performers have also taken up the issue. In 1995, for example, San Francisco lesbian performance artist Sara Felder's one-woman show at a Castro district club was titled "June Bride" and was based her own wedding some two years previous. And in

1996 an interracial gay couple from Minneapolis, Djola Branner and Patrick Scully, presented "Forever Hold Your Piece" in New York. Drawing on the complex cultural, racial, and political dynamics that surfaced as they planned their own ceremony, the two men's play offered a wry commentary on responses of their friends and families to their decision to stage a wedding ceremony. As these pages are written, diverse representations of gay/lesbian community interest in the theme of weddings and marriage continue to proliferate, becoming ever more prevalent elements of popular culture.

Back to "the Wedding"

None of the political controversies surrounding gay and lesbian marriage seemed very pressing as a huge throng of some five to ten thousand (2,600 couples signed up for official certificates marking the occasion) pushed forward to hear the speakers and participate in the service. But what followed, though formally somewhere between a generic Protestant marriage ceremony and a political rally, in many ways encapsulated the range of issues that have been delineated in both cultural and legal discussions.

Before the ceremony, speakers raised most of the central issues that have emerged in the debate over marriage both within gay communities and in dialogue with the wider society. Karen Thompson, for example, recounted the story, probably familiar to most of the assembled crowd, of the problems that followed after her lover, Sharon Kowalski, was seriously injured in an automobile accident. When Kowalski's family learned that the two women were lovers, they reacted both by denying that their daughter was a lesbian and by refusing to allow Thompson access to Kowalski. What followed was years of legal wrangling, finally leading to a court recognizing Thompson's right to be involved in the care and rehabilitation of severely disabled Kowalski. The lesson to be learned from this episode, Thompson emphasized, is that couples should create whatever legal documents are necessary, such as medical power-of-attorney, to allow them to be considered the primary person to be consulted in case of illness or accident. From a broader perspective, of course, it underscores the second-class status of gay and lesbian relationships; the rights routinely accorded to married heterosexual couples are denied same-sex couples, with potentially tragic consequences in cases such as Thompson's and Kowalski's.

Among the other speakers was an elderly male couple who had been together for some forty years. To sustained applause from the crowd, they spoke about the longevity of their relationship and the fact that there had been no social supports over the years—indeed, there had been many impediments—to their staying together. Their presence reminded the crowd that same-sex commitments are nothing new; only the demands for equity and recognition have changed the landscape.

At the heart of the various speakers' comments was a common theme, which while sentimental in its emphasis on love as the core value that united all the couples, also rested on a shared understanding of love and commitment as ordinary human impulses. All we want, speaker after speaker suggested, is acceptance for what already exists, and what already exists is merely what heterosexuals take for granted: the right to form legally acknowledged and culturally sanctioned marital bonds, to have all the resources of our families and the wider society marshaled on behalf of our relationships in the same way that heterosexual married couples do. Implicit in these demands was the notion that denial of such affirmation is tantamount to violence against gays and lesbians, permitting, as it does, a process that diminishes the public value of lesbians and gay men. The MCC's Reverend Troy Perry invoked the presence of the nearby Holocaust Museum, scheduled to open to the public the day after the march. "There is a museum a few blocks from here," he intoned. "It's the new Holocaust Museum. . . . We say to our government today, that building is an exhibit of why we're here today. As our Jewish brothers and sisters have said, 'Never again!' WE WILL HAVE OUR RIGHTS!"

At the same time that he likened actual or symbolic violence against homosexuals to a holocaust, Perry also raised images that evoked unity in spite of diversity, implying that gays share a sort of nationhood or ethnicity. Surveying the crowd, he observed, "We have Christians, we have Jews, we have Muslims, we have atheists, we have everybody, but we're gay and we're lesbian and we're proud, which is the most important thing." Perry's comments moved into a rambling exhortation about the cultural pressures placed on gay people to deny their natures, the likelihood that gay people will not encounter the kind of support and affirmation from their families that heterosexuals can take for granted, and the difficulties this creates for gays and lesbians as members of families. Nonetheless, his own experience, as one of five sons of a widowed mother, was that after his mother's death his relatives acknowledged that he had been the best and most devoted of the sons, despite his being "the gay one." The ability of families to eventually come around and see the truth, "as long as you don't apologize for your lifestyle," means that lesbians and gay men should accept their families' limitations, respect them and expect to one day win their respect in turn. This led him into an angry attack on the homophobic politics of the radical right. "Don't let the idiotically bigoted, right-wing Christian groups in this country, these right-wing religious groups, tell you that you can't be spiritual. Yes, you can!" With the crowd cheering, he prepared to begin the ceremony.

As the crowd pressed closer together, we began to notice our nearest neighbors, two white men, one probably in his forties, the other a bit younger. Although their presence at this event made clear that they were gay men, they hardly fit the glamorous stereotype promulgated in gay magazines. They had a southern rural air about them (confirmed when we heard them speak) and were dressed in virtually identical jeans and billed caps, T-shirts covering their ample bellies.

"Dearly beloved," Perry intoned, "we gather together here to stand before our friends, the larger society, and the United States government to proclaim our committed relationships. We do not make this proclamation lightly, but reverently, discreetly, and soberly. We stand before our nation and our friends because we wish to proclaim our right to love one another. We stand here knowing that love makes a family—nothing else, nothing less! We stand here knowing of the lies and untruths that have been told about us by some in the larger community. But we stand here pure of heart and unafraid in proclaiming that our concern and care for one another is as rich as that in any culture or community. It is with glad hearts this day that we stand in the light to proclaim our love one for another. We will no longer be silent about the love that dare not speak its name. We do this without hesitation in the full knowledge that we owe apologies to no one. We stand here today because we care. We stand today, many of us, in the valley of the shadow of death, realizing that this may be the last time we get to pledge our love one to the other in a public forum.

"We who are part of our community remember an ancient story in which two women pledged their love to each other. One woman said to the other, 'Do not ask me to leave you or to return and quit following after you, for where you go, I will go, and where you live, I will live. Your family will be my family, and your God shall be my God. Where you die, I will die, and there I will be buried. Only death shall part you and me.' Ruth and Naomi stuck together through great adversity. They traveled a long distance to stay together, looked after each other, and protected each other from danger. They expressed their love through physical affection in kissing and holding each other. They respected family and community customs and still retained the integrity of their love.

"We know of another ancient story of two men who did the same. Upon the death of Jonathan, David swore his eternal love for Jonathan and stated in 2 Samuel:26 that his love for Jonathan surpassed the love he had for the opposite sex.

"I remember the words spoken by lesbian feminist activist Kate Millett in Los Angeles in 1978, when she said, 'Never forget the nights of your love and the days of working for its freedom, its expansion to fill the world with the roses of those members out of time. An army of lovers makes a revolution.'

"It is on that foundation that we come today to again emphatically state our love one for another. We realize the prejudice that still exists in our culture concerning our right to live together, but we gladly challenge such prejudice rather than retreat into the shadows of despair and ignorance. We will not be stopped as we take our rightful place in this country as children of America. We shall be heard!"

As the Reverend Perry turned to administer the vows, the two men standing next to us moved closer together, eventually facing each other with their arms on each other's shoulders, foreheads and bellies touching. They gazed intently into each other's eyes, and after a few minutes I noticed that tears were streaming down their cheeks, especially the older man's.

"Participants," Perry continued, "is it your desire to take your vows of commitment at this time? If so, please respond, 'It is.'"

A roar of affirmation was raised from the crowd.

"As you are standing before me, couples, will the member of the couple who is standing to my right turn to your partner and do two things. First, tell them why you love them, and second, tell them why this ceremony is important to you." There was a pause, filled with a loud hum, as couples complied.

"I asked before this ceremony," said the Reverend Perry, "that each of you bring a token of your covenant. At this time I would ask that the individual member of the couple to my right take the gift, whether it is a ring, bracelet, pin, or other token—even if it is just a kiss of your affection—repeat after me, and then give your token of affection to your partner: 'I give you this gift as a token of our covenant,

vowing to live together in close friendship and love,
and to strive for fuller knowledge of your being
and to care for you above all others.
I pledge myself to recognize your needs
and to encourage your full potential
and to love you even as I love myself.
May love dwell between you and me forever.'"

Perry repeated the vows so that the partner on the left could also make them. Finally, he said, "Forasmuch as each of these couples have declared their love one for the other and have given tokens of their covenant each to the other, and have done this willingly before their friends gathered here, as well as before the larger American community, we proclaim together our rights as couples in hope that the day will come when not only will our own community recognize our relationships, but the laws of our country will also.

"Couples, you may kiss."[58]

After the ceremony, participants began to smile at each other, some hugging each other in congratulations, others just beaming in all directions as a sort of collective embrace swept through the crowd. We turned to the two men who had been standing beside us throughout the ceremony, now wiping their eyes but continuing to embrace and to gaze tenderly at each other. "It's been so nice to stand next to the two of you," I said, "you radiate so much feeling." "Yes," the younger man said dreamily, "we're pretty darned in love."

2

HEROES IN OUR OWN DRAMAS

The legal debate over same-sex marriage has grappled with questions of how to insure the expansion of full civil rights to lesbian and gay citizens and how to protect members of sexual minorities from abuse and discrimination. Besides the popular interest these questions stimulate, their political and ideological significance are just beginning to become central elements of a national debate that will no doubt continue and probably expand in the years to come. Controversy over the Republican-introduced Defense of Marriage Act, for example, burst into the headlines during the 1996 presidential campaign, as can-

Breaking the glass

didates Dole and Clinton sought to outdo each other's public commitment to the sanctity of heterosexuality as the foundation of marriage. This is just one of the intensely contested issues at the heart of public policy debates that reflect pervasive divisions in American cultural life.

But these disputes, and those that will follow the Hawaii Supreme Court's ruling in the *Baehr v. Miike* case, have little impact on the phenomena that are the crux of this volume—the private and public ceremonies lesbians and gay men create to celebrate, solemnize, and proclaim their relationships. Lesbians and gay men from a variety of backgrounds devise and stage commitment rituals or weddings despite the fact that no legal recognition awaits them. They enact these ceremonies even though members of their biological families may refuse to participate; certainly, as many of the couples I spoke with joked, few if any get married to please their parents. Same-sex couples almost always bear the entire financial burden of celebrating their unions, but even so, many create elaborate and costly events. Gay and lesbian couples who marry are less likely to receive the kinds of gifts their heterosexual siblings expect as a matter of course, and they make a public commitment with the knowledge that they will qualify for virtually none of the financial and legal benefits routinely associated with heterosexual marriage. But they get married, or proclaim their commitment, or affirm their unions, or celebrate their love nonetheless, and they will continue to do so in the future, as they have in the past, regardless of the outcome of the civic controversy over legalizing same-sex marriage.

I come to this discussion, then, less out of my active concern with the implications of the struggle to achieve legality for same-sex marriage than from a desire to fashion a cultural understanding of lesbian and gay weddings as powerful and complex ritual occasions. I bring (at least) two perspectives to this venture, that of a "married lesbian" whose personal life has been profoundly transformed by my own ceremony, and that of a cultural anthropologist with central interests in gender, sexuality, and ritual.

In this book, I will scrutinize same-sex weddings less in terms of determining whether or not people of good will should rise to their defense, or in terms of resolving the debates about their place in the unfolding gay civil rights struggle, but with the understanding that they simply constitute a reality, a piece of lesbian and gay life that exists in a late-twentieth-century American context. I will argue that these ceremonies embody complex ritual statements that make them meaningful beyond their particular significance for the shape of lesbian and gay culture. These events present challenges to our understandings of how ritual and political process meet in cultures. They force us to question easily accepted assumptions about how gay, lesbian, and queer sensibilities are formed and how they intersect with other sources of meaning in American life. They assault boundaries that have rarely been questioned.

Rituals of Rebellion and Resistance

The experiences I had in my own ceremony and those of other couples which I will detail in these pages are at once specific to lesbian and gay commitment ceremonies in the post-Stonewall era and part of the age-old repertoire of responses to ritual forms of all kinds. Rituals are all about transforming ordinary time into something special, about infusing the mundane with a hint of the supernatural. Their impact transcends particular historical moments at the same time that they draw their content from the cultural context in which they are situated. Rituals not only remind us of what is important in our culture but permit us to experience that as our own need and desire, as authentic and personal; as Victor Turner puts it, ritual "periodically converts the obligatory into the desirable."[1]

How do rituals do this? Anthropologists have defined rituals as formal action that is highly structured, repetitive, frequently redundant, and imbued with symbolization.[2] On perhaps the simplest level, rituals teach or reinforce the proper way to live, the values that a people hold in common, and the behaviors that are expected of them. In this sense, rituals act as tools that teach and reinforce *conformity*, imbuing it with intensity and personal meaning. Rituals do this, in part, by resolving or mediating contradictions and paradoxes that undermine structural integrity or challenge fundamental cultural principles. They achieve this effect, in general, not by presenting simple or unidimensional symbolic formulations but through their ability to evoke multiple meanings sequentially or simultaneously, what anthropologists call the *multivocality* or *polysemy* of symbols.[3]

Rather than necessarily communicating a particular lesson directly, then, a vital dimension of ritual symbolism is its ambiguity, the fact that the symbols deployed do not have a single precise meaning but can be understood differently by different people who participate in or witness rituals.[4] Because rituals affect not only those who are their subjects or performers but also communicate to audience and bystanders, their nonspecificity is a key element of their effectiveness.

Scholars have focused on this integrative aspect of ritual process from a variety of perspectives, a number of which inform my study of gay and lesbian weddings. The question that underlies all of these approaches concerns the mechanism or process whereby rituals and the symbols that constitute them have their effect or make their point. In a ritual, anthropologist Clifford Geertz tells us, "the world as lived and the world as imagined, fused under the agency of a single set of symbolic forms, turn out to be the same world." That is, symbolic systems generate a model, in Geertz's terms, both "of" and "for" reality. "Cultural patterns have an intrinsic double aspect: they give meaning, that is objective conceptual form, to social and psychological reality both by shaping themselves to it and by shaping it to themselves." Here Geertz speaks not only of religious rituals but of a wider class of phenomena that, following Milton Singer, he has called "cultural performances," occasions that merge audience and actors into a collectively (but, as I have already indicated, not necessarily uniformly) experienced event.[5]

"Genres of cultural performances," to quote anthropologist Victor Turner, "are not simple mirrors but magical mirrors of social reality: they exaggerate, invert, re-form, magnify, minimize, dis-color, re-color, even deliberately falsify, chronicled events. They resemble Rilke's 'hall of mirrors,' rather than represent a simple mirror-image of society."[6] Turner includes a range of narrated events as varieties of cultural performance— myths, rites, folk epics, ballads, dramas, and social dramas. In the words of another anthropologist, Barbara Myerhoff, these forms play out the plural "self-knowledge" of a group; they undermine the distinction between myth and reality, subjective and objective, and assure that "we receive experience rather than belief," combining elements to make a particular reality convincing, and validating such experience with the testimony of witnesses. "Cultural performances," Myerhoff explains, "are reflective in the sense of showing ourselves to ourselves. They are also capable of being reflexive, arousing consciousness of ourselves as we see ourselves. As heroes in our own dramas, we are made self-aware, conscious of our consciousness. At once actor and audience, we may then come into the fullness of our human capability—and perhaps human desire—to watch ourselves and enjoy knowing that we know. All this requires skill, craft, a coherent, consensually validated set of symbols and social arenas for appearing. It also requires an audience in addition to performers." As Turner notes, cultural performances may also be embedded in activity we think of as "play," which in many cultures has assumed functions otherwise acted out in the ritual domain; among these genres are carnivals and public festivals, and also games, contests, competitions, mimicry, and other theatrical events.[7]

These approaches help us to understand that the messages conveyed by rituals and cultural performances may not always be transparent. They may not only symbolize conformity to shared values and a commitment to meet the expectations of one's family and community; they may also act to oppose or parody the established order, but in doing so to vent hostilities as cathartic, "safety-value" mechanisms that, instead of overthrowing the existing system, finally act to preserve it.

Such rituals, which social anthropologist Max Gluckman termed *rituals of rebellion,* "entail dramatization of the moral relations of the group concerned" and are effective because they reveal "all the tensions and strife inherent in social life itself." Gluckman focused in particular on ceremonial events whose explicit messages are of opposition to or parody of the status quo. He classifies a number of different kinds of ceremonies in this way, but points out that all exhibit particular common features. "Whatever the ostensible purpose of the ceremonies, a most striking feature of their organization is the way in which they openly express social tensions: women have to assert licence and dominance as against their formal subordination to men, princes have to behave to the king as if they covet the throne, and subjects openly state their resentment of authority." These rituals emerge, Gluckman argues, when disputes really address the distribution of power rather than the nature of the system itself. "This allows for instituted protest, and in complex ways renews the unity of the system." The apparent discord, according to Gluckman and others drawing on the Durkheimian functionalist tradition, in no way actually implies opposition to the existing system; rather, rituals allow for the dispersal of resentments and stress so that in the end the system may continue and actually be strengthened.[8]

This concern with ritual's potential to dramatize and thus resolve points of strain in social systems has provided a foundation for an extensive literature in history and anthropology that offers compelling readings of such events, sometimes called *rituals of reversal,* in a wide range of cultures around the world and in various historical periods in the West. McKim Marriott's account of an Indian festival, for example, emphasizes the way the apparently riotous event could be viewed as ritualized reversal of everyday social stratification. High-caste men are abused on this one day by members of the low castes, and women, particularly low-caste women, deliver "beatings" to upper-caste men. Anthropologists who take these positions argue that pent-up hostilities need to be expressed so that opposing groups can continue to live together in relative harmony.[9]

All these approaches draw on a notion of psychological mechanics that represents frustration and the injustice which gives rise to it almost as physical forces that will destroy the equilibrium of a social system unless they are regularly vented. How a ritual of rebellion might expand to become an actual rebellion is not explicitly addressed in these schemes, though some scholars suggest that the relative fragility of the system in question might determine whether or not it can survive such symbolic challenges.[10]

But other scholars have approached the question of rebellion from a very different perspective. For those concerned with the conditions that work to undermine established authority, the study of rituals of rebellion shifts to the study of *rituals of resistance*, highlighting the actually disruptive effects of some ritual behavior. In his work on political ritual, for example, David Kertzer has emphasized the dual potential of ritual to have "both a conservative bias and innovatory potential."[11] This possibility for change comes from the constancy of rituals over time; that is, because memories associated with rituals color each subsequent performance, because they link the present to the past, they also can, by extension, represent a relationship between the present and the future. Invention and tradition become merged, as old materials are reshaped for new purposes, and history facilitates creativity.

Thus, rituals also offer mechanisms for symbolizing opposition to domination, *resistance* to hegemonic power. Jean Comaroff's work on the Tshidi of South Africa–Botswana provides a helpful account of the use of ritual as a medium both for resistance to and for compliance with colonial domination, bringing to light the complex relationship between these two dimensions of social action. Zionist Christianity among the Tshidi, Comaroff argues, reconfigures the meanings associated with colonial domination, turning "the structures of Western orthodoxy inside out, transforming marginality into esteem and subordination into defiance." While confrontations with the ruling powers may not be immediate or even readily traceable to the transformations generated by these symbolic means, they may set the stage for revolt at a later stage, though their most immediate, and perhaps superficial, effect may be to redirect dissatisfaction and ventilate anger, thus seeming to enhance people's cooperation with their rulers.[12]

Lesbian and Gay Weddings as Ritual, Rebellion, and Resistance

The tendency of these approaches to ritual has been to dichotomize resistance and accommodation as symbolic processes. But as the debate over whether the gay/lesbian civil rights struggle should move toward demanding the right to marry has developed, dispute has raged over whether same-sex marriage constitutes a callow effort to fit into the mainstream or a bold rebellion against the limitations of a rigid gender hierarchy. As discussed in chapter 1, while some proponents of gay marriage argue that it will convincingly demonstrate the underlying equality (and therefore equal value) of gay and straight relationships, other proponents favor it as a move that will aggressively challenge the assumptions at the heart of heterosexual marriage. Opponents bring similar concerns to the debate. Conservative adversaries of same-sex marriage claim that it will undermine the very foundation on which "family values" are built; radical foes of pursuing marriage believe that it will compromise the outsider status of gay men and lesbians, disrupting their ability to be "queer."

While focusing on resistance can alert us to the many strategies available to subordinated people to undermine the authority of their oppressors, this focus can sometimes suffer from a tendency to glorify virtually anything as "resistance," justifying this reading of behavior more from wishful thinking than from empirical evidence. Writing as an anthropologist, I submit instead that our task is to discover the meaning of symbols and other cultural materials from the "native" perspective, which may be more concerned with conformity and integration than with ironic transformations of cultural commonplaces. My priority here is to convey the meanings lesbians and gay men attribute to their experiences; while I will note the inconsistencies and contradictions that these meanings may generate, I will not attribute resistance to persons who are determined to conform, or assume conformity where persons perceive themselves to be subversive.

The intensely contested, politically charged atmosphere within which gay and lesbian weddings are performed ensures that everyone present, not only the immediate participants, will derive meaning from the events that are played out in rituals. In this latter group might be included not only the guests (typically, friends, family, coworkers) but the officiant (clergy or lay person) who performs the ceremony and the caterers, waiters, musicians, and other service providers involved in its realization.[13]

Unraveling Stories

This book is the product of a kind of ethnographic inquiry that profits from the view that texts (in all their verbal and written manifestations) may be considered as cultural materials as readily as observed behaviors. From this perspective, written texts, other cultural artifacts, observations, and interview data are significant not only insofar as they furnish explicit information about the community or other cultural unit under study, but as they themselves constitute examples of cultural process. As "accounts" or "stories" such materials may not be verifiable or replicable (in the sense of being scientifically reliable) even as they offer an authentic, though possibly fleeting, understanding of events and ideas. In other words, the literal accuracy of participants' stories is viewed here as less significant than what the crafting of the stories reveals about culture.

This approach owes much to recent developments in anthropology and in feminist and lesbian/gay scholarship. Though narrative analysis has had its most significant elaboration in analyses of literary works, its influence has been felt strongly in anthropology and ethnographic writing. In part, this approach has been inspired by efforts to examine narrative materials as equivocal and ambiguous products of particular historical moments; that is, informants tell stories not only to convey information but to express various kinds of truths. Writing about the Northern California Indian world in which he was raised, Greg Sarris has observed that stories emerge interactively, often juxtaposing elements outsiders may not understand to be connected and depending heavily for their realization on the social context in which they are produced. Stories are removed from their subject matter; an autobiography, he reminds us, "is not the life but an account or story of the life." In a similar vein, Renato Rosaldo has written of how the Ilongot of the Philippines craft hunting narratives that are not only about what occurred on particular hunting forays but that reveal fundamental cultural understandings. "Huntsmen in fact seek out experiences that can be told as stories. In other words, stories often shape, rather than simply reflect, human conduct."[14]

In my 1993 book *Lesbian Mothers*, I focused on the ways in which the *accounts* mothers produced of what it meant to be a mother not only described real events in their lives (which they sometimes did) but were also efforts to explain and define motherhood in interaction with a person (me) they knew did not share this identity. In other words, the stories mothers told me were both about how life was and how it should be; it was in their latter guise that the stories constituted or represented *culture*. William Leap, following Arthur Kleinman's usage, calls this process "retrospective narratization," referring to the ways in which "narratives reconstruct original action more than they actually reproduce it." Rather than seeking a literal recapitulation of experience, then, this understanding of narrative alerts us to its constructedness and potential variability.[15]

Making a similar point in *Families We Choose*, Kath Weston shows how ten coming out stories serve both as windows into actual events and feelings and as creations that meet particular formal and narrative criteria. Coming out stories have some obligatory elements: a discussion of whether one's family "knows" and how they responded if they do, illustrations of biographical continuity (i.e., evidence that one was "always" gay), and elaboration of negative or persecutory episodes, particularly if they have notable dramatic or suspenseful elements.[16] In other words, a coming out story not only relates a particular individual's experience of coming to terms with her/his homosexuality and making that information known to others, but reveals basic notions of what homosexual identity is all about: that the reaction of one's family of origin is a matter of great concern; that gayness is perceived as part of one's essential being; and that hostility from the outside world is an expected consequence of being known to be gay.

Narrative analysis of ethnographic materials has been particularly influential in recent works by feminist anthropologists and by some feminist scholars from other disciplines.[17] For example, Faye Ginsburg's *Contested Lives* allows fundamental parallels between the disparate accounts— what Ginsburg calls "procreation stories"—of pro-choice and antiabortion activists in Fargo, North Dakota, to emerge in their telling and thus to make a perhaps unwelcome cultural point convincing—that women representing these two conflicting positions share some fundamental similarities. In her study of Bedouin women's stories, *Writing Women's Worlds*, Lila Abu-Lughod uses the contrast between women's narratives and conventional categories of anthropological analysis to comment on the ways in which meanings are constructed in the course of explaining action. And

Margery Wolf's *A Thrice-Told Tale* makes clear how interpretation is a critical element of every presentation of a story, as her three versions—fictional, field notes, and anthropological article—offer different senses of authenticity and believability.[18]

In all of these works and in other innovative examples of ethnographic writing that draw on these techniques, narratives are examined as much more than evidence of cultural systems or as a way of finding out what people do under particular circumstances. Rather, the narratives stand on their own as a form of culture that has a life both as it is told and as it is written down and interpreted. Audiences witness and are instructed by narratives, and the relevant audiences are not only participants in narrators' cultures but observers (such as anthropologists) and those who read their interpretations. Perhaps the most significant witnesses, in a way, are the narrators themselves, for as they construct their stories they engage in a process of explaining their own worlds to themselves, thereby conceptualizing who they are.

Taking a Stance

Recent anthropological writings have insisted on the importance of making the investigator's position integral to the analysis. These writings have called into question the notion of neutrality or objectivity, and both positionality and reflexivity have come to be expected of the conscientious ethnographer. In part, this emphasis reflects a growing recognition of the instability of ethnographic data and the equivocal nature of what was once casually considered to be "true." Those promoting reflexivity have spoken convincingly of the collaborative nature of ethnography and have recognized that studies of the "same" culture by different investigators cannot be expected to replicate one another.[19] In marked contrast to earlier claims to absolute objectivity and the assumption that the ethnographer should be an "outsider" in every respect, anthropologists seeking to reduce the "orientalism" they believe results from such approaches have spoken in favor of investigators studying groups they themselves belong to.[20] The older disdain for "insider" research (sometimes) has been transformed into admiration for efforts to manipulate the position of native and observer into some semblance of the ethnographic gaze, a shift mirrored in the new literature on the dynamics and dilemmas of insider research or research by "native anthropologists."[21]

The valorization of studying "one's own" emerged with particular emphasis in the development of the anthropology of women, as feminist scholars sought to remedy the long silence of the ethnographic literature on women with a new ethnography produced by women themselves. Implicit in attempting this task was the notion that femaleness transcended geographical and cultural boundaries, and that women investigators would necessarily share some ineffable something with the women they studied. These expectations have also characterized the development of an anthropology of homosexuality; scholars working in this area were usually assumed by the rest of the profession to be gay themselves—who else, after all, would be interested in this unappealing topic? At the same time, gay and lesbian anthropologists unreflectively defined homosexual populations as their "tribe," reinforcing this same expectation and implying that incursions by "non-natives" into our territory smacked of colonialism and exploitation. Some lesbian and gay anthropologists have addressed these assumptions in recent essays on fieldwork, suggesting that other dimensions of identity, including the professional identity as anthropologist, insert difference into the relationship between ethnographer and subject.[22]

The uncertain identifications that insider research depend on are thus no less problematic for gay and lesbian studies. While some investigators believe that sharing the sexual orientation of their subjects promotes trust and allows them more ready access to the community,[23] others have made clear that being gay does not necessarily open doors or assure that they receive unhesitating cooperation, particularly when race, nationality, generational, and class differences loom larger than sexual orientation in defining notions of identity.[24] All of these field situations highlight the difficulties insider researchers experience in determining whether they fully share the meanings informants place on their behavior. As Stephen Murray has remarked, even the most intimate interactions between anthropologist and informant are not replicas of ordinary behavior in a culture; they tell us more about how the informant responds to the investigator than about what they might do under ordinary circumstances.[25]

Kirin Narayan has put a somewhat different spin on this issue, speaking of what she calls the "halfie"—the investigator who is both of and not of the culture she studies. On the one hand, the halfie may share characteristics such as race, nationality, or ethnicity with the people under study, but on the other hand, her immersion in an academic discipline (probably in a Western academic setting) compromises this identity and leads to a fluctuating or partial identification between native and observer. Elaborating on this insight, Lila Abu-Lughod calls for halfies, by virtue of their "split selves," to mediate between speaking "for" and speaking "from," taking their shifting and uncertain positionality into account so as to disrupt the tendency toward seamless descriptions of culture.[26]

Ethnographies animated by these approaches question the significance of boundaries and undermine assumptions about the stability, continuity, and reliability of the social units once at the heart of the anthropological imagination. These works confront the notions that the objects of ethnographic inquiry are necessarily what they seem to be and that actors are merely buffeted by the exigencies of culture rather than purposefully acting upon their environments. They demand, furthermore, that we ethnographers acknowledge our complicity in shaping and even inventing the phenomena we mean to study.[27]

Concerns about the place of the enterprise many have chosen to call "writing culture" in a world steeped in inequality and polluted by the heritage of colonialism have given rise to a questioning of form and expression that urges anthropologists to be more innovative and experimental, and above all, to be more reflexive in their writing. While the now-famous collection *Writing Culture* called on anthropologists to be self-conscious about how both their writing and the position from which it flows shape the object, or ethnography, that results,[28] a more recent feminist-inspired response[29] asks even more searching questions about how the identity of the investigator and the object of study intersect both in research and writing.[30] The incorporation of feminist perspectives into the theoretical repertoire of contemporary anthropology, then, has intensified these discussions, particularly as feminist scholars have insisted that reflexivity must be central to a properly situated ethnographic stance.

It should be clear by now, considering this changing ethnographic environment, that the methods used in this volume cannot help but have been affected by my personal experience of the ritual form I was investigating.[31] My earlier work on lesbian mothers was vitally marked by my own removal from the domain of parenthood: I had never been a mother and there were few mothers in my immediate social circle. As I soon learned, lesbian mothers tended to label both other lesbians and other women in terms of their maternal status; they assumed that non-mothers could not possibly understand the contours of their lives and that mothers and non-mothers differed from one another in terms of essential moral stature.

By the time I unraveled the narratives mothers offered me, I began to understand that among other dynamics they had formulated their stories for a non-mother. The mothers tended to emphasize the moral attributes of motherhood and the central part motherhood played in the way they constructed and conceptualized their identities, highlighting the ways that they saw themselves as fundamentally different from women who did not have children. How their narratives would have been shaped had I also been a mother I cannot know, but I feel sure that they would have been different, if not in substance, then in emphasis. I was an outsider in my research on lesbian mothers, and that fact shaped the narratives—the "data"—as much as the actual experience of the women I interviewed.

In the Field

My work on wedding and commitment ceremonies has a very different basis. As a veteran of a ceremony of my own, I always introduced myself to potential narrators by telling them briefly about my personal experience. I often injected humor into these opening comments, invoking the comical image of myself and my partner—two people with degrees in anthropology caught up in the experience of their own ceremony but still, perhaps perversely, driven to analyze its every detail. Some narrators asked me to tell them more about my ceremony, often after the interview was completed, effecting an exchange that at least in part equalized the encounter. In a number of cases, they invited me to bring my partner along on visits, or invited us to dinner, to their wedding, or to some other social occasion. Others had few direct questions, but simply understood that I was a sympathetic person, that unlike some others of their acquaintance, I would not regard their ceremony as bizarre, parodic, or illegitimate. Some narrators still in the planning stages perceived me instrumentally as an "expert" on lesbian and gay weddings and sought my advice about good locations for their ceremonies or persons who might officiate; many simply asked me about other gay couples' weddings, curious as to whether their experience was "typical."

Because the focus of this inquiry has been on a particular cultural phenomenon rather than on a geographically or behaviorally bounded community, I gathered information using both traditional methods of participant observation at lesbian and gay weddings and lengthy open-ended interviews with couples who had already had or were planning commitment ceremonies, with clergy involved in such ceremonies, with attorneys and community activists concerned with the civil rights ramifications of these events, and occasionally with other persons who have participated in lesbian or gay weddings in some capacity. Since many of the couples I interviewed had recorded their ceremonies using videotape or still photography, I have had access to videotapes of a large number of ceremonies and have been able to examine numerous photograph albums and other materials generated in connection with weddings: invitations, letters to family and friends, texts of vows and liturgies, ritual objects used in ceremonies, programs, guest books, and the like.

During the time I was working on the project, I also attended a number of political and public events related to same-sex weddings and the legalization of lesbian/gay marriage, including a conference for lawyers and law students concerned with the legal status of gay/lesbian families, the first ceremony for domestic partner registrants to be held in San Francisco, two workshops for couples planning weddings, an amateur play (put on by a local church) about a gay wedding, and a number of performance pieces by gay and lesbian artists which took up this theme. By the time I finished writing, I had interviewed twenty-two male couples and thirty female couples and attended eight ceremonies in person. Without a research budget that would have enabled me to sample systematically from various parts of the country or to interview a larger and more diverse group of narrators, I conducted most of my interviews in the wider San Francisco Bay area with people located through a variety of referrals and personal introductions, a technique sometimes called a "modified snowball."[32] The limitations of this method were exacerbated by the pressure I felt to complete the research as expeditiously as possible so as to contribute to the national discussion around the Hawaiian same-sex marriage case. These conditions all had an effect on the shape of the sample and are particularly evident in the racial breakdown of the participants, the majority of whom were white, though many couples brought together individuals of different ethnic, class, or cultural backgrounds. Nine of the couples were of mixed racial heritage, with three including an African-American partner, six a Latino/a partner, and one a South Asian. Participants' religious backgrounds were quite varied, with Roman Catholicism, mainstream and fundamentalist Protestant denominations, Judaism, Wicca, and Islam all represented.

Whenever possible, I took advantage of travel arrangements made for other purposes to conduct some interviews in other parts of the country: two in New York City, two in Atlanta, and one in a Midwestern university town, in addition to attending "the Wedding" at the 1993 National March on Washington (see chapter 1). Journalistic accounts, both in the gay and mainstream media, and several popular works published in recent years amply attest to the proliferation of same-sex ceremonies around the country and make clear that these rituals are not exclusively a big-city or a San Francisco phenomenon.[33]

Each of the ceremonies I witnessed and was told about, each of the weddings I will describe in these chapters has its own dynamic and rationale, its own particular style and flair, just as each illustrates the wider genre of American same-sex weddings. Though I am mindful of the artificiality and potential objectification that comes from freezing real-life experiences in the fiction of an "ethnographic present," unless otherwise indicated the accounts that follow will locate the interviews (which took place between 1993 and 1996) in a grammatically consistent present.

In contrast to my earlier experience working with lesbian mothers, who had serious concerns about confidentiality and anonymity, most of the couples I interviewed in this study were willing, and even eager, to have their real names appear in print. Many pointed out to me that by getting married they were, in effect, making a public proclamation of their identities that was not compatible with any form of concealment. Their openness recalled the desire for recognition expressed by the elderly Jews whose lives Barbara Myerhoff documented in her film, *Number Our Days*.[34] But even the most open informants sometimes hesitated before telling stories about other people in their lives, displaying a concern for the privacy of others that seemed to constrain their ability to be candid.

My preference, from the start, however, has been to adhere to the anthropological tradition of anonymity for informants, particularly because I was reluctant for the portraits of lesbians and gay men I present to be understood as solely about the specific people named or to be perceived primarily as history. I have, for these reasons, identified the cast of characters in these pages by pseudonyms, except for those few cases in which particular individuals have had well-known historical roles that would make use of such devices inappropriate or confusing. In those instances where pseudonyms are used, the first appearance of the name will be marked with quotation marks.

My argument in these pages is twofold. On the one hand, I will make clear that no single lesbian or gay wedding is typical or exemplary, since each event can and does articulate many different sorts of symbolic points. But at the same time, I will also contend that same-sex weddings are cultural constructions grounded in a particular social, political, and historical context in which gender is an embattled domain and inequality based on sexual orientation has become visible to a perhaps unprecedented degree. As such, these ceremonies draw on related sources of meaning and stand together as coherent reflections of what it means to be gay and American on the eve of the millennium.

This analysis of lesbian and gay weddings is arrayed around five key themes that can be enacted or elaborated in particular same-sex ceremonies. Using extended narratives and descriptions to launch my discussion, I view ceremonies in terms of the salience of one (or more) particular thematic elements. Other themes might have been selected; I make no claim to crafting an exhaustive analysis of these exceedingly rich rituals. But I will, at the very least, argue that the five themes I do elaborate—tradition, family, community, authenticity, and resistance—have been central both to the articulation of gay culture as it has unfolded in recent years and to the definition of American culture.

Chapter 3 takes up the theme of *tradition*, demonstrating some of the varied ways that lesbian and gay couples come to understand the commitment rituals they construct either in terms of their rigorous conformity to something they understand as established tradition, or in terms of their insurrection against such tradition. In both cases, the articulation of tradition is revealed to be a strategy for conveying particular representations of the self, or for making statements about the place of one's relationship in the wider social constellation. The symbolic elements lesbian and gay couples devise for their ceremonies reveal both novel representations enriched by humor and wit, and seemingly straightforward reliance on tried, true, and conventional depictions of marriage and family.

In chapter 4 I consider the representation of *family*, looking in detail at the ways in which gay and lesbian commitment ceremonies celebrate or delineate specific concepts and expectations about the bonds of kinship. Weddings can make these statements in a number of ways. Rhetorical strategies use ceremonial texts and liturgical elements to declaim on the subject of family. At the same time, inspection of the guest list and of actual participants in the ritual can reveal couples' beliefs and ideals about the constitution of family; who is invited, what they are asked to do, and how couples react if invited relatives fail to meet specific expectations can tell us much about the definitions and meanings that attach to particular kinship categories.

I move on to the complicated question of *community* in chapter 5. Weddings are often occasions that enable actors to express particular ideas about community boundaries and membership. Because some couples define themselves as coming from different ethnic or racial backgrounds, for example, their weddings may offer the opportunity for them to claim either the indissolubility of these diverse origins or to propose ways to collapse and resolve differences. Here a variety of expressive solutions may be brought into play: costumes, language, and music may recall ethnic or cultural traditions and may be used in varied ways to comment on couple's affinities, reminding participants of how they imagine their identities to be constituted. At the same time, affiliations may also be visualized as amounting to community membership. Here such sources of personal identity as politics, sexual preferences, and particular cultural interests may emerge as ways of defining the self (and the couple) comparable to ethnicity and race.

Chapter 6 is concerned with the ways in which lesbian and gay weddings describe and define a domain that I call *authenticity*. Since same-sex marriage is not recognized legally and rarely receives the legitimation extended to heterosexual unions, establishing that their relationship is what they claim it to be—that is, a marriage—is a problem that faces every gay and lesbian couple. Same-sex weddings typically deploy and elaborate the key symbol of "love" to remind guests and actors that the celebrants partake of the most important element in American marriages. It might be argued that in the absence of easy expression of either "blood" or "law" (the central symbols of American kinship identified by David Schneider),[35] "love" takes on a salience it might not otherwise require. At the same time, the blessing and support of God (or some other spiritual force) can also be called upon to reinforce the connection between the union in question and a more inclusive domain of the divine. Such symbols make an end run around stigma, arguing that the sacred support revealed in the ceremony supersedes or invalidates secular disapproval.

Finally, in chapter 7, I argue that lesbian and gay weddings can also excel at representing *resistance* to gender conventions and heterosexist hegemonies. In some cases, the playful and humorous devices actors use to construct their ceremonies offer a vehicle for expressing basic opposition to mainstream society. Couples may understand such representations as primarily consisting in the display of a "queer" sensibility, while at other times (or simultaneously), they manipulate ceremonial content to invoke particular political messages. Perhaps paradoxically, perceptions of the symbolic directions taken in ceremonies may vary among participants; here we see that couples' stated intentions may sometimes be contradicted by the interpretations of guests and other actors and that couples may not necessarily agree on the meaning of specific ritual moves. Symbols couples intend to invoke resistance may instead suggest complicity with cultural norms, while other symbols explicitly meant to suggest conformity may be understood to subvert and undermine heteronormativity.

This approach will make clear that an analysis of gay/lesbian weddings is more than what it first appears to be. Beyond a simple description of the ritual content and process, an examination of these performances facilitates three projects: (1) an enhanced understanding of the dynamics of North American lesbian and gay life in the post-Stonewall era; (2) more generally, a window into significant features of American cultures as they take shape on the eve of the twenty-first century; and (3) a further development in the ongoing anthropological study of ritual processes.

We will see, as well, that these multiple interpretative goals may be reached even though (or perhaps because) lesbian and gay weddings (like other cultural phenomena) are neither consistent, coherent, nor seamless. They embody contradiction and contentiousness, and as such are apt vehicles for understanding the seemingly incoherent expression of the diversity and competition that are defining features of postmodernity and its symbolic representations.

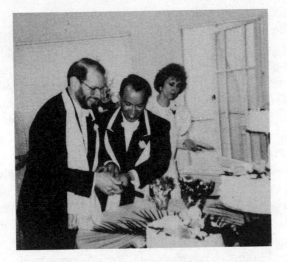

3

OLD SYMBOLS, NEW TRADITIONS

I t started off as a theatrical performance, a series of sketches generated by the ensemble at Theatre Rhinoceros, a gay/lesbian repertory theater company in San Francisco. *Jumping the Broom*, the production that played at the theater in the fall of 1993, celebrated and lampooned the politics and culture of gay weddings and relationships, offering vignettes and monologues on domestic partnership, formal weddings, making contracts and wills, and a host of other topics suggested by the wider theme of gay marriage. While the show was ignored by the mainstream press during its successful run, it was lauded by gay critics and played to enthusiastic audiences from around the Bay Area.[1]

Associate artistic director Doug Holsclaw's expectation at the start of the three-year process leading up to the final production was that the

Cutting the cake

show would be largely comical in tone, but also that by presenting a wide
variety of lesbian and gay commitment practices it would reveal a distinctive and presumably subversive gay and lesbian sensibility at odds
with heterosexual wedding conventions. But after eliciting work from
gay playwrights around the country and refining their submissions during months of improvisational workshops, he and his colleagues found
they had to acknowledge that something quite different from what they
had anticipated seemed to be going on. "What we found out, to a certain
extent, was not how *different* we are, but how the *same* we are in some
ways," he told me. "There was something old-fashioned, wholesome, and
traditional that did seem to be at the core of wherever we looked. . . . We
tried to have a well-rounded show, but there wasn't any getting away
from that kind of romantic, idyllic thing that people shoot for." Holsclaw
expected to find political issues at the heart of the marriage question, but
was surprised to find that religious and family concerns loomed at least
as large for writers, actors, and audience members alike.

Theatre Rhino's artistic director, Adele Prandini, was the first to think
of creating a situation that would allow life to imitate art. "Neil Roberts"
and "Dennis Gilmore" didn't really expect that they would ever have a
commitment ceremony when they found themselves conversing with
Prandini on opening night of *Jumping the Broom*. The two men had been
together for over ten years but had never actively entertained the idea of
getting married. But as Neil explains,

> We were talking about the play and gay marriages and all, and we had
> maybe mentioned that our friends were after us [to have a ceremony],
> and we just never really took the initiative and did anything about it.
> And she said, "I've been having this thought of having at the closing
> night . . . a real ceremony." And she said, "How would you like to do
> that?" And I was the first to raise my hand and say, "Yes, let's do that."

The spontaneous decision to celebrate their union in the context of a
theatrical event evolved, by the end of the play's run, into a life-imitating-
art spectacle that combined playfulness, politics, and sentiment and lent
the Theatre Rhino production a unique element of veracity. Neil had
grown up attending a Pentacostal church, and he explained that this background made him uncomfortable with the idea of appropriating what he
felt was essentially a religious experience. But he also was a sometime
actor, and when the possibility of carrying out the ceremony in a theatrical context presented itself, he "ran with the ball." As long as the ceremo-

ny was entirely secular, he explained, "It was fun for me to come up with something that I actually felt and that wasn't religious but would still communicate the feelings and the connections and emotions and commitment and love and all of those things that we have ... so others could understand and experience it."

Although neither Neil nor Dennis has talked about homosexuality explicitly with his family, they explained to me that both sets of relatives are extremely accepting of their integrity as a couple. They are always included in family celebrations and holiday observances, though because Dennis's family lives in the Bay Area and Neil's in South Carolina, their involvement with the Gilmore clan has been more frequent. Dennis's nieces and nephews call Neil "Uncle Neil" and Dennis's father usually greets Neil with a huge bearhug whenever they meet. They both feel fortunate that their families are so accepting, and are perhaps a little amazed that this is the case considering the Gilmores' longtime involvement in a Pentacostal church and the Roberts' Catholicism. While they told me that they have every intention of putting together wills and other legal documents that will protect the survivor in case of his partner's death, they also have no fear that their families will fail to respect their wishes should they never get around to completing these arrangements.

Since their ceremony at Theatre Rhinoceros was organized as "a continuation of the play," however, they never imagined it as an occasion that should include their families. (Moreover, Neil's relatives are all back East, so fairness dictated, as they explained to me, that Dennis's relatives not be included either.) Dennis and Neil received ten complementary tickets to that night's performance for a contingent of friends, who settled strategically in the front row, but the "attendants" were made up of cast members, who lined up on each side of the stage after their curtain calls, framing the couple in an arrangement reminiscent of bridesmaids and groomsmen in a conventional wedding. The remainder of the audience, more than one hundred strong, who had been notified at the intermission that this "real" ceremony would occur at the conclusion of the play, remained in their seats, instantly transformed from audience to witnesses and community.

Dennis and Neil's attire, devised by Neil, was intended to nod at the usual wedding formality of black and white, while actually being casual. They wore black Levi's and white shirts with, in Dennis's case, a silver and black knit tie and casual black jacket, and in Neil's a gray and white striped vest. Dennis explained that while their outfits harmonized, they were intentionally not the same, conveying the "uniqueness of each of us." The message of unity-with-individuality also determined the use of three candles in the ceremony. At the beginning of the ceremony, each man lit a single candle, showing, as Neil told me, that "we were separate and we were joining in a union, and we lit the one [center] candle together at the end. But it didn't mean we were one person." They self-consciously defined the event as a "commitment ceremony," seeing the term *wedding* not only as the province of religion but as being inalterably "heterosexual." Nevertheless, Neil relied upon what he described as a vast array of wedding-related sources to devise the text of the ceremony. "I did whatever I could to make it unique, and not be so heterosexual, and yet there were still some aspects of it that would probably still be considered traditional."

Adele Prandini, from Theatre Rhino, officiated. She began by welcoming the audience.

> Let us join in celebration. We have been invited to share the joy of this moment with Neil and Dennis. We are their family and friends and together we form a community. Let us witness their commitment. Today you are presenting yourselves in the context of community to declare your intention of uniting your lives voluntarily and on record. The achievement of this purpose will require officiation of each other's abilities and virtues, forgiveness of each other's faults, unfailing devotion to each other's welfare and development. I encourage you to share willingly and sympathetically your joys and your wounds, your successes and your struggles, and to be neither conceited by the former nor depressed by the latter. Whichever may prevail, cling closely to each other, that defeats may be met with united strength and victories by united joy.
>
> Neil and Dennis, before you lies a future with its hopes and disappointments, its successes and its failures, its pleasures and its pains, its joys and its sorrows. These hours are mingled in every life and are to be expected. Do you affirm your purpose in a deeper union whereby you both shall know joy and fulfillment as one?
>
> Neil and Dennis, in unison: We do.

The two men then offered each other brief vows in which they promised to share life's sorrows and joys, to respect and forgive one another, and to instill hope each in the other. They then exchanged rings "as outer pledge and symbol of [our] promise to fulfill the vows that we have taken." The exchange of rings was followed by the lighting of the single "unity" candle, and then by a kiss.[2] At this point, the audience burst into applause, cheering the couple as a large wedding cake and bottles of champagne were brought onto the stage.

Looking back on that night several months later, Theatre Rhino's Doug Holsclaw remarked on the unanticipated power the brief ceremony had on actors and staff.

> It was a fairly traditional little thing, very short and simple. But it had this great feeling about it. It was silly, because I hadn't anticipated this reaction. But there was something almost like Christians-in-the-caves-doing-something forbidden, you know. They said their little thing. And they were all dressed up. And they did their things, and then they kissed, and Adele went like "Yes!" And the audience, the roof just went off the place. Because it was just . . . I don't know. It wasn't silly anymore. To use these overused words, there was something kind of empowering about just claiming this and doing this and it really was a nice feeling. . . . There was a kind of excitement that was much more so than I had anticipated.

Are Lesbian and Gay Weddings Rituals of Queerness?

Many discussions of the developing shape of Western cultures in the last decade of the twentieth century have focused on the extent to which new forms represent an amalgamation or pastiche of disparate elements drawn from a variety of sources. The inconsistencies and contradictions that characterize these forms coalesce in the aesthetic of "postmodernism," what Fredric Jameson describes as "that pure and random play of signifiers . . . which . . . ceaselessly reshuffles the fragments of preexistent texts, the building blocks of older cultural and social production, in some new and heightened bricolage: metabooks which cannibalize other books, metatexts which collate bits of other texts—such is the logic of postmodernism in general, which finds one of its strongest and most original, authentic forms in the new art of experimental video."[3]

These approaches have made us more conscious of departures from what were once assumed to be the basic building blocks of cultures and more attentive to instances in which they seem to have lost their relevance. Sociologist Judith Stacey, for example, has labeled the social form that is the outcome of "domestic upheavals" in California's Silicon Valley as "the postmodern family," by which she refers to a structure that in her view is crafted mainly by women to meet the exigencies of life in a new, unsettled terrain of divorce, drug culture, feminism, disparate spiritual quests, and economic uncertainty. According to Stacey, families manage these levels of indeterminacy by tolerating heightened variability in both form and behavior as new members are absorbed into the kinship constellation and compromises are fashioned to meet novel challenges. Echoing anthropologist Colleen Johnson's analysis of postdivorce kinship relations in another suburban outpost of the San Francisco Bay area, Stacey seems more impressed with the changes in family personnel that her informants report than in, to continue the metaphor, their job descriptions. Thus, the fact that families are constituted differently after divorces or in the face of particular economic pressures looms larger in these analyses than the fact that they remain "families" with all the meanings the culture attaches to that concept.[4]

Recent work in queer theory also draws on these perspectives. Particularly for those who posit "queer culture" as a unique concatenation of subversively incongruous elements, the self-consciously innovative, "brave new world" aura that attaches to presumptively distinctive gay/ lesbian cultural and social forms is more attractive than their possible resemblance to elements of the familiar. Creativity, in this reading, implies the overthrow of tradition, what Michael Warner calls "resistance to regimes of the normal." Thus, such scholars as Judith Butler (essentially reconfiguring the earlier insights of sociologists like Erving Goffman, Mary McIntosh, and Howard Becker) posit a performative foundation to gender that questions how substantial it really is. Butler calls for a reconsideration of our understanding of "woman," arguing that "there is no gender identity behind expressions of gender; that identity is performatively constituted by the very 'expressions' that are said to be its results."[5]

Earlier work on drag moves us toward a somewhat more subtle understanding of performativity and gender. In her classic ethnographic study *Mother Camp*, Esther Newton proposes that the professional drag queens she studied in the 1960s are engaged in a complex process of identity formation through the symbolic resources offered by drag. On the one hand, their representation of femininity allows them to claim that despite having men's bodies, their inner selves are "really" those of women. Conversely, and seemingly paradoxically, however, the very same symbolic strategies also permit a different assertion: that despite the female appearance they project with their costumes, their bodies, or their authentic selves, are those of men.[6]

Some social-psychological approaches to gender, notably a fascinating study by Suzanne Kessler and Wendy McKenna, support this performative reading of gender. Inspired by Howard Garfinkel's famous ethnomethodological study of the transsexual "Agnes," Kessler and McKenna argue that the biological insignia of gender, the characteristics that have conventionally been called "sex," are in many ways the product of a cognitive process of gender-labeling.[7] That is, we decide whether a person is a "man" or a "woman" and then ascribe particular biological features to that person. These characteristics may or may not be objectively present, but that has little relevance to the process Kessler and McKenna call "gender ascription."

Such questioning of the objective reality of gender has been amplified in recent years by two perspectives. The recent heightened visibility of queer identity and culture has emphasized gender classifications considerably more fluid than those derived from dichotomous notions of male and female.[8] Meanwhile, another vocal challenge to the reality of basic gender dichotomies has been posed by the transgender movement—or what one of its leading spokespersons, Leslie Feinberg, evoking a notion of history and perhaps even nationality, calls "transgender warriors."[9] Proponents of both these viewpoints have written across the spectrum, undermining the divisions of academic production and popular cultural representation (at least on those occasions when their theories are accessible to ordinary readers). We have come to a point where challenges to the conventionalities of gender and assumptions about the biological foundations of dichotomous sexual categories seem to be everywhere, and where "queerness" of all complexions presents itself as the heart of the current rebellion against gender conventions.

At first glance, gay and lesbian weddings would seem to epitomize the postmodern sensibility and the constructedness of cultural forms that these analysts have alerted us to. The process of creating a ceremony, of planning who will say what, who will wear what, and what everyone will do, is one that many gay men and lesbians understand as open and innovative. There are no rules, it seems, for what has to happen, particularly considering that from a legal point of view gay marriage doesn't even exist.

Organizing a ceremonial event can draw on the performative creativity that is a hallmark of gay culture, particularly as it has been elaborat-

ed in the camp sensibility of some gay men.[10] Rituals call for many theatrical mechanisms, and particularly the "dressing up" conventions of
weddings offer the opportunity to generate innovative gender expressions through manipulations of costume and decor.[11] The couple whose
relationship is the theme of the wedding are not only making a commitment to each other but representing themselves to a selected group of
witnesses—an audience, in essence. What they say, what they wear, and
how they choose to represent the connection between their ceremony
and conventional, heterosexual weddings, are all critical dimensions for
the construction of ritual.

But even as creativity is the star of many gay and lesbian weddings,
with startling and self-conscious versions of customs taking center stage,
celebrants tend to naturalize their choices, to understand them in the
framework of what they often call, without even a hint of irony, "tradition." The pastiche that results may summon up images of postmodernity, of parody, and camp, but experientially it is something else. The sort
of irony that also plays a role in postmodern expression and the tongue-
in-cheek bitterness that is frequently a trademark of camp are no more
characteristic of these ceremonies than they are of the families Stacey
studied in the Silicon Valley. While their *structure* may be postmodern,
then, the affect associated with them and hence the *meaning* to actors is
not. The creative process that shapes lesbian and gay weddings often con-
structs naturalness and authenticity; once construction is completed, it
is experienced as though it couldn't possibly have been otherwise.

Symbolic anthropologists have often reported that ritual recycles and
reconfigures old images even as it may intend to devise something new.
Observing that symbolic formulations are characterized by "multiplicity
of meaning," for example, Abner Cohen in *Two-Dimensional Man* points
to the process whereby "old symbols are rearranged to serve new purposes under new political conditions." This "conservative" characteristic
of symbolic systems is in some ways a contradiction; as Cohen concludes
from his examination of ethnic struggles and revolutionary movements,
"social change is effected through continuities." Old symbols may be retained, even as they come to have different meanings and functions. Recent Northern Irish economic and political struggles, for instance, may
be symbolized through a religious idiom with deep historical roots, just
as ethnic distinctions in the United States may come to be represented as
specific religious practices. Cohen also points out that symbolic evocations of family and kinship can be powerful vehicles for defining eco-

nomic relations in both developing and industrial societies, implying that particular ways of mobilizing networks are not only utilitarian but right, true, and natural.[12] Thus well-established kinship symbols come to be employed in very different contexts than in the past.

An examination of the meanings enacted in lesbian and gay weddings offers what may seem to be an unexpected site for a questioning of recent theories of performativity. These ritual occasions would seem, after all, to constitute textbook instances of the radical interrogation of nature, gender, and cultural order that has been celebrated in these analyses, to be performances that subvert tradition and sow disorder where stolid convention had ruled. But I will contend that no such clear tendency can be uncovered in these ceremonies, and that a close examination of their content and spirit will instead reveal processes whereby presumed outsiders make claims that both change and preserve tradition.

What's in a Wedding?

Religion or spirituality is conventionally a part of American weddings, even for couples who have little other involvement with organized religion. Catering halls and hotels often supply their clients with referrals to clergy willing to perform weddings for couples not affiliated with their denominations or with specific congregations. Churches—particularly in mainline Protestant denominations—may be wedding sites for couples who have no ordinary connection with them, and many churches, in fact, depend upon wedding rentals (along with rentals to twelve-step groups, community organizations, and child care centers) for part of their financial base.

Many lesbians and gay men also tend to imagine their weddings as occasions that demand some sort of religious or spiritual component. This dimension often functions as a way to elaborate a sense of connection with other sources of identity—ethnicity, race, and family tradition—beyond those derived from sexual orientation. (See chapter 5 for a more detailed discussion of these strategies.) But insofar as many religious denominations have negative or at least complicated views about homosexuality, establishing a relationship with many such institutions may require diplomacy, flexibility, and a host of symbolic strategies and reconfigurations of meaning.

Along with variations in the sort of religious expression deemed appropriate or desirable, gay and lesbian weddings, like heterosexual wed-

dividuality of the celebrants and which are historically and culturally specific. But just as the particular formal expressions that make up a commitment ritual stand alone at the moment of their performance, the explanations offered to account for them and the strategies celebrants seem to be pursuing reveal consistency and pattern.

"The Real World"

At first glance, the "celebration of union" for "Eric Alvarez" and "Allen Waters" held at San Francisco's First Unitarian-Universalist Church on a Saturday afternoon in June 1995 seemed like a pretty conventional affair. While I knew the reputation of Unitarian churches for almost limitless liturgical and doctrinal openness, and I was aware that the Unitarian-Universalists have championed the cause of same-sex marriage perhaps longer than any other mainstream denomination,[16] entering the massive stone edifice I still felt awed by the scale and momentousness of the place. The resonating organ intensified the "high church" sensation, a perception that was further dramatized when the large choir began to sing from its position in the loft overhead. Tuxedo-clad ushers offered programs and welcomed the guests. Liz and I filed in and quietly took our places in one of the pews. The crowd appeared to be mixed—gay and straight, male and female, old and young. Most were dressed in conservative but festive attire, suits and ties for men, sleek silk dresses and pantsuits for women. Formal flower arrangements decorated the altar.

The two grooms, both members of the choir as well as of this church, made their first appearance in the loft, each performing a tenor solo with the organ. We next saw them when they walked down the aisle hand in hand, after the minister, dressed in formal robes, and the best men—one of whom was Eric's brother—had entered and taken their places in front of the altar. Allen and Eric were wearing tuxedos, with white silk scarves draped over their shoulders; their boutonnieres, like those of the attendants, were white roses.

The acting pastor of the church officiated. The readings he selected, in characteristic Unitarian fashion, drew on diverse sources: a reading from Chief Dan George that dealt with love and its importance as a source of creativity and sacrifice, a poem by Walt Whitman, and the famous quotation from Corinthians (1 Cor. 13:4) on love, "Love is patient; love is kind; love is not envious or boastful or arrogant or rude. It does not insist on its own way; it is not irritable or resentful; it does not rejoice in wrongdoing, but rejoices in the truth. It bears all things, believes all things, hopes all things, endures all things."

In his homily, he commented on the ancient Chinese symbol of yin and yang to raise the question of how opposites can work together in dynamic interaction with one another. Using the image of a car battery with its two poles, he suggested that the spark between these poles offers recognition of the inherent oneness of the universe and reminds us of the power and energy that result from that underlying unity. Opposites in this example generate a positive tension, suggesting that there is greater personal potential to be achieved by bringing these opposites together than can exist for any individual struggling alone. By bringing their lives together, he concluded, Allen and Eric are responsible to the highest expression of self within each of them, the essence of I/thou. Following this homily, the choir sang J. S. Bach's "Alleluja."

At this point, Allen and Eric turned to face one another and grasped each other's hands. Allen, speaking in English, and Eric, speaking in Spanish, made identical vows, each promising his commitment to the other in this life and forever. Allen spoke first.

> My dearest Eric, this is my commitment to you: To always be here for you, in comfort and in joy, for good, for better, and for best; to always value your thoughts and feelings, even when they may differ from my own; to always be honest with you, even when that honesty may be hurtful; to always respect you as my best friend, my one and only love, and my soul mate, in this life and hereafter; and to never let anyone or anything become more important to me than this, our mutual bond.[17]

Continuing in Spanish, Allen completed his vows.

> Eric, mi amor. Si tuviera cuatro vidas por vivir, las cuatro viviría contigo.

Eric repeated this vow in English.

> Allen, my love, if I had four lives to live, I'd live them all with you.

As they exchanged rings, the minister led the two men in these vows:

> I give you this ring as a token of our covenant, vowing to live together in close friendship and love, and to strive for fuller knowledge of your being, and to care for you above all others. I pledge myself to recognize your needs, and to encourage your full potential, and to love you even as I love myself. May love dwell between you and me forever.

After reminding us that the rings are cast in the shape of a circle, symbolizing the sun, the earth, perfection, and wholeness, the minister turned to the congregation, asking for our vows as witnesses to this union. Once these had been made, he returned to Allen and Eric, leading them through the lighting of a unity candle. He pronounced their union to be complete and binding, and closed the ceremony, as the choir sang the benediction. The couple, the minister, and their attendants walked up the aisle to an organ recessional, the "Toccata" from the Second Symphony for Organ by Charles-Marie Widor. A number of the guests, turning to watch the recessional, were now weeping, others smiling and hugging. We filed out after the recessional, stopping to shake hands with the grooms and the wedding party at the door to the sanctuary. A reception, held in the spacious home of a lesbian couple who are close friends of Allen and Eric, followed the service.

On our way out of the church, I ran into a longtime acquaintance who had also just attended the service. She was clearly very moved, and I asked her what she thought of the ceremony. "When it first started," she told me, "it looked like any other traditional wedding. I mean, when they walked down the aisle, I almost had to look twice to see that it was two men. So I was a bit skeptical. And then I looked at them standing up there with the minister in his robes and it hit me that they were doing this *here*! This institution is supporting them. It's really amazing. I'm overwhelmed."

What did Allen and Eric seek to achieve in this celebration? The two men, both natives of Texas, had been together for about eight years when they decided to set a definite date for a commitment ceremony, something they had been discussing on and off for about four years. They had moved to the Bay Area seeking a more tolerant social climate and had joined the Unitarian Church as part of that quest. Allen, forty-two, had grown up attending Methodist churches and had served in a number them as organist and choir director. Eric, thirty-eight, had had a Roman Catholic upbringing, though in recent years he had only attended church when visiting his parents. They wanted to belong to a church together that would fully accept them as gay men and as a couple as well as one that was not rigidly doctrinal. But their desire to find a gay-positive church did not mean that they wanted to belong to an exclusively gay congregation, so they decided against joining either of the local MCC churches. Eric's prior experience with MCC (in Texas) convinced him that it was a pleasant enough place to meet one's friends, but that it wasn't as "spiritual" as he felt a church should be. Allen agreed, feeling strongly that church was a place where he wanted to see a more varied group of people.

> My feeling was [that belonging to a gay church] is not living in the real world. I've never been a person who wants the whole world to be gay or lesbian or anything else. I want people to be people, and just accepting the way they are. And that's why I think a church like [the Unitarian], you know, they have everything. . . . And to me that's the way the world is. It is a cross-section. And I think you go to things like that so that you can experience the world.

Following from this notion of "the real world" and their place in it, Allen thinks of the ceremony as a way to say something about the similarities between their hopes and those of heterosexual couples, but also argues that having a commitment ritual does not imply that they are trying to emulate straight marriage.

> I think you have to live in the real world. And I think that we're not trying to be a straight couple, because we're not. But there are principles and ceremonies and things like that that are in the straight world that there's no reason that they shouldn't be able to be carried over to the gay world. I mean, we're not copying anything. We're doing this because of the way we feel about one another. About the commitment that we have. To me, I've never thought of it as trying to copy what my parents had or any other married couple. Most of the gay couples and lesbian couples that I know that have been together are together a hell of a lot longer than most straight couples that I know. We know lots of couples that have been together fifteen, twenty years. Which I think is fabulous. So I guess it's kind of like a public statement that yes, gay people are just like anyone else. We have many of the same dreams and goals and aspirations and why not have a public ceremony saying that?

Allen's statement suggests that he has merged two seemingly distinct perspectives by both asserting a difference between gay and straight relationships and also believing that all committed couples are, beneath superficial differences (such as sexual orientation), the same. In a sense, he argues that these seemingly dichotomous views actually overlap: if gay and straight couples share the same dreams, then the whole issue of imitation becomes moot. But he also believes that gay and straight couples are not the same with respect to their rights and visibility, and that, therefore, gay couples have needs that rarely arise for straight couples. The commitment ceremony, then, can serve the conceptually distinct aims of providing gay couples with support and recognition they find it difficult to acquire while also revealing underlying similarities between these relationships and those of opposite-sex couples. This potentially serves the larger political goal of helping straight people to understand the "normalcy" of gay people. As Allen put it,

> I want [our guests] to know, if they had any doubts whatsoever, that gay and lesbian people are just like regular people. That this will help to get this out of their mind, show them that love is love, that we get up in the morning and do our thing, just like anybody else. I guess I want them to see our normalcy. And by seeing the way that we feel, maybe that will help. Granted most people who I think we will invite will be very supportive to begin with, but some people may be a little on the fence about it, and those are the ones that I'd like to reach out to, to let them know that we're not freaks.

These ideas were given play in the realization of the ceremony. On the surface, its form and setting denied specialness; it was, in every sense of the word, an "ordinary" (or "traditional") Unitarian wedding. But while that appearance startled some of the guests, it spoke powerfully of Allen and Eric's concept of "the real world" as a place where inclusiveness would make imitation unnecessary and indeed illogical.

When the two men told me about particular decisions they had reached about details of the ceremony, however, they emphasized how a specific ritual feature would be "original" or "unique," even as they acknowledged the use of many of these same symbols by heterosexuals. They decided, for instance, to wear their wedding rings on their right rather than their left hands. Characteristically, Allen explained the decision both in terms of their desire to differentiate themselves from opposite-sex couples and as evidence that they are part of the mainstream.

> I think that was something *not* to be straight. A conscious effort that most American straight people wear it on their left hand. But I've also noticed a lot of straight couples out here wearing it on their right hand, because it's more of a European influence, I guess.

Their decision to have a ceremony was also influenced by the worsening state of Allen's health. They had both known he was HIV positive since the beginning of the relationship, but about a year after moving to

San Francisco his health declined to the point that he had to stop working as a corporate travel administrator (though he has since then kept up an active schedule as a volunteer for AIDS organizations). Eric, who is HIV negative, works as an insurance administrator for a large corporation. He knows that Allen's future health is uncertain and wants to make a statement about their commitment to each other as life partners extending even beyond their lives. "It's a commitment for after death, for me," he said, "It's really like forever." Though neither man sees Allen's illness as the primary motivation for having the ceremony, they also talk at some length about how staging a celebration of their life together will enable them to accentuate the positive, to affirm their happiness together.

Probably the most explicit indication of the tone they felt the event should have emerged in their decision to wear matching tuxedos. As Allen put it, "That's the kind of feeling that we want to have for the service, that it's special. That it's formal, but not stuffy. Just special." As they moved through the months before the wedding, their sense that they were doing something "special" was confirmed by the warm and interested responses of people they knew at church. They told me with particular pleasure of an elderly (heterosexual) woman who sings with them in the choir and who was angling for them to design a specific role for her in the ceremony. Allen described her excitement with some amusement.

> She probably wants to do cartwheels down the aisle, knowing her. But it's also nice to see that kind of support from the straight community. . . . They actually see two people who care a great deal for one another, and that's all that's important. . . . It's nice to have that kind of support. And I guess I'm idealistic enough to hope that that spills out beyond that community and goes into the community at large.

Both men invited a large number of current and former coworkers, very few of whom were gay or lesbian; they estimated that the ratio of gay to straight guests was about fifty-fifty. But Eric and Allen's involvement with "the real world" also made them vulnerable to painful exclusions. Eric's family, despite their ardent Catholicism, had a history of being quite accepting of his homosexuality, but before the ceremony he was unsure and somewhat apprehensive about how they would deal with this new test of their tolerance. His fears were well-grounded. His mother accused him of "breaking her heart," and refused to relent even after Allen called her to try to explain the importance of her and Eric's father's presence. Eric's brother, "Robert," and his wife, did attend, with Robert serving as Eric's best man. The day after the wedding, they came to a barbeque the two men threw for all the visitors from Texas, and though they were the only straights there, Eric was pleased that they seemed to be at ease in that milieu. He described their presence that weekend as "supportive."

Allen's relations with his father, whom he had only just informed of his HIV status, had been strained for some years. His father cited health reasons for declining the invitation, and in the months since seemed to avoid the topic of the ceremony as assiduously as he avoided acknowledging his son's AIDS. Allen's struggle to make his father aware of his precarious health condition alternated with his desire that his father understand the happiness and satisfaction his relationship brought him. Neither message seemed to be easy to communicate.

Eric and Allen's ceremony encapsulates a number of themes that are central to other lesbian and gay weddings, whether or not these take place in mainstream religious settings. In accounting for particular symbolic strategies, they both seem to claim that their union is morally equivalent to a heterosexual marriage, and that they are therefore not significantly different from straight people, and that their relationship is special and embattled, and therefore intrinsically distinctive. This shifting consciousness of their ties to convention is characteristic of lesbian and gay commitment ceremonies, and though it seems to be paradoxical, I will argue in these pages that such ambiguity is at the heart of these rituals.

Allen and Eric's experience also points to the fragile politics of kinship that planning a commitment ceremony instigates. In the months leading up to the wedding, the two men devoted considerable energy to deciding how to broach the subject to key family members and what to do if they encountered rejection. Once the ceremony was over, they were preoccupied, at least to a degree, with both the acceptance and rejection they experienced, and continued to struggle with the meaning of their relatives' behavior. Besides being concerned with their families' responses, they also elaborated the participation of heterosexuals in the ceremony, remarking on their numbers or enthusiasm in describing the occasion. They attributed the supportive response of this wider community to their understanding that "love is love," and that gay people are therefore fundamentally the same as everyone else. Their interaction with the nongay world, then, is mediated by their ability to substantiate claims to legitimacy as a couple, using symbolic evocations of "love" to demonstrate their authenticity.

"As the Goddess Wills"

"Cynthia Kelly" and "Alisa Rosenberg" faced a complex task in planning the wedding they held in June 1995. Although they laughingly described themselves as "goddess gals," or devotees of the feminist spirituality movement, they take the ideas of goddess worship extremely seriously, placing the spiritual orientation they also refer to as "pagan" or "Wiccan" at the heart of their lives.[18] But they felt as well that it would be vital to represent both of their family heritages—Celtic and Czech in Cynthia's case and Eastern European Jewish in Alisa's—in the construction of their ceremony and to incorporate practices of varied origins they had observed at other weddings. So the task they set themselves in planning the event was to create a delicate balance between their spiritual priorities and the multiple layers of identity they wanted to invoke in making a public commitment to one another.

I first met with Cynthia and Alisa in their sunny Sonoma County ranch house about a year before their wedding. Both women have long histories of involvement in feminist circles, with early commitments to what Cynthia characterized as "a real radical feminist lesbian experience which said, 'We don't do it this way! This is very patriarchal'" in relation to marriage. In recent years, Alisa and Cynthia's feminism has moved them to embrace the feminist spirituality movement as well as to become active in twelve-step self-help recovery programs.[19] Alisa, forty-three at the time we first met, teaches at a nearby community college. Cynthia, forty-seven, is a nurse who now evaluates geriatric health facilities. I had been referred to them though a convoluted web of mutual friends, and they immediately drew me into the planning of the wedding, enthusiastic about contributing to a research project. I attended their ceremony a year later, and a year after that, joined them for their first anniversary party.

Cynthia and Alisa's decision to have a public ceremony grew directly out of their awareness of the emerging significance of marriage as an issue on the gay and lesbian rights agenda. Alisa was the first to raise the issue—proposing was something she was inspired to do at particularly romantic moments—but Cynthia initially was uncomfortable with the image of marriage, a concept firmly linked in her mind with heterosexuality. Cynthia continued to think about the matter, however, and about a year after Alisa had first broached the topic, it began to make more sense to her, largely in relation to the struggle for domestic partner rights and recent legal developments in Hawaii. After reviewing her retirement plan at work, she also began to realize that Alisa would never be entitled to most of the varied benefits accorded a legal spouse, and became incensed at the injustice of the system. She told me that she changed her mind

> basically because of . . . what I was reading in the papers. It started to really get to me that yes, I deserve this. This is what I want. This is what I've truly wanted—I don't know, I mean you think about it, of course I want to seem like everybody else. . . . I mean I want to fit into the mainstream of life. And I *am* part of the mainstream of life. Well, why not? Let *me* enjoy the gifts of this too.

This growing feeling of entitlement became particularly compelling for Cynthia when she and Alisa participated in a public commitment ceremony held in conjunction with Sonoma County's Gay Pride observances.

> We were the focal point of the whole parade at the picnic afterwards and at the rally, all of us that were getting married. And there were many people who wanted to make this commitment who came forth. . . . And we were all in front of everybody. And it was like, *yes!* This is really very significant. I mean, I know I want to do this, but now I really feel how this empowers you and makes you feel totally different about the experience.
>
> ELLEN: Can you say what made it feel that way?
> CYNTHIA: First of all, there was the community. And they were giving total support. These people were *cheering.*
> ALISA: Everybody was cheering us.
> CYNTHIA: Yes! Yes! It was like oh, yeah!
> ALISA: We don't get that kind of validation very often in this society.
> CYNTHIA: And so it was very validating and it was like saying, yeah, our ceremony is going to be this way, too. Our friends are going to be there. Our family.

For Alisa, the sense that getting married would give her access to sources of validation normally available only to heterosexuals became most convincing as they made decisions about their wedding rings. They embarked on the selection of rings as a major research project, reading up on different kinds of gold and mulling over the economics of buying diamonds. They visited store after store and speculated about whether they could get diamond rings and remain within the boundaries of good taste and their budget. Alisa laughingly explains the contradictory feelings she had about diamonds. "I went back and forth about a diamond. I felt like it was kind of pretentious, but I wanted it 'cause everybody at school has one! All the straight girls I know have these diamond rings."

They eventually located a jewelry shop that displayed a special setting for the diamond that wouldn't "stick up" (i.e., be ostentatious) and that also had two matching, and not excessively large, diamonds in stock that could be used for their rings. They were able, then, to avoid overstepping their notion of good taste while also being able to afford the rings by purchasing them on layaway. While the diamond and eighteen-carat gold rings they ordered would be the equal of anything a straight girl could expect, they also saw these rings as special. The setting was patented and available nowhere else in the United States, and the store had to negotiate with the jeweler, they explained, before an agreement was reached about making the rings with these particular stones.

As we talked about their plans for the wedding, Alisa and Cynthia described their expectation that the ceremony would generate a palpable experience of "community," a force that would essentially rise up at the wedding to affirm and support their relationship. As an example of how this sort of feeling might be generated, Alisa described other experiences she had had at weddings, both gay and straight, in which the assembled guests were called upon in some fashion to collectively witness a couple's union. She was particularly impressed with a Quaker wedding she had attended where all the guests signed a wedding document and with a Unitarian ceremony where the minister asked the guests to verbally swear to their willingness to support the couple.[20] As she explained, "For me, it's wanting the Goddess to be involved. You know, say it in front of the Goddess. Say it in front of our families. And I guess it's about wanting to be taken seriously. It's wanting to make that spiritual commitment. And that community commitment."

The wedding was held in the Russian River resort town of Guerneville on a sunny Saturday afternoon about a year after our first meeting. On the grounds of a large Victorian farmhouse festooned with balloons, guests were invited to take their seats in a semicircle on a lush lawn behind which towered a stand of redwood trees. Each guest received a program detailing the "order of ceremony," listing the roles of ritual participants and their names, and including a sort of glossary, labeled "Customs

Explained," that defined and briefly interpreted some of the proceedings.
A *chuppah* (the canopy traditional at Jewish weddings) draped in white
and purple had been set up in front of the trees, under which a small
table, also covered in purple and white, held a variety of ritual objects, including pictures of close friends and relatives now deceased. (The program defined the *chuppah* as follows: "Jewish wedding canopy, representing here a return to the sacred groves in which our ancestors
honored the Goddess.")

To a guitar accompaniment, a procession of eight women filed in,
dressed in robes of various colors. (The program explained that they
were the officiating priestess, three assisting priestesses, and four "druzicky," defined as the "Czech name for bridesmaids.") These women were
followed by Alisa and Cynthia—both dressed in off-white dresses, carrying bouquets, and wearing tiny white flowers in their hair—who joined
the other women under the *chuppah*. Once they were assembled, the
priestess welcomed the guests and explained the ritual of purification as
aiding participants to be "centered and present" and as creating a transition "from where we've been to where we are going." As she blessed each
of them with a few drops of salted water from a bowl on the table, she directed the assembled guests to do the same using the bowls that had been
placed under chairs in each row. She asked the guests to hold the bowl for
their neighbors, passing it on to the next person as each mutual blessing
was completed. The priestess blessed Alisa and Cynthia with salted water
while attendants walked around the standing guests, creating a "sacred
space" by sprinkling water.[21]

Next, the priestess and her assistants moved around the space, to the
accompaniment of two drummers, "casting a circle" by "honoring the
four sacred elements of life: earth, water, fire, and air." She explained to
the guests that this process creates a sacred space in an area that has other
ordinary uses, such as an outdoor space. The "claiming and transition" of
that space is ritualized by the use of the four elements to create a suitable
environment for the goddesses to gather. As she moved around the circle, stopping at each of the cardinal points and chiming her bells, the
priestess chanted, "I purify this space in the name of the Goddess." Moving around the circle, one assistant scattered water, the second carried a
candle set in a small holder in the shape of the Goddess, the third played
tiny cymbals, and the fourth scattered salt. As they arrived at a point facing each of the cardinal directions, the priestess chanted to invoke the
blessing of the forces of that direction.

Once this process was complete, the priestess announced that the circle had been cast. The drums stopped playing, and she and her assistants began to "call the directions." They moved to each of the cardinal points in turn, beginning with east, and there chanted the names of the Goddess associated with that direction. Once all four directions had been called, the priestesses returned to the *chuppah* (north). The drums resumed, now joined by the sound of rainsticks and chimes, and the guests were led in a chant that repeated the names of goddesses ("Isis, Astarte, Diana, Hecate, Demeter, Kali, Inanna") and then shifted to an incantation of the names of the brides, Cynthia and Alisa.

Turning to the guests, the priestess explained that Cynthia and Alisa were entering a sacred marriage. Because the state does not recognize the validity of their union, they need their assembled friends and relatives to witness their commitment. "This is a joining of heritages," she continued, connecting the brides' Jewish, Celtic, and Czech origins to their commitment to the Goddess and the twelve-step spirituality they have embraced.

At this point the priestess invoked a series of seven blessings, constructed on the model of the *Sheva B'rachot* (Seven Blessings) of Jewish wedding tradition but adapted to fit into the pagan framework of the ceremony. (The program explained the Seven Blessings as "the essence of the Jewish wedding liturgy, intertwined here with the Wiccan tradition of honoring the earth.") The priestess began by asking the Goddess to bless the wine, first reciting a variant of the Hebrew blessing for wine (*B'rucha Yah Shekina, Ma'yan Chayim borayt p'ri hagafen*) and then translating, "Blessed are you, Goddess, Spring of Life, who created the fruit of the vine." As Cynthia and Alisa each drank in turn from a single glass, they said to one another, "May you never thirst." Next, another attendant said, "Blessed are you, Goddess, source of life, who created the fruit of the earth." As they each fed one another from a plate of fruit, the brides both intoned, "May you never go hungry."

The third blessing, based (according to the program) on a Celtic blessing, invoked the Goddess of the sun and the moon. "In the name of Brigit, Flame of Beauty, Flame of Love, Flame of Life, Goddess of the Sun and the Moon, May the blessing of light be on you, light without and light within. May the blessed sunlight shine on you and warm your two hearts 'til they glow like a great peat fire." The fourth (identified in the program as the "blessing for healing the planet: Tikkun Olam")[22] was as follows: "May the joyous hope of a better world inspire all people to work for justice and thus for peace, so that the homeless will have homes, the hungry will be fed, the persecuted and oppressed will be free, and all people will learn to live in peace with each other and in harmony with their environment." In the fifth blessing, the priestess called on the Goddess to bless, honor, and affirm the two women in their commitment to each other, and in the sixth and seventh she asked the families and friends, respectively, to also affirm that commitment. The guests responded, "We will."[23]

The next portion of the ceremony consisted of the exchange of vows. Alisa turned to Cynthia and spoke with tremendous emotion.

> *I looked for you and hoped for you for many years. Soon after we met, a voice inside told me clearly, "You're the one," though I had little idea then what that meant. Now I know you are the perfect partner I longed so much to find, my soulmate, my playmate, my heart's true companion. Your generous kindness, your tender passion, and steadfast honesty fill me with joy, and I thank the Goddess every day for the blessing of you in my life.*

Going on, she said to Cynthia,

> *I promise to love, honor, and cherish you, to stand by you through good times and hard times, in sickness and in health, one day at a time, for this life and beyond, as the Goddess wills.*[24]

Turning to Alisa, Cynthia gave her account of their meeting.

> *My dearest Alisa, I searched for you for many years, then one day on the way to a housewarming party in January 1990 a dear friend told me I would meet the love of my life at the party. And when you sat down next to me and gently touched my arm, after I told you of my recent operation, your kindness, your sweetness touched my heart. You are my heart's purest desire, friend, my soulmate, my lover, and now spouse. I love you with all my heart, and I promise to love, honor and cherish you, to stand by you through good times and hard times, in sickness and in health, one day at a time, for this life and beyond, as the Goddess wills.*

Following these vows, the priestess called on the Goddess to bless the rings, and to facilitate this she asked the audience to hold hands, sending love to the rings and creating a "circle of energy" that would "charge the rings." One after the other, the two women said, "*With my body, I worship you. With this ring, I wed you and pledge my faithful love.*"

Returning to the four directions, the priestess called on the goddesses of the north, west, south, and east to bless, honor, and affirm the union before their departure. "May the circle be open, but unbroken," she cried. As the drummers began a rhythmic serenade that opened the circle, the priestesses and *druzicky* together chanted, "Leave if you must, stay if you will." The priestess then placed two cloth-wrapped glasses at Cynthia and Alisa's feet, saying, "To shatter homophobia, fear and hatred, and to affirm your love."[25] The brides stomped on the glasses and, as they broke, the sound of applause and cries of "Mazel tov" (congratulations in Hebrew) mingled with the drumbeat of the recessional.

The guests followed the two women and their retinue back to the house, and after greeting the brides near the reception area, each was invited to sign the *ketubah*, Cynthia and Alisa's version of the traditional Jewish wedding contract. According to the program, following "Quaker tradition, everyone present signs as a witness." The *ketubah* was hand-calligraphed and was designed so that the signatures would radiate out from the center, like the spokes of a wheel.

Cynthia and Alisa created a ceremony that sought to unravel and bring together the tangled threads that they viewed as constituting both their individual identities and their sense of how they were connected to a series of overlapping communities. Conceptualizing all these affiliations—whether defined by ethnicity, feminism, spirituality, or recovery—as "traditions" allowed them to commingle seemingly disparate elements drawn from each, fashioning a notion of heritage specific to the occasion. Rather than viewing these varied sources as standing in conflict or as potentially contradicting each other, they effectively claimed the right to appropriate aspects of all of them, and thereby both affirmed their links to each component tradition and argued that these traditions are complementary rather than incompatible. This meant, then, not only exalting their current spiritual affiliations with the Goddess and the twelve-step movement (by using them as the central idiom of the ritual) but also invoking the past to suture its interruptions and soften its incongruities.

"Starting a New Life"

"Bob and Mark Herron" met in a San Francisco leather bar in 1992, and within a week or two they had begun to date quite seriously. On their second date, a dinner at Bob's house, there was a knock at the door just as they were sitting down to eat, and when they answered it, the woman who lived next door rushed in. Bob describes the scene:

> She said, "My husband's just had an accident in Vallejo. . . . Could you take care of my baby while I rush up to Vallejo and get my husband out of the hospital?" I said, "Sure." So we sat down and had dinner . . . and spent four hours with the baby. And both of us talked over how we both wanted to have kids and everybody that we were interested in didn't want to have children. And that was one of the things that brought us real close together real fast. Not a discussion of how to do it, but soon after we got started seeing each other it was yes, we'd like to do that.

Even three years later, the two men can't resist describing every romantic gesture—sunsets and candlelight; picnics served with china, silver, and crystal, cracked crab and sparkling cider—that punctuated their courtship. Recollecting each detail with fond nostalgia, they take me through the story of how they met, fell in love (practically at first sight), moved in together, registered as domestic partners, and got married. Mark, who is thirty-two, tells me: "He's a romantic. Which is one of the things that swept me off my feet. I'm an incurable romantic. I still believe in the shining knight on the horse. And I found him. I couldn't say no to him. He's just so good-looking and so wonderful."

About a month after their first date, Bob took Mark out on his motorcycle to a spot where they could watch the sun setting over the San Francisco skyline. He proposed, and Mark immediately accepted. As Bob, now forty-seven, says, "So we decided early on that we were for each other."

About six months later, they registered as domestic partners in San Francisco, and then began to plan their wedding ceremony. The domestic partner procedure allowed them to make clear to their friends that they both considered this a serious commitment, even as they were setting up what they call "a unique family" with Mark's former lover, "Frank Smith," as their roommate. Since both men, employed in law enforcement fields, are municipal employees, they have access to the health and retirement benefits that San Francisco extends to domestic partners of its workers.

As they tell their story, Bob and Mark's decision to not only marry but to choose a new surname to mark the formation of their new family stemmed from their intention to have children. (A close woman friend has volunteered to serve as surrogate for this venture.) As Mark explains, after describing the difficult relationships both men had with their fathers:

> Neither of us was very happy with our father, obviously. And the idea of having to raise a child, whose name do we give the child? So we said, well, neither of us is thrilled with either of our names. Let's make a new one. That was a way of us making a commitment to each other, and starting a new life. Letting it be known that we are together, we are choosing to be together the rest of our lives.

The two men agreed that having hyphenated names would be awkward, and both also felt strongly that there would be nothing positive about passing on their family names to a new generation. Their solution was to use a Scrabble set to devise names that combined three letters from each of their former surnames, "Mather" and "Browne."[26] After coming up with more than one hundred possibilities, they finally settled on Herron, which "sounded right," and took the various steps necessary to make the name change official and legal.[27]

Mark and Bob told me that they planned their ceremony with the goal of making it "as traditional as possible." They designed invitations and inserted them in cards bearing pictures of Japanese cranes, birds that they regard as symbolic of their relationship. According to Mark, who explained the significance of the particular species of crane that provides a decorative theme echoed throughout their home, "They choose one mate and they mate for life. And if their mate dies, they spend the rest of their life alone."

But the two men also used their ceremony to make clear the importance of their belonging to the leather community. "Leather" refers to a style or sensibility characterized by a focus on homosexual masculinity, a sexual preference for S/M or fetishism, and a choice of sexual partners who also identify as manly men. Its most visible expression is achieved through various sorts of costuming. The clothing leather fanciers wear to symbolize their maleness draws on key American images of masculinity associated with motorcycles, the West, and the working class. Thus, leather men are likely to sport motorcycle jackets and boots, Western wear, or blue-collar workingman's clothing, or particular items associated with those styles, including the insignia of various clubs and fraternal organizations to which leather men belong—most commonly motorcycle clubs and uniform clubs.[28]

Uniform clubs are among the many kinds of fraternal organizations that have sprung up in the gay men's community, particularly since the 1950s. At club events, members dress up in military or police uniforms, taking care to do so with as much authenticity as possible. Like the motorcycle clubs, these organizations sponsor social events, always with a uniform theme, many of which benefit gay community charities (in recent years, usually, but not always, AIDS-related).[29] Aside from their specialized sexual connotations, these organizations are functionally not unlike fraternal organizations favored by men outside the gay community (e.g., Elks, Masons, Lions) in that they offer opportunities for socializing, networking, and community service while also allowing for masculine fellowship and providing occasions for dressing up in organizational regalia.

Bob and Mark identify both as leather men and as "uniform enthusiasts," and they are active members of a local uniform club. On the day of the wedding, they decorated their San Francisco house with flowers and draped the Gay Pride and Leather Pride flags[30] over the doorway that led to the tented backyard where chairs for the eighty-five guests had been arranged on the grass. Using the back porch as a stage, they made their entrance down the back stairs, under the flags, accompanied by their attendants. Dressed in matching tuxedoes, the men invoked their involvement in a uniform club by wearing their trousers tucked into knee-high police boots and in the leather community with black leather bow ties, tying, as Mark explains, "a very formal look into leather." Four attendants accompanied the two men onto the porch, two "maids-of-honor" in matching dresses and two "best men" dressed in tuxedoes with matching lavender bow ties and cummerbunds.

Many of their gay guests came in attire that symbolized their identification with particular gay (male) subcultures or sensibilities—leather, uniforms, drag, rubber accessories—but their families, and particularly their two mothers, were dressed in a fashion Bob characterizes as "conservative Midwestern." And although Mark's family is considerably more liberal and generally accepting of homosexuality than Bob's rather rigidly Catholic relatives, both men have their origins in the Midwest, and they noted with some amusement the almost uncanny similarities between the two families. "The funny thing was our mothers are dressed in different colors," Mark said, "his mother's in red, mine's in blue, but their dresses are almost identical. And it turns out, even stranger, they were born in the same small town in Minnesota." Mark went on to explain that these strange and unpredictable convergences simply confirm what they already felt about each other. "We both believe in fate. And there's too many coincidences that have happened in this relationship that tell us it's not a coincidence. Somebody decided we are supposed to be together."

Both men describe themselves as being "very religious"—Bob, in fact, spent six years in a Catholic seminary studying for the priesthood, and Mark was active in the Metropolitan Community Church (MCC) before moving to San Francisco—but they rejected the notion of having anyone play the role of officiant at their wedding or of having any explicit religious content in the ceremony. Bob and Mark view their religious faith as a private matter, best conveyed without the intercession of organized religion, so while they count gay clergymen among their friends (there were at least two in attendance as guests), they saw no need to insert explicit religious content into their wedding. As Mark put it:

> We'd already done our peace with God. This is a destined relationship. We're fated to be together. . . . The only way I'm religious is [that] God for whatever reason chose me to be gay. And for me to go against that wish would be in my mind committing a sin against God. And the only true way that I can show my love is by sharing my life with another person. And this is the person that was chosen for me.

Not only was it essential, then, that they marry themselves without the intercession of religious authority, but it was vital to the two men that the ceremony take place in their home. As Bob explains, "We didn't want to have it someplace else that wasn't important to us. And we wanted this to be shared with our closest friends, and acquaintances, and family."

The ceremony itself was short and simple. Bob welcomed the guests and asked them to witness their vows and pledge to help them to live "as a committed and bounded [sic] couple" and to support them with their love and friendship. Then Mark read his vows.[31]

> I guess you could say in some ways I've always loved you. That doesn't sound right, I know, because I haven't always known you. But I've always known certain qualities that were important to me, and in my heart I've always carried an image, a fantasy, a wish, I guess, of a wonderful person I could love totally. You've given me what I've always wished for, fun and laughter, concern and understanding, a friend to depend on, a lover to cherish, a partner in everything I do. Thinking about you, how you make me feel, how I feel about you and all that you are, I realize that all my life I've always loved you in my dreams. Now that you've come out of my

*dreams and into my life, I can tell you that I've always loved you and that
I always will.*

Bob's vows came next.

*Mark, I do solemnly swear before all of these friends and family gathered
here today the following: I, "Charles Barrett Mather," do love you with
my whole heart, soul, and mind. I want to spend the rest of my life with
you, and you alone, as my soulmate. I will do everything in my power and
abilities to make our lives together as good as possible. When the rough or
bad times do come, I will be there with you all the way through them. I
promise that when we do fight, that we will fight fair, and that we will try
to compromise and make up as soon as the issues are resolved. I promise
that we will try to make our family grow in love and in size.*[32]

Bob continued.

*I will ask all here present to witness that I am giving this ring to you as a
symbol of my love for you. The ring is also my promise to you that I will
love you until death does part us temporarily.*

After they had made their vows to each other, and the guests had
vowed to support their relationship in the years to come, one of their
maids-of-honor, who also had been doubling as emcee, followed the
form common at the conclusion of heterosexual weddings when she announced to the crowd, "Ladies and gentlemen, I'd like to introduce you
to Mr. and Mr. Herron." Though their close friends already had been informed of their plans, this was the first time any of their relatives had
heard that they were choosing new names. Both men laugh as they describe the open-mouthed amazement of their mothers and siblings
("They were totally aghast!"). While Mark's family, which had always
been positive about his homosexuality, has since embraced his chosen
name, most of Bob's family has refused obstinately to accept it, possibly
because he not only changed his surname but his first and middle names
as well.[33]

The incorporation of the name change into the wedding offers a particularly dramatic symbol of Bob and Mark's understanding of their
wedding ceremony as the occasion that would mark their change in status from two individuals to a committed family unit. They characterize
their wedding and their relationship as "traditional," referring to the
value they place on permanence and fidelity as well as their conviction

that their union was preordained, part of the natural, God-given order of the universe. Bob and Mark's concept of "family" symbolizes their commitment to one another, a commitment they hope to concretize with the eventual birth of a baby girl.[34]

Their understanding of themselves as "traditional" is highlighted, as well, by their emphasis on the diversity that characterized their wedding. The eighty-five guests, they were quick to point out, included men and women, gays and straights, friends, family, coworkers, and neighbors. Although limited space prevented them from inviting all their neighbors, they were proud of the attention the ceremony got on the block and particularly that many of the neighbors they didn't invite expressed interest and disappointment at not being among the guests.[35]

Bob and Mark's wedding pictures also speak eloquently to their claim of adhering to "tradition." They showed me an array of photographs they identify as "traditional pictures"—cutting the cake, feeding each other pieces of cake, opening their many presents, along with formal group portraits of their two families separately and then together. They registered for gifts at several department stores and proudly pointed out some of the varied housewares and decorative pieces their friends bought them.

But the wedding also highlights their involvement in the gay (male) subcultures of leather and uniforms, a sensibility that intersects with "tradition" at every turn. They wore their police boots with their tuxedos and sported leather bow ties. Some of their gifts reflected these themes— one package, for example, was wrapped in black leather with chains as the ribbons. (The package contained nothing more transgressive, however, than a clock.)

Bob and Mark's wedding demonstrates the tendency of many such ceremonies to depend on the juxtaposition and intermingling of materials drawn from multiple, and sometimes apparently conflicting, sources. The two men sought to convey respect for, and even immersion in, something they called "tradition" by reproducing images they associated with mainstream American weddings—represented most notably in their tuxedos, their choice of attendants, the cake, and their intention to have a child. But they also proudly disrupted the consistency of those images with specialized gay amendments, particularly those that evoked their involvement in the leather and uniform communities. The mingling of these apparently contradictory representations highlights Bob and Mark's claim that they are both part of the gay world and well integrated into the wider society, as evidenced by the diverse guest list and their discussion of how their families, neighbors, and coworkers joined in the festivities.

The two men's understanding of the meaning of their relationship and, particularly, their view that a force beyond their control has fated them to be lifelong companions points to another rendition of the theme of authenticity. In Bob and Mark's case, authenticity is elaborated in their choice of their home as the setting, their decision not to have a member of the clergy officiate, and by their reiteration of the "uncanny" similarities between their two families, viewed as evidence of the mystical sources of their union. Their intent to solidify their "family" with a child recalls anthropologist David Schneider's analysis of American kinship as a system of cultural symbols.[36] "Love," in Schneider's reading can represent either of the two substances believed to constitute kinship—blood and law—as procreation offers evidence of the presence of love and also extends love into a new generation.

The Eighth Blessing

Incongruity and contradiction can be played out in weddings that make subversive gestures at the same time that they maintain connections with wider traditions and communities. For these lesbian and gay couples, an acknowledgment or assertion of difference is inserted within forms that are squarely located in their view of "tradition." These strategies enable the celebrants both to make explicit claims to inclusion in a wider community or kinship group and to underscore their difference from ordinary couples.

"Miriam Kaufman" and "Hannah Levine," San Francisco residents in their early thirties, went to great lengths to construct their wedding using traditional Jewish elements. Miriam said:

> Especially because it wasn't legally recognized, this was our opportunity to create something that was exactly what we needed. You know, that was really a gathering in of all the support that we had in the world. And something that for the rest of our lives we would look back on when we needed strength.

Jewish culture, and connectedness with their families of origin, is of tremendous importance to both Miriam and Hannah, who met each other through their mutual interest in klezmer music. Once they fell in love, they felt strongly that this relationship would be permanent, that marriage was "right" and the direction they both were moving in even before meeting each other. As Miriam put it, "We were both looking for the partner for a lifetime. We both felt that, like mallards, you know, we just mate for life."

In planning what they would wear to their wedding, Miriam and Hannah initially reached a decision to either both wear pants or both wear dresses. "We decided we didn't want to do something that would sort of look butch-femme, and look like there was a man and a woman." They finally settled on two white dresses (neither identical nor traditional wedding dresses), though Miriam laughs when she relates this; she sees the final choice of clothing not so much as a commitment to a "wedding" theme as a practical response to the problem of finding similar outfits they both liked in their two different sizes.

Their decision to have traditional Jewish wedding rings—unbroken bands without stones—made for the ceremony was, in their view, more conscious. Miriam explains:

> We're pretty traditional. And I think in a lot of ways we wanted, to the extent that the traditions made sense to us, we wanted to stay as close to a traditional wedding ceremony as we could, a traditional *Jewish* wedding ceremony. And I think in terms of being in the world, too, it's nice to have something that's sort of universally recognized. And then people can make assumptions [that we're married to men], and if they do, they can be corrected.

Both Miriam and Hannah felt that it was important to have a traditional Jewish ceremony:

> [This] was one of several occasions in life where you feel drawn to the tradition, that the collective wisdom of centuries has something to offer us. . . . We pretty much wanted it to be as close to traditional as it could be. And make whatever few changes were necessary to accommodate the fact that we were both women. We also felt, since we had been living together for a while, and since we had a [private] commitment to each other that we considered to be binding, that the ceremony was also for us a ceremony through which we entered the Jewish community as a family, and that linked us to the Jewish people, as people. . . . So we wanted it to be traditional, and we felt entitled to the same words and wisdom and everything that any other Jewish couple who was making this commitment both to each other and to the community would have.

What this meant for Miriam and Hannah was adhering to the traditional form of a Jewish wedding as much as possible, but also consciously departing from these forms when they felt it necessary to make a point about this ceremony uniting not a man and a woman but two women. They had a *chuppah*, a *ketubah*, and followed the standard liturgical form typical of Jewish weddings in the Reform or Conservative movement. But while they had the rabbi provide a traditional translation of the *Sheva B'rachot*, the Seven Blessings, which interpret marriage in the context of the seven days of biblical creation, they added an eighth blessing (placed between the fourth and fifth blessings), one that they described as "explicitly gay," and slightly amended the seventh blessing by feminizing its wording.

1. *Blessed is Ha Shem, Source of All Creation, creator of fruit of the vine.*
2. *Blessed is Ha Shem, Source of All Creation, creator of the universe.*
3. *Blessed is Ha Shem, Source of All Creation, creator of humanity.*
4. *Blessed is Ha Shem, Source of All Creation, creator of human beings in the divine image. Blessed are You, Adonai our God. You endow each of us with life, with the power of creation, with a bond to all humankind through Your Oneness.*

4a. **Blessed is Ha Shem, Source of All Creation, creator of love and passion between woman and woman, man and man, woman and man. Blessed are you, Adonai our God. You open our hearts to love, and strengthen us to walk with dignity among those who are different from us.**

5. *May the dream of Zion inspire us to create a life of goodness, wisdom, and generosity, a world of compassion, justice, and peace. Blessed are you, Adonai our God. You rejoice, as a mother reunited with her children, when the promise of humanity is fulfilled.*
6. *May the perfect joy of the Garden of Eden envelop these two beloved companions. Blessed are you, Adonai our God. You sanctify the rejoicing of these unique souls united in love.*
7. *Blessed is the Mystery, Source of All Creation, creator of joy and gladness, lover and beloved, awe and exultation, pleasure and delight, love and harmony, peace and friendship. Soon may we hear from the streets of every city and the paths of every field the voice of joy and gladness, the voice of the lover and the voice of* **her** *beloved, the voices of* **brides** *rising from beneath the* chuppah, *the voices of celebrants lifted in song at their wedding feasts. You Abound in Blessings, Adonai our God. You rejoice with these lovers united in marriage.*

Getting married is itself something that Miriam and Hannah viewed in the context of Jewish history: "This idea of marriage . . . is part of a continuum of thousands of years" that links their relationship to the ongoing history of Jewish life. Still, both women were acutely aware of the difference between their situation and that of a heterosexual couple, particularly since their marriage would not be legally recognized. Miriam explained:

> We wanted to have a traditional Jewish wedding, but we didn't want to pretend that we weren't gay. And so, we wanted to acknowledge the fact that the marriage wasn't going to be legally recognized. And we thought about doing it in the ceremony, and we thought that it would be inappropriate to sort of turn it into a political thing. So what we decided was to include it in the invitation, and to have this postcard to the governor urging legalization of gay marriage. . . . It was hard to find the right place to do that. Not to ignore it, and also not to let it take away from what we were doing.

Miriam and Hannah acknowledged the contradiction their marriage presented both to Jewish tradition and to the wider society and built it into the heart of the ceremony. But their articulation of gay/lesbian marriage as a potentially controversial political issue was kept at the margin of their ceremony, so that they could focus more directly on the ways in which their goals corresponded to the historical concerns of the Jewish people.

"Chapel of Love"

"Carmen Gómez" and "Eileen O'Hara" spent months planning every aspect of their wedding. It was particularly important to them that the event be unambiguously "gay," even though their image of the event was clearly drawn from experiences at many other family weddings. Carmen's Mexican-American family had always been extremely accepting of her lesbianism, and the plans called for large numbers of her relatives to have key roles in the ceremony. Eileen's more conservative, upper-middle-class Irish-American family had been sharply hostile to her coming out, and she fully expected that she would end up getting married without a single one of them in attendance. She was so estranged from her family, in fact, that she and Carmen had begun to discuss her changing her name to Gómez, both to symbolize the unity of her new family and to make clear her break from the past.

The ceremony, held at a catering establishment in downtown San Francisco, was presided over by a Presbyterian minister (whom the couple had met when he had officiated at his daughter's lesbian wedding) and was attended by more than a hundred family, friends, and coworkers. Despite the formal seating arrangement around a central aisle, the small jazz ensemble that played discreetly for the guests as they took their seats, the massive floral displays, and waiters circulating after the ceremony with glasses of champagne and trays of hors d'oeuvres, the appearance of convention broke down at a number of points. Not wanting to "mimic" the style of a traditional wedding, both women wore dark formal clothing that suggested a night at the opera more than a marriage ceremony. Along with a succession of attendants that included a ring bearer and a flower girl, two men dressed in matching floral-pattern vests carried baskets of flowers which they tossed into the crowd. They were the "flower fairies," according to Carmen and Eileen. The music that accompanied the procession was the 1964 song, "Chapel of Love," sung by the Dixie Cups; the couple and their attendants literally danced down the aisle to the cheers and laughter of the spectators. At a key moment in the ceremony the congregation not only was asked to swear to uphold and support the marriage in the years to come (a common feature of Protestant weddings) but was requested to rise and vow to oppose homophobia wherever it might be encountered.

Family members, wearing boutonnieres to distinguish them from other guests, were seated at the front. Time was taken during the ceremony to mark the attendance of both brides' relatives, noteworthy in Carmen's case because of the large, multigenerational Mexican-American contingent who appeared and in Eileen's case because a group of her relatives had come all the way from the East Coast after earlier turning down her invitation. Immediately after the ceremony, while the guests were sipping champagne and nibbling hors d'oeuvres, the couple spent nearly an hour posing for formal photographs with their families. The wedding ended with a sit-down dinner, dancing to live music, and celebratory toasts. A honeymoon in Hawaii followed.

Carmen and Eileen's ceremony demonstrates the kind of concatenation of diverse elements that some theorists would identify as "queer" and that others would label "postmodern." Despite the fact that both women were raised as Catholics, they diverged from what might be construed as their own traditions both by staging a Protestant ceremony and by inserting irreverent gestures at every turn. The stately, almost generic,

Protestant ritual evoked a claim to the American mainstream while playful references to popular culture undercut the wedding's solemnity and,
from Carmen and Eileen's perspective, expressed their loyalty to the gay
community. But the couple also used the wedding to elaborate their ties
with their blood relatives; although a few friends were chosen for inclusion in the formal portraits taken after the ceremony, the photographs
mainly documented the participation of family from both the Gómez
and the O'Hara sides.

Inventing Traditions

The material details of ceremonies constitute the arenas in which partners' assertions that their unions are legitimate and worthy of respect are
most palpably expressed. Material culture, as anthropologists have long
argued, can be mined for clues to the social relations, beliefs, and values
that are the more ineffable stuff of culture. The varied indicators that tell
us that a particular occasion is a wedding also constitute a site where creativity and conformity intersect, and sometimes become indistinguish-
able from one another.

This is the domain in which each decision about clothing and decor
tells the audience how the gay or lesbian couple understand their experience in relation to a set of diffuse expectations they and their guests conceptualize as "tradition." Tuxedos or similar formal wear, white bridal
dresses with veils, ornate flower arrangements, multitiered white wedding cakes, engraved invitations, ushers who seat guests on the right or
the left depending on which partner's side they represent—all of these
gestures evoke participants' associations with the generic wedding. If gay
and lesbian couples can make their invocation of "wedding" convincing,
then they may also be assured that the audience accepts their claims to
authenticity. The absence of these elements, or their rejection, also sends
a message, of course, as couples who wear more casual clothing, make
their invitations themselves, have potluck receptions, or do without the
services of a formal officiant deliberately situate themselves at some distance from these wedding conventions.

My view of lesbian and gay commitment ceremonies as instances of
people "inventing traditions" clearly depends on the pathbreaking work
of Eric Hobsbawm, Terence Ranger, Benedict Anderson, and Raymond
Williams, all scholars who have offered ways to think about the constructedness of cultural forms and the flexibility and indeterminacy of

both history and tradition.[37] As Hobsbawm explains, " 'Invented tradition' is taken to mean a set of practices, normally governed by overtly or tacitly accepted rules and of a ritual or symbolic nature, which seek to inculcate certain values and norms of behaviour by repetition, which automatically implies continuity with the past. In fact, where possible, they normally attempt to establish continuity with a suitable historic past."[38]

The media through which tradition is invoked can, according to these formulations, vary enormously, including such devices as linguistic usages that imply continuity with the past; food, music, and decor that recall particular readings of history; and other forms of expression that constitute claims to tradition. These significations, as Benedict Anderson argued in his work on nationalism, are "cultural artefacts," attributes that signal particular assertions of identity. Their flexibility above all demonstrates Raymond Williams's portrayal of hegemony as a "lived process" that complicates attempts to understand domination and subordination as one-dimensional or static.[39]

The power of Allen and Eric's ceremony, for example, flowed directly from its straightforward placement in a formal church setting. Congregants' reactions depended on their absorbing the novelty of the occasion, on their counterposing the reiteration of the "traditional" Christian wedding against the fact that a nontraditional couple was being blessed and accepted in this setting. No further commentary needed to be made; the only note of incongruity resided in the identity of the couple, a departure that was barely discernible in the scale of the ceremony.

In a somewhat different approach, Cynthia and Alisa claimed their right to define their tradition to suit their particular histories and sensibilities. Drawing on elements they understood as "heritage" or "tradition" meant that newness and oldness merged into a reality that was at once innovative and conservative. Bringing a diverse group of guests into their reality, largely defined by New Age spirituality, reverence for the Goddess, and adherence to the principles of the twelve-step/recovery movement, Cynthia and Alisa were able to experience their ceremony as a tribute to both their individual and shared traditions, but also to efface the differences between their personal histories by presenting them within the common framework they drew from the Goddess. In a sense, their ceremony transcended their lesbianism as a specific focus, enfolding this aspect of their identity in a wider understanding of their spiritual roots; it became just one component of their experience of nature.

But while the representation of tradition may contribute to the overall shape of an event, the desire to identify the wedding as "gay" may demand the inclusion of features not evocative of heterosexual ceremonies. The creation of Hannah and Miriam's eighth blessing, for example, insists upon legitimation for their being not just a couple but a *same-sex* couple. In a related strategy, Carmen and Eileen intended their campy march down the aisle to the tune of "Chapel of Love" as a demonstration that their wedding was "gay" even as they strictly adhered to other conventions typically associated with heterosexual weddings. But in a somewhat different fashion, Bob and Mark's ceremony depended on a fusion of elements associated with specialized gay communities, particularly as it invoked symbols of leather and uniform fetishism. Nevertheless, the two men conceived of their union as being rooted in "tradition" because they were reinventing their identities within the context of a new family unit, symbolized on several levels but most assertively with the announcement of their new, shared surname.

Lesbian and gay couples who create commitment ceremonies or weddings, then, tend to conceptualize "tradition" both as something they can appropriate from the wider society and as something they are in the process of creating for themselves. The process of constructing or inventing traditions sometimes leads couples to assume seemingly ambivalent stances vis-à-vis elements they view as typical of heterosexual ceremonies. Even while appropriating these features, couples sometimes argue that the use of these very elements provides evidence of their originality, particularly to the extent that they are not the expected forms for a same-sex wedding. Moreover, features that seem to depart most clearly from the image of the generic American wedding are often mentioned as evidence that could be viewed as indicative of the couple's having been accepted by straight society. This was the case, for example, with Mark and Bob's allusions to leather and uniforms, which because of their positioning in proximity to "traditional" matrimonial symbols were transformed as markers of acceptance by (at least a part of) the wider society.

Like other rituals anthropologists have examined, these events are dramatic occasions that, to quote Barbara Myerhoff, "cope with paradox by mounting the mood of conviction and persuasion which fuses opposing elements referred to by their symbols, creating the belief that things are as they have been portrayed—proper, true, inevitable, natural." To the extent that they employ sacred symbols and configure themselves as "traditional," these rituals present their contents as (and here I again draw on Barbara Myerhoff) "beyond question—authoritative and axiomatic."[40] Just as heterosexual weddings convey to couples their place in the history of their families and remind them of the contribution they will make to the continuation of their line, so lesbian/gay weddings symbolically claim that lesbian and gay couples are not estranged from the values of the wider communities to which they consider themselves affiliated, but that they are also capable of framing tradition however they like.

These ceremonies do not depend on a single definition of tradition to make their impact even as they all manipulate the powerful image of "tradition." Some seem to strive to keep tradition intact; others reconfigure it playfully or solemnly. Some celebrate their involvement in a specific gay/lesbian subculture; others assume that they are simply family members and marrying couples, no different from any other. But each of these weddings makes the claim that the marrying couple are members of the wider community, both the communities in which the couples have their origins and the implied community of the married, even when they acknowledge that they must continue to struggle for recognition of their status. While a strictly formal examination of the ceremonial elements couples deploy may lead us to see these rituals as exemplary postmodern assemblages, celebrants clearly interpret them not as synthetic but as natural symbols to which they have an authentic claim.

Gay and lesbian couples who stage wedding rituals revel in their ability to devise inventive ceremonial solutions to the particular requirements of their situations, to self-consciously craft their identities in the specific features of their presentations. But these couples also use these same tools to establish claims "that gay and lesbian people are just like regular people," as Allen phrased it, to reiterate the legitimacy and authenticity of their unions, and to elaborate their conviction that their love flows from the force of nature, unmediated by artifice. Religious or spiritual references can be used in service of either or both of these agendas, as well as to demonstrate the couple's integration in a nexus of racial and ethnic bonds that work with sexual orientation to constitute their identities.

4

THIS CIRCLE OF FAMILY

On a sunny Saturday afternoon in September 1994, "Bonnie Martin" and "Barbara Hall" spoke their vows to one another in the presence of about one hundred family and friends who had gathered to support them. The ceremony was presided over by two ministers, a Methodist pastor whose church Bonnie's family had attended for many years and a Presbyterian whose openly lesbian stance has stimulated tremendous controversy within her church both locally and nationally. Held outdoors on the lush grounds of a Northern California conference center, the ceremony was followed by cocktails, a sit-down dinner, music and dancing, all in a romantic poolside setting. As the guests arrived and found their way to the glade where the ceremony was to be held, musician colleagues of Barbara played chamber music. During the ceremony, other music was provided by friends of the couple, one of whom had written a humorous song about them and their relationship specifically for the occasion.

Bonnie, thirty-two, and Barbara, thirty-seven, both have their roots in small towns in the Midwest, though Bonnie's family moved to the Bay Area when she was young and she grew up in the suburbs of San Francisco. In describing the process through which they decided to have a ceremony, both women stress having been raised by parents who had long-term, stable marriages.

> It's kind of like Bonnie says. Her parents have been together for a long time. My parents were. So that's what I got used to, this thing that had been publicly acknowledged, this thing had been recognized, and I don't know why it is, but I think that sometimes going against the grain of the societal norms and the societal rituals is not as empowering as just *doing* them. So for me, to actually go through the process of having the marriage, because that's what society knows, then that gets a whole other echelon of approval that it wouldn't get otherwise.

Bonnie shares Barbara's desire to replicate the stability of her natal family and sees the urge to make a strong commitment as a significant part of her personal identity:

> I really feel that that's the kind of person I am. That I make a commitment to one person and get past all the surface stuff and make a deeper connected relationship. That's always been my goal, to find a person that would be willing to kind of wade through all the shit with me and go forward. So that was much more important to me than dating or doing a two-year relationship, breaking up, two years, breaking up. I could see myself going through life changing jobs and doing things, but I didn't want to keep changing relationships.

The decision to have two ministers—one a Presbyterian and the other a Methodist—perform the wedding had less to do with loyalty to these particular denominations than with a desire to bring together elements of their past and present. The Methodist minister who officiated had known Bonnie's family for years. She explains: "He was a good friend of my parents. So he was a good friend of our family. He had participated in family events like baptisms and weddings. I had a good feeling from him. And I wanted somebody that represented my faith and my family."

Barbara had known Janie Spahr, a Presbyterian minister whose business cards identify her as a "Lesbian Evangelist," for some years and felt that her presence would be essential; because she would bring such a strong spiritual element to the ceremony, her participation would be a "blessing."

The service started with "George," the Methodist minister, talking about family. He invited Bonnie's parents to come up to the front and quoted comments Bonnie had made about the "abiding love" she grew up with and the "kindness, courage, strength" she learned from her parents. Following this, Janie invoked the spirit of Barbara's parents, who are no longer living (or in her words "on the other side"), inviting them to join "this circle of family" and reading from letters they had written which indicated approval of and support for this relationship. She also read a selection of sayings that Barbara's mother had assembled as a wedding gift for her older daughter, along with words of wisdom from her father, explaining that they are "really here in spirit," pleased that their daughter is truly loved by another person. This was an emotional moment in the proceedings; Barbara began to cry, as did some of the members of her family seated in the front.

George then took his turn, talking about marriage as a holy covenant, a celebration of the mystery of great love. He said that marriage and love are not always easy and that a couple has a responsibility to grow, keep their love alive, have a sense of humor, and be flexible. From individual love, he concluded, flows love for all creation.

At this point, Bonnie and Barbara turned and talked to the congregation about love. They described the process that led to the ceremony, the months of meeting with Janie and George and the "homework" Janie assigned them to prepare for the ceremony and for their future together. Janie followed their remarks with her own observations of their growing spirituality during the process, marked especially by the way their dogs sat nearby listening with particular sensitivity. With Bonnie and Barbara looking slightly embarrassed, Janie mentioned some of the things they described to her that are important in their relationship—their walks with their dogs, hikes, the process by which they "let each other in," making a place for each other in their lives, becoming increasingly intimate, and "learning not to be afraid." Janie asked, rhetorically, "Why marriage, holy union?" The answer, she explained, is about respect, sharing values, and the desire to share family. She reminded the congregation that these are "Midwest people with Midwest backgrounds!" (At this, the crowd broke into applause and appreciative laughter.) "What is wonderful about being in a lesbian relationship?" Janie asked, and then as an aside to the audience, "I want you to know they are lesbians!" Lesbian relationships, she explained, benefit from the likeness of two women, their softness, the fact that their similarities limit the need for explanations.

Bonnie and Barbara then spoke of a grounding spiritual balance, inspiration, strength, support to be themselves, and to create a synthesis, to combine their love to make a new entity: "us." Janie acknowledged their comments, reminding the congregation that they are here to "witness their love." The two women spoke their vows in unison, exchanged rings, and kissed.

The next part of the ceremony was announced as a time for sharing. Both family members and friends stood up to make comments, some clearly prepared in advance, others off the cuff. The first to speak was Bonnie's mother, who read a poem she had written. It spoke of love and support, blessings from God, and welcomed Barbara to the family, saying that she fits right in because her name starts with "B" (like all the names in their family) and because, like the Martin family, she comes from Iowa.

At the end of the ceremony, Bonnie and Barbara carried out a ritual they explained as a symbol of the unification of their two families into one. Each of the family members who was present was holding two roses. Bonnie's family's flowers were dark pink and those of Barbara's family light pink. The two women moved through the rows where family members were seated, speaking briefly to and embracing each person who then gave each of them one rose. At the end of the process, they each held a mixed bouquet of dark and light pink roses tied with purple ribbons, symbolizing the new family that the ceremony would create, a combination of two formerly separate units.

Bonnie and Barbara understood their ceremony as marking a reaffirmation of family. Since primary kin from both sides were eager to help them celebrate their relationship, there was no need for them to reconfigure a definition of family; indeed, the similarity in their backgrounds made it possible for Bonnie's parents to serve as surrogates for Barbara's deceased mother and father. Their wedding seemed to enshrine a construction of family that already existed, making it stronger perhaps, but doing so by clarifying attributes already in place.

Do Gay People Have Families?

Much recent writing and scholarship on gay/lesbian culture and history has been concerned with documenting their creativity, vigor, and continuity, and with seeking to justify the logic of the forms they have taken while implicitly assuming their boundedness and integrity. Studies of lesbian/gay life have tended in particular to characterize such social entities as relatively impermeable—though reactive to antagonism from beyond their boundaries—and as interesting insofar as they generate their own cultural rationale.[1] Such approaches have, of course, been essential to formulating a cogent response to the emphasis on deviance and stigma that long dominated the field,[2] as well as to articulating an intellectual stance that might enhance the development of political consciousness among gay men and lesbians.

Susan Krieger's early ethnographic study of a lesbian community in a Midwestern city exemplifies these assumptions. Though her discussion of the role of gossip in the formation and maintenance of community faithfully evoked the flavor of 1970s lesbian feminist society, she only occasionally hinted that the women in the community might have significant ties beyond its boundaries. Certainly the notion that these extra-lesbian connections might form as vital a part of women's existence as the rules and expectations of the lesbian community is never explored. Tellingly, Krieger called the two chapters that dealt with family and work connections "The Outside World I: Work" and "The Outside World II: Families, Friends, and Straight Society." The implication of this organization is that there are boundaries around the lesbian "identity community" that are tangible, mutually agreed upon, and persistent through time, and that the terms "inside" and "outside" describe a lived reality. That the scheme she devises for describing the "community" rests on a geographical metaphor also is revealing, in that it reflects definitions of "community" that are implicitly (if not explicitly) territorial.

Similarly, other sociologists who have examined gay life in the United States, such as Stephen Murray, have placed "community" at the center of their theoretical armamentaria. As I will discuss more thoroughly in chapter 5, Murray's survey of the varied uses of concepts of "community" in studies of lesbian and gay life confirms the reliance most scholars, including Murray himself, place on assumptions of territoriality or at least some geographical referent in defining their terms.[3]

The growing field of gay and lesbian history has also tended to concentrate on intragay experience to the (often unintentional) detriment of studies of relations across boundaries. When the specter of the "outside world" is invoked in much of this scholarship, it is couched in images of reactivity; that is, community studies chronicle the way that gay men and lesbians shape their social lives to shield themselves from the hostility of heterosexuals, be they family, coworkers, or neighbors. These representations assume that relations beyond the presumed boundaries of the gay or lesbian community are fundamentally stressful and antagonistic, though how pernicious actual connections may be varies with historical conditions.[4]

At the same time that this body of work, and the vast outpourings of a growing popular gay/lesbian/queer literature, have contributed to a heightened identity and an increasing sense of entitlement and pride among younger gay people, some recent thinking can help us question the premise of a uniformly separate cultural entity. Kath Weston's pathbreaking work, for example, on lesbian and gay ideas about kinship has demonstrated a reliance on kinship ideology from the wider culture as the foundation for the construction of ideas of gay family, or "families we choose."[5] The gay men and lesbians who appear in her study conceptualized themselves as members of both biological and chosen families but drew their classificatory systems for chosen families from their knowledge of blood-based kinship. And while the existence of reliable, interdependent links with gay kin to some extent offset rejection and disappointment suffered at the hands of biological relatives and promoted what might be characterized as a critique of kinship conventions, they not only never replaced these ties but were conceptualized by gays and lesbians as an adjunct to these other forms of relationship.

My book on lesbian mothers made similar suggestions. Not only did lesbians who were mothers tend to place "motherhood" at the center of their identities, and to regard their lesbianism as secondary to motherhood in explaining "who they were," but these mothers' social networks reflected significant permeability between gay and nongay elements, with blood kin relations continuing to take center stage and to be regarded as more reliable, predictable, and "natural." Lesbian mothers, in other words, not only did not organize an alternative culture once they had children but instead anchored themselves more firmly within an ideology that privileged blood ties and directed suspicion at links not based in biology.

Christopher Carrington's study of gay and lesbian domesticity makes a related argument.[6] He shows that the extent to which the social networks of lesbian and gay couples are kin-centered or friendship-based has much to do with their financial status and social class, sometimes mediated through gender. More affluent couples tend to interact with larger groups of friends and to count more gays and lesbians among them; their circles also overlap significantly into their economic lives as friendship bonds often become the basis for professional or financial dealings. Less affluent couples, in contrast, have smaller, more kin-centered networks and are less likely to mobilize friends to provide specific sorts of assistance. To the extent that female couples are more likely to have lower incomes than male couples, they are also more apt to find themselves in more constrained and more kinship-defined networks. Carrington does not locate distinctly gay or lesbian domestic forms or identify interpersonal dynamics in same-sex couples that could be considered apart from other components of their identities.

In a different vein, William Leap's innovative study of "gay men's English" focuses in part on the overlapping codes that characterize specialized communication devices in diffuse and shifting social arenas.[7] Gay men's English is not a separate language or even necessarily a distinct argot; instead, Leap argues that effective communication between gay men on topics apt to be of mutual interest (such as their shared gay identities) can be framed without departing from standard English usages. Rather than being the product of a localized speech community, as are other kinds of dialects, gay men's English is constructed in fleeting interactions, formed by manipulation of connotations and associations that evaporate as soon as they have been used.

All of this recent work recognizes a lack of boundedness between lesbian and gay life and the cultural nexus in which it is situated. Just as lesbian and gay culture cannot be characterized apart from an understanding of the class, race, ethnic, gender, historical, and other variables that act on the range of choices individuals can make, so we find that treating these cultures as isolated or impermeable entities is as flawed as imagining other sorts of cultural units in this way. Anthropologists have come in recent years to be intensely suspicious of notions of boundedness when applied to tribal, ethnic, or cultural foci, and similar insights need to be applied to the study of sexually defined communities as well.[8] Gay people do, indeed, have families.

"The Child Who Didn't Grow Up"

It took many phone calls, messages, and delays before I was able to finalize plans to talk with "David Barber" and "Bill Edwards" about their wedding. Since their 1990 ceremony, David and Bill have adopted three infants, and as the children are still only toddlers, their schedule is very much dominated by the exigencies of child care, bedtimes, bathtimes, and naps. David and Bill live in San Francisco's relatively conservative Monterey Heights district, a neighborhood of gracious single-family homes where a virtual maze of curving, tree-lined streets wind their way up and around steep hillsides. Though it took less than ten minutes for me to find my way from my Noe Valley Victorian to their stucco split level, I felt as though I had traversed several time zones in transit.

David greeted me at the front door, showing me into a large living room in whose picture window the last rays of daylight faded over the Pacific Ocean. Besides the comfortable couch, club chairs, and oriental rug, all in softly harmonizing pastels, the room contained a vast array of baby and toddler equipment—strollers, play pens, blankets, clothing and toys, all heaped wherever space was available. The mantle displayed numerous framed photos of the children, but David had to climb over a stroller and several boxes to reach them when he wanted to show them to me. Baby things were also piled up on the table in the adjoining dining room and in the other visible corners. The children were asleep upstairs.

David, a psychotherapist in private practice, is tall, thin, and quite fair, forty-six years old, with an angular clean-shaven face marked by high, prominent cheekbones. Bill had worked late and arrived a few minutes after I did. Thirty-nine years old, he is shorter and stouter than David, with thick brown hair and a full mustache. Bill is a medical administrator. Both men have also been involved in real estate investing over the years, separately and together, and they eagerly talk about the properties they own in addition to this house.

David and Bill spoke to me at length about their two families. David grew up in the Pacific Northwest and was raised Presbyterian; Bill comes from a large Irish-Catholic clan in New England. The overlapping stories that composed their wedding narrative meticulously traced the sequence of how they met, how they came out to their families, and how these benchmarks of their relationship intersected with details of their family's histories and with their many joint and individual real estate ventures. For three years after their relationship began in 1982, they maintained a bicoastal relationship, with Bill living in New York and the two men having twice-daily phone conversations. After Bill moved to San Francisco in 1985, the two men lived separately for several years, but once David had begun to spend all his nights at Bill's house, they decided to buy a home together. Bill accounts for this decision as growing directly from the values he learned in his family, explaining, "I really am traditional, and it didn't feel right. . . . He moved in, but it didn't feel right, because the motto I came from was 'you go buy a new home together.'"

Once they moved in together, it was only a matter of time before they would make more explicit statements about their relationship to their families, and how they accomplished this was a matter of central concern to both men. A major "turning point in terms of being more visible" involved their attendance at Bill's sister's wedding. Although it was held on the East Coast, Bill invited David, and his presence started the family talking. Bill's account of these events, like his comments about virtually every other aspect of his and David's life together, draws on his understanding of his place in his family to make sense of his choices and decisions. David and Bill agree, for instance, that it was "natural" for them to decide to get married once they had a home together. As Bill explained, "We both come from very strong marriage models. . . . Maybe it just felt natural because we bought a home together. . . . Because all of a sudden furniture was being combined." He adds that they had begun to visit frequently with David's parents and even to take vacations with them. "That solidified it," he said.

Right after moving into their current home, the two men had a huge party and invited virtually the entire neighborhood to join their gay and lesbian friends for a housewarming. The positive response that followed from this gesture was further confirmation of the naturalness of their connections. Bill explains his feelings at the time:

> It was very amazing. And that was rather reassuring and psychologically it was *very* important for me because I had no history of anyone in my family being gay. No relatives. Didn't have exposure to gay people myself, so it was very supportive and reassuring that . . . you could be out and comfortable [and that] it was no big deal.
>
> ELLEN: Including among people who were not gay?
> BILL: Right. We're right on the fence. We have many straight friends.

Around the same period, Bill initiated a discussion about having children and David quickly agreed, even though he says he'd never before given serious thought to parenthood. In contrast, Bill explains that his desire for children was lifelong, but that it began to feel more urgent during the time they were planning their ceremony. "I came from a large family. . . . I didn't know how it was going to happen . . . [but] I came from a family in which love of God and love of family was important." Even as they were preparing for the ceremony, Bill started exploring private adoption resources in the Bay Area and finally located a suitable birth mother in June, just a month before the wedding. Her delivery date was in August, so as the date of the wedding approached, the two men knew that they would be becoming parents only a month or so later. Not wanting to "up-stage" their wedding, they kept the impending birth to themselves.

At the time that Bill first told his mother about their commitment ceremony plans, she urged him to make the event modest, something that could be held in his home. While she made it clear that the family would never consider anything other than full participation, she also seemed to be somewhat embarrassed at the prospect of being publicly labeled as the mother of a gay man. Her embarrassment surfaced most clearly in constant suggestions that he reduce the guest list, particularly among her relatives and friends, and in her insistence that a simple, at-home ceremony would be the most tasteful way for the two men to mark their union.

But Bill and David did not want a simple ceremony in their living room. They wanted to do something big and elegant, and to have their ceremony in a church. David says, "We decided that we wanted to make it really fabulous." As Bill explains: "It was a big issue for us. . . . Why wouldn't we go to the Fairmont? We were professionals in income, and [both] our parents . . . had . . . a lovely wedding. . . . They didn't go to a funky garage when they were getting married. And my sisters all went to lovely spots." The two men felt that they were known in their social cir-cle for entertaining graciously, and their expectation for their wedding was that it should surpass events they had held in the past.

Bill's mother's hesitant, but eventually supportive, response stood in stark contrast to the reaction of David's family. He wrote letters to his parents and to his sister and brother-in-law some six months before the ceremony, letting them know that he and Bill were planning a commit-ment ceremony. But as he explains, "My brother-in-law wrote back on behalf of my sister and himself, saying that they didn't want to be in-volved in any way. That they thought this was between the two of us. And they would appreciate our not including them. So that was that. And then I got a letter from my mother saying that my father and her, that they also would not have any involvement in it." David reports that even though previous antagonistic interactions with his parents over his sex-ual orientation made him anticipate a response like this, "It was very

painful. I remember crying about it. . . . So we then went forward knowing that my family wasn't going to be participating in any way."

Everything about their commitment ceremony was planned in order
to facilitate the full participation of family and friends. They chose a Saturday in July so that family members with children could incorporate the
wedding into their summer vacations. Since many of Bill's family members could not easily afford to come cross-country with their children,
David and Bill put all of them up at a downtown boutique hotel, ultimately booking thirty rooms for two days. They also paid the airfare for
some relatives and bought formal dresses for two of Bill's sisters. A rented bus transported these guests from their hotel to the large Unitarian
Church where the ceremony was held and then to the elegant Nob Hill
hotel where a dinner-dance reception for 225 had been arranged. In lieu
of a standard rehearsal dinner, the night before the ceremony Bill and
David (whose favorite vacation destination is Hawaii) hosted a lavish
luau for about sixty out-of-town guests at their home. Virtually all the
guests at this event dressed, as instructed, in Hawaiian-theme clothing.
The hosts draped them with leis as they entered the party; entertainment
was provided by a troupe of hula dancers.

Just a week before the ceremony, David's parents and then his sister
and brother-in-law suddenly announced that they would attend after
all, but that they would not bring his sister's children along with them.
All four arrived on a late Friday night flight, just allowing them to appear at the house for the very end of the luau. Even so, after staying only
a short time, David's father announced that they had to go. When David
asked his father to make sure his mother got some rest the next morning, so that she would have plenty of energy for the ceremony, his father
balked, arguing that she wouldn't need much energy for the minimal
role they were planning to play in the festivities. On the way out, he
scornfully pitched his lei into the shrubbery. Their participation in the
commitment ceremony itself, the next day, was as limited as they had
predicted. They refused to pose for family portraits at the church, and
left the reception, apparently scandalized, when David and Bill got up
for the first dance.

Both David and Bill describe the ceremony itself as an intensely emotional experience. Bill's account revolves around the participation of his
family members and his efforts to structure the ritual on the model of a
Catholic mass. Only the benediction and consecration, according to Bill,
were omitted. The Catholic mass provided a particularly apt structure

for their ceremony, he explained, because it offers numerous opportunities for participants to read prayers and so allowed them to have many different people take active ritual roles, people, David emphasizes, who had been important in supporting their relationship and whom they wanted to honor and acknowledge.

David's description is more focused on his emotional response to the ritual. "I cried through the whole thing, from beginning to end. Nonstop through the whole thing. For an hour, I was crying." Just before they walked down the aisle, the minister gathered the two men and their witnesses together to hold hands. She set a very emotional tone (all Bill could say about it in retrospect was that it was "very lovey-dovey"), and not only David but most of the witnesses began to cry at this point.

David also explained that "we wanted to acknowledge how long couples had been together, straight and gay," and that they inserted some readings into the text that would remind the witnesses that their relationship fit into the larger category of other committed relationships, whether homosexual or heterosexual. To emphasize that message, it was important to David and Bill that all their 225 guests know the story of their long relationship and something about the process that had led to their commitment ceremony. They prepared a statement that was displayed at each place setting so that every guest would have a copy of their story as a souvenir of the day.

Once upon a time a charming fair-haired Yankee ventured to the city of St. Francis seeking renewal in that spectacular land of seven hills above the sparkling waters of the Golden Gate. On the final day of his journey, he met a tall, friendly cowboy. With glad hearts, they quickly got acquainted, danced the night away, and then all too soon, the Yankee flew away in a big, roaring jet.

The very next day, the Yankee had a yearning to call the cowboy and thank him for his Western hospitality. Then the next day, he decided to call again. And the next day, too. The day after, he called in the early morning rather than in the evening. Just to be different, on the fifth day, the Yankee called the cowboy in the morning and in the evening. Three thousand miles seemed so far away and yet it felt so close, thanks to AT&T.

It has often been debated whether long-distance relationships are worth a thin dime. The arguments against it [sic] are very convincing and have been raging for years. You read about the difficulties of bicoastiality in the

press. You hear about it on TV. Everyone seems to have their own har-
rowing story. It really has become very popular thinking that if you meet
someone identified as being from far, far away, you shouldn't dance but
one dance, and certainly not tell your real name. Yet with all due respect,
it seems that the new, incredible power of the telephone has not been fac-
tored into these almost fool-proof arguments. It must seem a surprise that
the telephone can make you feel like you're right there with the most distant of callers. You actually can reach out and touch.

The Yankee and the cowboy found that to be so. Before long, they were
telephoning every day, both morning and night. Not a day was missed.
The Yankee called at 9 A.M. Eastern Standard Time, and the cowboy
called at 8 P.M. Pacific Standard Time, and sometimes in between. The
highlight of the week was calling on Saturday nights to read the Sunday
New York Times out loud on the phone with Frank Sinatra crooning in
the background on the radio.

This went on for an astonishing one thousand and ninety-five days.
AT&T stock soared. People watched the stock go up and didn't know why.
AT&T truly did cultivate the relationship between the Yankee and the
cowboy. Though, of course, periodic bicoastal visits helped some too. But
these trips were made so much easier by the daily calls.

Despite terrible odds and powerful social mores, the relationship flourished. The cowboy had indeed lassoed the Yankee, or was it the other way
around? The Yankee packed up his bags, sold his furniture, gave notice at
his place of employment, and hardest of all, said goodbye to his wonderful, large family. He then set out, spending ten days traveling across the
land, visiting ex-Easterners along the way. Meanwhile, the cowboy picked
up fourteen suitcases at the airport that had been sent out ahead. The
cowboy knew now for sure that the Yankee was due.

As the Yankee returned once again to the magic of the seven hills above
the sparkling waters of the Golden Gate, there was much excitement in
the air. The cowboy met him with great happiness and helped him to set
up a new life in the windy hills. There was so much to do: a new condo to
renovate, new furnishings to choose, new friends to meet, a new job to be
found, and new extended family to greet. Before long, the Yankee desired
a bigger house and a larger garden. The cowboy helped him move into a
quiet neighborhood at the foot of one of the hills. And then shortly there-
after, the Yankee and the cowboy decided it was time to settle into a home

together. So they searched the city high and low wondering where they could find a home that could hold all of their happiness. There had to be a very special place.

Nowadays, the cowboy and the Yankee can be found perched high over the Western slope of the city of St. Francis entertaining their neighbors and friends with music and good cheer. Every night, they watch the sun set over the sparkling waters and feel blessed. Who would have guessed that it has been eight years since they first danced the night away? And every day, at dawn and at dusk, the telephone still rings, now delivering happy voices of the Yankee's family and friends, three thousand miles distant, but close in the hearts of these men. So if you ever find yourself gladdened by the acquaintance of someone who lives far, far away, don't believe that age-old thinking. Don't be fearful of the distance. Trust your heart. And most important of all, trust in AT&T. You, too, could find your dreams come true.

This account of the events leading up to David and Bill's decision to marry situates their relationship in a narrative reminiscent of a fairy tale or romance novel. Against all odds, particularly those presented by distance, the Yankee and the cowboy's love grows and flourishes until they finally decide they must unify their lives. But even that decision requires triumph over adversity, as the Yankee must bid farewell to his loving family, pack his numerous possessions (the fourteen suitcases), and make his way across the breadth of the entire country. Their emphasis on the importance the telephone had in facilitating their romance, reflected in their joking reference to its beneficial effects on AT&T stock, is a bit harder to fathom. An association with AT&T—that bulwark of American business—reminds the audience that their love is utterly respectable; this is amplified by their allusions to the home they have established together and to their continuing (AT&T-mediated) intimacy with the Yankee's distant family.

Not only the content of the ceremony, but its size and grandeur, were essential to its successfully conveying the couple's (especially Bill's) new relationship to biological family. Bill has much to say about the complicated arrangements they made for the ceremony and for their guests' comfort, and is particularly vocal about the considerable expense they went to in bringing his relatives from the East Coast (as well as about their good fortune in having their ceremony coincide with a period of airline fare wars). Many in his family had never flown before and had certainly not visited California, so his generosity loomed large in making the entire weekend memorable and in endowing the ceremony with an aura of glamour. The reception alone, which included drinks, a salmon dinner, a band, a harpist, and a chocolate bar for after-dinner nibbles, cost about $16,000, and the bill for the entire commitment ceremony reached $26,000. Bill was the undisputed author of this largesse.

But probably even more important, the commitment ceremony allowed Bill to claim parity with his heterosexual siblings—not in a political or subversive way, he was careful to emphasize, but in a way that would allow him to make a personal statement of adulthood and to demonstrate the progress he had made in life.

> BILL: I guess for me, every one of my siblings had weddings with people present. No one ran off and got married. And so it was the final separation stage for me to go through in my own family context. . . . Because I think before that happened, there were some issues. I was the oldest son. And I hadn't completely separated. And that got taken care of on some level when [the commitment ceremony] happened. I think that's the one thing I usually find myself saying to other people. That definitely gets clarified in a commitment ceremony. So if the parents can deal with it enough, the one thing that does happen is that they realize that their child has finally separated. And has a partner now. And whether they like it or not, take away the gay issue, that does come out.

> ELLEN: And without having done that they still saw you in some ways as . . .

> BILL: Theirs. The child that didn't quite make it. Or have happiness. Didn't grow up. So what happens is that it's thrown up in [your parents'] face that [they] may not agree with [your] lifestyle, but it gets really pushed in their face that [your] life is working and [you] do have a relationship and that it's moving ahead. So it does bring it in a very, very dramatic way back to the parents.

Their closeness with Bill's family increased after the ceremony, even as their relationship with David's parents continued to deteriorate. The news that the couple would be adopting outraged David's parents.

> DAVID: When my first son was born, I phoned. The birth mother went into labor and I felt very connected to my parents. You start feeling like a parent. And you feel it in your body. So I phoned home and I said, "We're going to the hospital now. The baby's com-

ing tonight." And my father said, "This is the most disgusting thing I've ever heard in my life. Is this baby *black*?"[9]

BILL: And then your mother came onto the phone and she said, "Don't call us back."

In stark contrast to David's family, Bill's mother was thrilled by the arrival of their son six weeks after the commitment ceremony and accompanied them and their baby on their "honeymoon" a year later. Each of the three children have been christened both in the parish church Bill and David belong to and in Bill's family's parish in New England. When Bill and David talk about their desire to get legally married in Hawaii in the event that same-sex marriages become legal there, Bill is clear about wanting his mother and other family members to share in the event. He views legal marriage not only as a move that would simplify the complicated financial and legal issues that have become ever more pressing since the men became parents, but sees it as another opportunity to enhance family solidarity. As further evidence of their acceptance by his family, his narrative is filled with stories of various relatives, many of them staunch Catholics and political conservatives, congratulating him months after the ceremony.

The story of Bill and David's wedding returns repeatedly to their view of themselves as individuals who have done something that is mainly important just because it's what they wanted to do. They are pleased that their commitment ceremony might incidentally benefit other gays, but they don't see themselves as having set out to make dramatic political statements. David explains how this view determined their resolution of what would potentially be the most volatile part of the ritual. After their vows and ring exchange, "the big deal was were we going to kiss or not kiss. And given that we had just gone through the coming out . . . so we decided to just hug. And that's what we did. . . . We're pretty private anyhow."

It is only when they describe the enormous number of gifts they received and a series of misadventures with Macy's Bridal Registry that a hint of rebellion creeps into their narrative. After spending Saturday night at the hotel, they came down to the lobby in the morning wheeling a huge cart heaped with the gifts that guests had brought to the ceremony. Both men laugh as David tells the story:

So we roll this thing into the elevator piled up with gifts, two men. And other guests get in the elevator. And they say "Oh, it must have been a big wedding last night." And it's Bill and me in the elevator.

BILL: I think you got wise and told them. Yeah, we did get married. The wife just about dropped her tongue.

DAVID: Just totally. And then we . . . get in the car and this porter is loading up our car with all these wedding gifts and all the hotel guests are standing out there watching this. And you and I get in this car with all these gifts.

Their laughter shifts to annoyance as they recount the misunderstandings and instances of apparent homophobia that accompanied their efforts to register for gifts at Macy's. Friends and relatives who called the store were told they had to have the "bride's name" to use the service, and some Macy's personnel insisted that it was impossible for two men to be registered. But even this mild pique evaporates in their descriptions of the multitude of gifts—mainly china, glassware, and silver—that continued to arrive each day in the weeks following the ceremony, even as they began to prepare for parenthood.

BILL: We got tons, and tons, and tons of gifts! Unbelievable. We had over a hundred gifts.

DAVID: More than that. They just kept coming. And coming.

The gifts transparently signal their friends' acceptance. That most are the formal articles that are the conventional symbols of respectable married life is central to their value; they stand as concrete reminders of the approval and support David and Bill felt they got on the day of their ceremony from almost everyone of importance in their lives, approval that was expressed after their exchange of rings and hugs with a huge round of applause from the guests. Even though the ceremony marked the further deterioration of David's relationship with his parents, it also stands at the symbolic heart of Bill's increasing centrality in his family, now that he is no longer the only "unmarried" child and that he and David have three children. The ceremony is now a memory that is shared with his relatives, and he feels the strength of those memories each time he joins his family for a holiday or life-cycle celebration.

Bill and David were in the process of generating a new definition of family at the point when they held their wedding. As their first adoption drew near, they anticipated the dramatic reorganization of their life together that children would bring. Moreover, each man faced a different challenge in seeking recognition for the relationship from his family of origin. For David, this meant disentangling his notion of family from his ties to his parents and sister, while Bill's task focused on taking his place among his other siblings as an adult—that is, as a married man, a person of substance. The wedding provided an opportunity for him to demonstrate that he had arrived, a message facilitated by, and indeed, symbolized by his economic achievements.

"Over Forty of You Are Related to Us; the Rest Are Our Chosen Family"

"Marcia Weiss" and "Betty Appelbaum," East Bay Jewish lesbians in their early forties, also used their wedding to elaborate definitions of family and belonging. Marcia and Betty struggled for the first few years of their relationship over whether they should even consider putting on a commitment ceremony. At issue for the two women, who were both very active in a Bay Area synagogue with a predominantly gay and lesbian membership, was less whether they could frame their union in sufficiently "ordinary" terms to make it fit some traditional idea of a Jewish wedding, but whether they could create an event with sufficient drama to make it uniquely meaningful to all who attended.

Betty's graduate degree in theater gave her a particular awareness of the performative elements of ritual and how they could, if skillfully deployed, engender a transformative experience for all involved. But both women also had trouble justifying the expense that would be necessary to stage a wedding as elaborate as they had envisioned. And as they were entering their forties, they also had some concerns that this sort thing wasn't really appropriate for women their age, that they had somehow passed the time in life when people get married. As Marcia put it, "I wish I was thirty years old going through this. I mean it seems a little ridiculous in some ways, you know, we're in our forties, and here we are running around like twenty year olds."

Marcia also explained that Betty sometimes thought it would be much more meaningful to have a ceremony "after we had our family." The two women had been trying, without success, to conceive through donor insemination for some time, envisioning their family as ideally including two children, with each of them the biological mother of one. She said that Betty "could see having a commitment ceremony after we have our kids and have our kids be part of it." But Betty hastily explained that this had a lot to do with trying to justify asking friends and family to make the trip to California. "I could see more rationalizing bringing everybody out from the East Coast to celebrate, because I'd want every-body to meet our child, so then we'd just all work it into one big visit." Betty wasn't sure she could ask people to travel so far just for the wed-ding of two middle-aged lesbians, no matter how supportive she consid-ered her family and friends.

Still, both Marcia and Betty wanted to create an occasion that would reinforce the notion that they could start a family just as a heterosexual couple could. Marcia felt that if she ever got pregnant, her family would congratulate her personally and not understand that both she and Betty were going to have a baby. "I think if we had some ceremony like this it would be very clear that they would get it. That we're a family. That if I'm having a kid, she's having a kid, too. That kind of thing."

Marcia and Betty finally decided that they would have a ceremony, even before achieving their goal of having a baby, and in April 1994 my partner and I found ourselves driving to a nearby college campus for their Sunday afternoon wedding. The day was sunny, with bright blue skies and a soft breeze. The whole campus seemed to be in bloom; aza-leas, rhododendrons, and flowering fruit trees filled every vista. As we ar-rived at the college chapel, two men wearing boutonnieres handed us programs and directed us into the imposing redwood and stone struc-ture. The ceiling arched up into a dome and sunlight streamed in through a skylight at the top; even the whispered greetings of the arriv-ing guests echoed through the room.

In the center of the chapel (covering what was probably a baptismal font), the ritual table had been set up under a large *chuppah* made of white fabric with a lace border that draped over freestanding poles. Lavender ribbons were wrapped around the poles and looped up in bows at each corner. Large flower arrangements, mainly in white, separated the rows of seats from the *chuppah*. On the ritual table stood two silver can-dlesticks with candles and a goblet. Guest seating was in semicircular rows facing the table in the middle; a raised area behind the *chuppah* (probably used as the pulpit for Christian services) was not in use. De-spite the fact that this chapel was clearly designed to be used for Christ-ian ritual, there was a distinct absence of intrusive Christian symbolism in its decor.

The ceremony started with the playing of Eastern European music by a small ensemble. The rabbi from Marcia and Betty's synagogue entered, greeting many of the guests who were also members of the congregation. In his opening remarks, he explained the meaning of the *chuppah* as a symbol of family and said that in order to extend its boundaries to include the entire chapel and everyone in it, the ribbons would be brought to each of the four corners. Four people went up to do this as the rabbi explained the intent to "have a sacred space and fill the space with sacred words." This was a tremendously emotional moment, and a number of guests dabbed at tears. A man and woman guest then came up to the front and after some quick instructions led the congregation in singing a *nigun*, a traditional round. The chapel was filled with the sound of two hundred voices softly chanting the melodies of the *nigun*.

This signaled the bridal procession. With several relatives leading, Marcia and Betty entered the chapel together and moved slowly down the aisle. Both women wore simple off-white dresses and each carried a single, long-stemmed white rose. As they reached the *chuppah*, they turned to welcome the guests to the ceremony. Marcia spoke first, noting that "over forty of you are related to us; the rest are our chosen family." She spoke of the importance of their wedding in terms of providing a basis for future lesbian and gay weddings.

She also noted the fact that people had come from near and far to share this occasion. Pointing out her father and stepmother, Marcia said, "Your presence means more to me than you'll ever know." Betty briefly mentioned that her father had been "unable to come," but acknowledged other important relatives, particularly her sister and her aunt, who had traveled a great distance to be present. Marcia and Betty invoked the memories of their mothers, both deceased, who they said they wished to honor with this ceremony. A married heterosexual couple, relatives of Betty's, were then beckoned to light the candles, using (according to the program) candlesticks they gave Marcia and Betty when they first began to live together.

The rabbi then commented a bit on the notion of someone being someone else's "intended," a concept that emerged thematically at several points as the ceremony unfolded. He pointed out that God has been making matches since creation, and "this union is part of creation." The singers who had led the *nigun* returned at this point to sing a song entitled "Bashert" ("meant to be," in Hebrew), composed for the occasion by Betty. This provided another emotional moment, as a number of guests sitting near me began to weep. This was followed by the first cup of wine, and the *Shehehiyanu*.[10]

At this point, the rabbi gave his *d'rash* (a religious insight, often drawing on a Torah text, similar to a sermon or homily). He talked about this wedding as a community gathering, an occasion for the reaffirmation of connections, and as a political statement about our right to freedom, to hold these ceremonies, and of the way that we are all strengthened by the possibility of finding commitment in our lives. He noted the fact that quite a few of the guests present were couples who had also had ceremonies (many of which he had presided over) and that sharing these events constitutes the beginning of a new community. He mentioned that Betty and Marcia had originally met at the Magic Kingdom in Disney World, and that they had taken risks in having a long-distance relationship, risks that he related to Jewish life in general. Right now, he explained, in the weeks following Passover, we are in the time of counting the *omer*, a time during which Jews didn't know what they were missing (i.e., they were waiting for Sinai) until they got there. This is comparable to not knowing how good a relationship can be until you "get there." Counting the *omer* means counting ahead to Sinai, a time of commitment. Marcia and Betty's commitment, he suggested, draws several lessons from Sinai: (1) that one must stick with one's commitment; (2) that there are many different interpretations of what happened at Sinai; (3) that Jews are stubborn and determined; and (4) that caring is a key Jewish value. Marcia and Betty also have something that they can teach the Jewish community—to "lighten up" and understand the value of humor. He described the two women as models of *menschlikeit*, of how to live a Jewish life, and urged them to continue to look for the best in each other. In the world to come, he added, one must give an accounting of all the pleasures one did not take advantage of; for this reason, we must celebrate their taking advantage of their relationship.

The rabbi's comments were followed by the singing of "Dodi li" (from the Song of Songs) and then by an exchange of vows and rings. The vows drew on both traditional and modern sources, with two small children acting as ring bearers. After the vows, a guest read a poem by Adrienne Rich, and then the rabbi read the *ketubah*.

The next part of the ceremony, the Seven Blessings, involved seven pairs (or in one case, a foursome) of guests offering interpretations on the traditional Hebrew texts. For each blessing, the Hebrew was chanted by a male guest to a nontraditional melody composed by Betty. Then the interpretations were offered by a combination of family and friends. The two women who had originally engineered Marcia and Betty's meeting started by telling the story of the cross-country matchmaking that led to their forming a relationship. Their partnership was described as equivalent to heterosexual marriage, a central moment in the continuity of Jewish history, while the speakers also emphasized how Marcia and Betty's shared Jewishness strengthened their match and would enable them to make important contributions to the wider community.

Marcia's brothers and sisters-in-law offered the second interpretation. Their comments focused on the addition of Betty to their family. They were followed by Betty's sister and aunt, who talked about how Betty has long been a person who has brought members of their family together and how characteristic it is that she is now bringing Marcia into their family.

The fourth commentary was offered by a lesbian couple who spoke on the theme of continuity and wished that Marcia and Betty be blessed with a child. A gay male couple, originally friends of Marcia's, spoke on the fifth blessing, focusing on the theme of *bashert*. They underscored the intendedness of the two couples in becoming friends and quoted from the Talmud by humorously invoking the text of a refrigerator magnet: "When joy is shared, it is magnified." Their emphasis was on "community." The sixth blessing was interpreted by another gay male couple, one of whom is an old friend of Betty's. They emphasized the central and essential role they believe couplehood plays in the gay community.

The final blessing was offered by a lesbian couple who had had their own wedding a year or two earlier. One of them described her long friendship with Betty, going back to their college days, and their shared experiences of coming out and "at last finding our heart's true home." Marcia and Betty had made a major contribution to their wedding, leading the Seven Blessings and the *Shehehiyanu*. These comments brought this wedding into the context of others before and after and emphasized the creation of tradition, all of which proclaim the joy of commitment.

As the Seven Blessings were completed, a Jewish lesbian songwriter well known in the San Francisco area invited the congregation to join her in the singing of "L'Chi Lach," a song she had composed based on the story in Genesis where God sends forth Abraham to lead a great nation, promising to bless him and the generations who follow. The rabbi next pronounced a blessing, reiterating Marcia and Betty's hope to have "non-sexist children." He took out a tallith (prayer shawl), wrapped it around them, and had the congregation hold hands, so that they were symbolically embraced by the entire assemblage.

The final moment in the ceremony was the breaking of the glass. Five sample interpretations of this custom were offered in the program, with an invitation to each guest to make up her/his own midrash (interpretation). The congregation then sang "Siman Tov U-Mazel Tov" (the words of which were translated as, "Auspicious signs and good fortune, may these be unto you and to all Israel").

After the ceremony, the guests walked across campus to the faculty club, where drinks, a buffet lunch, and a dance floor had been set up using indoor and outdoor spaces. The band, "The Shetl Blasters," played klezmer, traditional Hebrew, and Motown selections. The brides, seated on chairs, were cheered and toasted as they were bounced over the heads of the guests. Hebrew folk dances alternated with sedate fox trots and rock 'n' roll numbers. In between turns on the dance floor, guests were called outside to pose for formal photographs; besides many pictures of the brides' relatives, various groups of friends were summoned by the photographer, including a large group to sit for a portrait of members of the gay and lesbian synagogue.

Betty and Marcia's wedding is memorable as an occasion that merged notions of family and friendship into a much broader and more inclusive idea of community, symbolized most powerfully with the extension of the boundaries of the *chuppah* to include the entire congregation. Jewishness—the women's involvement with the gay synagogue, and the synagogue members' extensive participation in the celebration—was not just a tradition appropriated for the day, but evidence of the vitality and validity of their relationship. Each person who attended the wedding was implicated; while family (in the sense of kin) played a special role in the day's activities, which greatly strengthened the legitimacy of the proceedings, virtually everyone else who was present was essentially invited to become a family member. This strategy of inclusion was especially marked in the assignment of roles during the *Sheva B'rachot* and the organization of formal photography.

"Who Could Object to Such a Boring and Conventional Life?"

"Margaret Barnes" and "Lisa Howard" held their wedding in a luxurious outdoor setting, a historic Victorian inn in Northern California's wine country. The springtime ceremony was held on a verandah overlooking a formal garden, with both women wearing subdued pastel dresses (mail-ordered from Talbot's) in delicate shades of pink and green. Margaret and Lisa had begun their relationship some ten years earlier when they were students in business school. They shared similar backgrounds, coming from well-off families on the East Coast, and both had attended elite colleges and graduate schools. Now working for conservative investment firms, the two women seem anything but "queer." Their comfortable San Francisco home is far from the gay ghetto, and their demanding work schedules leave little time for participation in gay community events.

Margaret and Lisa's decision to have a wedding was largely inspired by their friends Jeff and Paul, who had held a rather elaborate party a year or two earlier to celebrate their registration as domestic partners. Margaret and Lisa were coming close to the tenth anniversary of their relationship and wanted to celebrate their having endured many challenges to its survival, particularly those posed by years during which conflicting professional obligations had prevented them from living in the same city. A close friend of theirs, actually the man who had introduced them, had died of AIDS shortly before they began planning the ceremony; their experience at his funeral convinced them that they didn't want to wait until the end of their lives for their family and friends to meet. Their conception of their wedding, then, was not only as an occasion for their families and their large circle of friends to support and celebrate their relationship but also as an opportunity for all the important people in their lives to get to know each other and form lasting connections.

Margaret's family had had a difficult time accepting her lesbianism when she revealed it to them some years earlier, and she was concerned that they might refuse to participate. Long before plans had been finalized or formal invitations sent out, she wrote them a letter describing the kind of event that she and Lisa were planning and explaining why the family's involvement was essential.

> I really hope that you will be there too, and to the extent that you feel comfortable, will participate in our celebration. For Lisa and me, this is as close as we can come to a wedding, so it is terrifically important that all our loved ones are there for this once-in-a-lifetime occasion. You know I have always loved weddings because I love the gathering together of all the people who have been really close to the couples over the years. . . . It's a really joyous occasion, and it seems appropriate to gather together all the really important people in your life to witness your commitment and to express their support for you as a couple.

In an effort to acknowledge the problems she felt her family would have with the ceremony, Margaret continued:

I know that it has been hard for you to become comfortable with my being gay and not following the path you had always expected for me. But I also know that you are fond of Lisa, and I believe that at some level you realize that our path is not really so very different from yours, or from that of my sister and brothers. A year from now Lisa and I will have been together for ten years, and our lives are pretty much like that of our married friends—we work hard, we pay lots of taxes, we entertain some, we give as much time as we can to volunteer work, we're faithful to each other, and we take care of each other. Under the circumstances it is sometimes amazing to us to think that we can't be married legally; who could object to such a boring and conventional life?

To facilitate the kind of socializing they hoped would occur, Lisa and Margaret planned the wedding to include a complete weekend of activities in the vicinity of the inn where the ceremony was to be held. In addition to the ceremony itself on Saturday afternoon, those who came for the entire event arrived on Thursday night, spent all day Friday together, shared an informal dinner on Friday, and took an excursion to local wineries on Sunday.

Margaret and Lisa's simple Protestant wedding was led by a Unitarian minister, the same minister who had officiated at Jeff and Paul's ceremony. Lisa and Margaret exchanged nonmatching rings, chosen specifically, they told me, to not look like wedding rings that might stimulate questions about spouses in their workplaces.

In planning the text of their ceremony, Lisa and Margaret modeled their vows on those used by two lesbian friends whose wedding they had attended the previous summer. Each of them read the following statement:

> *On this day before God and our family and friends, I reaffirm the commitment I have made to you. I join your life with mine in righteousness and justice, in love and compassion,*
> *I will be your loving friend as you are mine.*
> *Set me as a seal upon your heart, like the seal upon your hand.*
> *For love is stronger than death; it is the flame of God.*
> *I will cherish you, honor you, uphold and sustain you*
> *in all truth and sincerity. I will respect you,*
> *and I will love you with all my being.*

The ceremony was followed by a dinner, with toasts from family and friends, dancing, and a traditional wedding cake. The two brides took a short trip afterward and returned to their jobs a week later. Though Margaret's firm offers an extra week of vacation to employees who get married, Margaret had not requested this time off, instead taking regular vacation time she had accrued for the wedding and honeymoon. In other words, everything about this wedding was calculated to be in good taste and compatible with family standards for such occasions, but also was intentionally discreet and low-key. For while they wanted very much to celebrate their relationship in a public manner, both Margaret and Lisa were apprehensive about drawing attention to themselves and about coming out to non-gay colleagues. Only a few carefully selected coworkers were invited to the ceremony. In composing their guest list, Margaret and Lisa had to consider not only their own preferences but to keep in mind which of their lesbian or gay guests might be closeted. They had to be careful not to invite anyone whose presence would inadvertently "out" one of their guests.

Margaret and Lisa's ceremony used somewhat different strategies than Marcia and Betty's, but also sought to intensify bonds with biological family while collapsing the distinction, to a degree, between family and friends. Like Betty and Marcia's wedding, adherence to family tradition made the occasion familiar and comfortable for relatives in particular, facilitating the two women's claim to "a boring and conventional life." While they avoided any hint of insistence in setting a tone for the ceremony, however, Margaret and Lisa tacitly established a basis upon which they would be able to demand recognition for their relationship, something which (as we will see in chapter 7) would preoccupy them more in the months to follow.

"Before God and Before Our Families"

"Steve and Tom Rosenthal-Baker" were married in a Saturday night ceremony in June 1993, the night before San Francisco's Gay Freedom Day Parade. Originally from Southern California, they had moved to San Francisco about a year earlier, inspired by a romantic weekend they had spent together in the city, which marked the beginning of their commitment to one another. Steve and Tom had met through their common involvement in a twelve-step organization; Tom had almost immediately become convinced that Steve was the man of his dreams and pursued him relentlessly, sending a barrage of flowers and letters, and calling on the phone several times a day. Though Steve had just ended a relationship that left him wary about getting involved again, he eventually found himself unable to resist Tom's charms. By the time their weekend in San Francisco was over, they had resolved to move there so that they could spend their lives together in what they regarded as a "gay-positive" city. To their amazement, Steve's company proposed a transfer to San Francisco only a few months later, so they were able to make the move under secure financial circumstances and with at least one job assured.

Tom explained to me that he had always wanted to find a life partner and settle in to a permanent, committed relationship.

> That's always been my dream. To find somebody who you can just tell that it's going to be a fairy tale. I basically wanted . . . what my parents had. And I didn't separate the fact that here is a man and a woman. I just saw the relationship. . . . I felt that if I was going to marry somebody, another man, it would either be in a church, in a synagogue, or it would be in my backyard [with] just us saying " 'til death do us part." That's always what I've wanted.

Tom had never felt that being gay would prevent his achieving this dream, though he had not yet met any man who he felt sure was "the one." But when he met Steve, he knew immediately that he had found the person he wanted to spend his life with.

> I loved his honesty. And I could just tell by looking at him that he didn't buy into a lot of what I would characterize as the stereotypical gay male agenda. . . . He didn't go out to the clubs. He didn't buy into all of that. He wasn't petty and he wasn't catty. And he wasn't campy. He was Steve. And there was something extremely refreshing about that. And even though I didn't fall into the catty . . . I was sometimes campy, [and] I've always been a fashion victim. And it was just really nice. He was so opposite that I was just drawn to him.

Shortly after moving to San Francisco, Steve and Tom joined the gay/lesbian synagogue and started preparing both for Tom's conversion to Judaism (something he said had been a long-cherished dream) and for their wedding. Tom felt strongly that his conversion process should be completed before their wedding, so that they could begin their life together with "a Jewish household." He explained, "We were really making a big commitment to each other and it wouldn't be a Jewish commitment until I was Jewish as well. . . . I wanted to make sure that I was wearing tallith [the Jewish prayer shawl, worn by men after their bar mitzvah] before we went down the aisle." On Gay Freedom Day of 1992, they sealed their commitment with an engagement ring. A week later they registered as domestic partners, considering that to be "our legal piece of paper."

Steve and Tom's wedding was designed to be what their rabbi called "high church." As Steve explained, "We wanted it to be as close to an orthodox wedding as we could possibly get without compromising who we were." Tom interjected, "Without one of us having to marry a female." Working with the rabbi, they included elements that "would help to make it closer to ritualistically pure." These included circling around each other at the beginning of the ceremony, the *chuppah*, the Seven Blessings, the *ketubah*, breaking the glass, wearing tallith, and going to the *mikvah* (ritual bath) together the day before the ceremony. Tom's conversion also took place the day before the wedding. He went to a *moyel* (ritual circumciser) who drew a drop of blood from his penis to symbolize his entry into the Covenant, was examined by a *bet din* (rabbinical court), and then went through a conversion ritual in the *mikvah*. Once these procedures were complete, he and Steve stayed at the *mikvah* for their prenuptial ritual bath. There they recited the *Shehehiyanu* together. Steve explains the importance of doing this.

> It was important to us, because we honestly believed that we entered a covenant with God. We honestly believe that our sexuality and our identities were preordained by God. And that in God's eyes, we are legitimate, that our relationship is legitimate, and that our ceremony and our actions leading up to the ceremony also had to be legitimate in the eyes of God. And so that's why it was so important for us to add every [traditional] element we could.

When I visited Steve and Tom in their Glen Park district home, they spoke at length about their hopes to adopt a child, even showing me the future nursery that they had already begun to decorate. Not long before, Steve's mother, who lived in Los Angeles, had reached retirement age and so decided to relocate to San Francisco, buying a two-flat building with them and moving into the downstairs unit. The two men very much felt that this established their home as a kind of extended family, which would provide a particularly good situation for raising a child. The decision to hyphenate their surnames was also tied to the project of making themselves a family. Steve explains:

> Both of our last names are ties to our lineage. And I think that we both are very proud of what we came from, so I don't think either one of us

would have wanted to lose our identity. But, and this is something that Tom and I talked about a lot, we also feel that, especially me, knowing now how I grew up viewing gay relationships, I wanted our relationship to be a beacon of hope to people that have had difficulty coming out. I wanted it to be an example of what could happen if that's what they desire. It went against the grain of a lot of older gay people. We got a lot of flak from people.

Except for Steve's father, who is divorced from his mother and with his new wife has separated himself from his previous family, nearly all the two men's relatives participated enthusiastically in their wedding. As she would have for any other siblings, Tom's sister made matching dresses for all the women in the wedding party, and all his siblings brought their spouses and children with them. Neither of Tom's parents were living, but he placed pictures of them on the *bimah* (the raised platform in the synagogue from which the Torah is read and from which worship services are conducted). Steve's two brothers and Tom's two sisters held up the *chuppah*.

When I asked them what they wanted people to know after the ceremony, Tom said:

> For me, that I wanted my family to know that this is your brother. Because basically the people that were there were my brothers and sisters. This is your brother, as "Mike" (who is my brother-in-law), he's my brother, he's my family now. And that any children that we bring into our family will also be your nieces and your nephews. It works that way. And it's been great. My nephews have always called him Uncle Steve. . . . I wanted them to know that this is my family and this is now your family, too.

Their mutual fascination with their family histories led them to decorate their living room with an enormous display of family photographs representing both sides, some dating back to the nineteenth century. The arrangement mixes both sides of the family and historical periods, making the point that they have merged themselves into one new family unit that is directly continuous with the past. "We specifically put these together so that you couldn't tell family from family," Steve said.

Tom and Steve's wedding, and the steps they have taken since that time to reorganize their lives as a married couple, speak to an understanding of marriage founded on the merging of families. Once they had taken their vows, they set themselves the task of erasing boundaries between their two family histories. Tom's conversion to Judaism is perhaps the most powerful mark of that transformation. Their understanding of the inevitability of their union stands for its authenticity, a characteristic also attested to as they become full and accepted members of their respective families and make plans for the future that will assure their inclusion in a single family unit.

"It Was Like the Earth Being Raised Up"

"Muriel Parker," fifty-four, and "Carol Lang," thirty-seven, held their ceremony in the spring of 1993 in a San Francisco redwood grove. What they had originally planned as a party to celebrate their having registered as domestic partners some months earlier gradually had evolved into a wedding as they expanded their guest list and finally decided to hire a caterer. Since Muriel is active in goddess worship activities and is a member of a crone circle (a support group of women over fifty who get together to perform pagan rituals), there was little question that the ritual would need to be constructed on a pagan model. But Carol identifies as a Roman Catholic, and wanted there to be some touches in the ceremony that would recall "traditional" Christianity.

The ritual was performed in the middle of the redwood grove, around an altar that represented the four directions and their four associated elements with four candles and four symbols. The officiant, a woman minister who is heavily involved in the feminist spirituality movement, introduced herself as "one of the celebrants" as she welcomed the participants to the ritual. She began:

> It was Jesus who said that wherever two or three are gathered, there will spirit be also. Let us acknowledge the sacred circle we create. Let us recognize that this space is holy and that our intentions are good. Let us look around the circle of those who are gathered and let us say in one voice: Peace and greetings to all.

She continued by invoking the spirit:

> Oh, Holy One, wise and loving nurturer, be present for us today. Bless this circle we have created and make it sacred to you. Hecate, Mother of our souls, destiny caller, come to us today, share your wisdom as we celebrate. We come in celebration and thanksgiving for this gift of love which you have given Muriel and Carol. Help us to love as courageously. Help us to

live as boldly. Help us to be as unwilling to sacrifice our happiness to convention. Dwell in us and expand our vision to see your endless possibilities and our hearts to encompass your boundless opportunities. We ask you to bless this ceremony of heart as it unfolds today and the life these two women will live together. Be with us, share with us. Come, holy spirit, come. Blessed be.

North, associated with earth, was symbolized on the altar with a crystal globe and a green candle; east, which means air, was represented by a feather and a yellow candle; south, meaning fire, was symbolized by two dragons and a red candle; and a container of water stood for west; its element was water and its candle was blue. The seventy guests were seated in a circle around the altar, and the minister had everybody stand to "call the directions," which Muriel and Carol described as the start of all pagan rituals. After invoking blessings from east, south, west, and north, the minister said:

Sky above and earth below, we acknowledge the power that you share with us. We open ourselves to the lessons you will teach us. Bless us, guide us, strengthen us as we gather to celebrate this union and our love for these two women. Blessed be.

Since the two women are frequent participants in drumming workshops, they brought drums and rattles to the ceremony and had a local drummer well known in their circle participate. At one point in the ceremony, the drummer and her assistant picked up their drums and came and sat right behind Muriel and Carol, inviting the guests to come up and circle the couple, and to join in by drumming and shaking rattles. Muriel describes "everyone rattling and shaking and drumming and banging. . . . Oh, my god," she said, "it went on and on and on. It was like the earth was being raised up."

The symbolic focus of the ceremony came through the repetition of a single word, *namaste*, which has become a kind of totem for the couple. The word is a respectful Indian greeting derived from Sanskrit,[11] but Carol and Muriel told me that they didn't know exactly what it meant, aside from their suspicion that it comes from "some Eastern tradition, Hindu or Buddhist." During a trip to Hawaii, they saw the word over the picture of a rainbow, and on the spot decided that their finding it was "fateful," and that it contained "the spirit of what we wanted to say to each other."

Even without knowing what the word actually means, Carol explained the meaning they have decided it has for them: " 'I honor the place in you in which the entire universe dwells. I honor the place in you which is of love, of truth, and life, and of peace. When you are in that place in you and I am in that place in me, we are one.' What 'namaste' really means is mutual respect for where you are." Besides having Muriel and Carol repeat the word with various permutations, the minister talked about the importance of friends and family supporting the couple and had them chant, "Namaste, we hear you. Namaste, we see you. Namaste, we celebrate your love." Carol says, "And to have everyone you knew saying . . . that was part of the participation thing of validating in the same word that we use to validate to each other. That's a word that to us says that we really respect each other's place."

This part of the ceremony was followed by a "handfasting," a ritual in which the couple join hands in a way that suggests the infinity of a circle, symbolizing "the entirety of the universe as represented in relationship." In explaining this part of the ceremony, the minister alluded to evidence that women's unions were once celebrated in Europe "in the same way that the unions of heterosexual couples were."[12]

In assembling the formal elements of their wedding, Muriel and Carol freely drew not only on traditions they could trace through their own personal histories, but appropriated fragments of other traditions that came their way. Some of these appropriations were anchored in a mystical sense of their relationship's significance, a certainty that any symbols that they associated with their love and commitment to one another ought to be elaborated and celebrated. Their (inaccurate) use of the Indian word *namaste* was one such instance: their awareness of this word coincided with an incident that they understood to be a key moment in their romance and thus was forever transformed into a symbol of their love. In a somewhat different way, their inclusion of a version of the pagan handfasting ritual spoke to a claim for historical validity, bolstered by their understanding of new research on early Christianity. Both elements linked their wedding and their love to global and perhaps cosmic forces; from their perspective, neither temporal, historical, nor cultural boundaries could undermine the transcendent truth of their love.

Muriel and Carol talked with me at length not only about the shape the ceremony eventually took but the "organic" process by which they created it. To demonstrate, they presented me with a copy of the book they used to record all the ritual elements, pointing out the numerous corrections and crossings out as evidence of the event's development. Some of Muriel's changes to the ceremony had to do with deleting anything that seemed "too political." She explains:

> There was mention made [that] I'm a lesbian and some political statement about justifying the fact that it's okay. I didn't want that in there. Because I didn't feel it was necessary to acknowledge that I'm taking a political stand as a woman loving a woman. I was acknowledging publicly my love for this person. Not because I'm a lesbian, not because she's a lesbian, but because we are one and we love each other. And that's purely and simply what I wanted to say.

While the process of creating the ceremony helped Muriel and Carol define their relationship and what was important to them, their negotiations with family members over who would attend the ritual were filled with acrimony. Muriel, who had been married to a man for some twenty years, has three grown children—two sons and a daughter—and six grandchildren.

> About a week before the ceremony, my older son called and said he and his wife didn't feel that their children should be exposed to that kind of thing. But he himself would be glad to come because I'm his mother and he would like to honor me that way. And then followed an hour or so later by my other son with a similar story. And so I thought about it overnight. And I called them both back the next day and told both of them that I didn't want either one of them at the ceremony if that's the way they felt. They were going to come by themselves without their wives and more particularly, without their children.

Muriel reminded her sons that she did not need social approval to follow her conscience. As a young white woman marrying a black man in the 1950s, she had endured the hostility of her family and community and had not given in. She had raised her mixed-race children under circumstances of tremendous adversity, and she thus found her sons' conventional attitudes particularly ironic. Muriel went on:

> At one point my daughter, who did come with her two oldest children, didn't want to come for the same reasons. And I just told her, "What the hell do you think we do at home? Roll around on the floor naked in front of your children, or something? You think that sex governs our lives, that's all we're about, is sex? You know, we live a normal life. We

want to make a public statement of our love." She capitulated. And did come. And participated.

Muriel's daughter and foster daughter both came and sang a song during the ceremony. On the morning of the ceremony, this daughter, accompanied by her teenage daughters, arrived early to give them "something old, something new, something borrowed, something blue." She then told Carol, "You're now part of our family," which left everyone in tears.

Carol also had problems with her family. She is an only child; her widowed mother has remarried and now travels around the country in a recreational vehicle. They are not close. Carol explained:

> My mother and I have a very complicated relationship about me being gay. . . . What I decided to do was send her the invitation with a letter explaining that this was a really important step in my life and this was something I wanted to do. And she called me from somewhere and said, "How could you do this to me" basically. . . . And I tried to explain to her how important this was for me and that I was only planning on doing this once and how there were a lot of other people . . . that she knew that would be there. All the straight people that she knew that would be there. You know, sort of like, they can support me and you can't. And her whole thing was about how this was so terrible and her husband is very religious and how immoral this is. All this stuff. And so that was the end of that. My fourth-grade teacher and her husband who I've stayed in contact with all these years came as my surrogate parents for me.

The group of people that came together at the ceremony was diverse, including Muriel and Carol's lesbian friends, their friends from other times in their lives, and a few coworkers.

> One of the things that we wanted since we were having such an eclectic group of people coming—we had straight folks, we had gay folks, we had folks that had never heard of a ceremony between women, we had radical lesbians that probably this was the first time they had been in the same room with men for a while. We had a lot of different folks together.

It was particularly significant to the two women that there were a number of children in attendance, and that many of the guests later described the ritual as the most moving and meaningful one anyone could recall. Carol sums up her feelings, "It was like being in a cocoon of love and excitement and joy."

For Carol and Muriel, family was a problematic component of their ceremony. Carol's family's refusal to participate continues to be painful for her but led to a redefinition of her teacher and childhood friend, who did attend, as surrogate kin. Muriel was forced to confront her daughter and sons, and while the results with her daughter were rewarding, her relationships with her sons continued to be strained long after the event. Their ceremony reminds us that lesbian and gay weddings are, more frequently than heterosexual weddings, occasions that mark the collapse or the unreliability of family ties more than their resiliency, leaving resentment and sorrow that may persist long after the ceremonies themselves have passed into memory.

How Rituals of Commitment Construct Family

That weddings are rituals that reenact significant family ties and celebrate efforts to continue and sustain those ties in the future is certainly not a novel observation. But for gay men and lesbians, family bonds, particularly those connections defined as being based on "biology," can be fraught with uncertainty, standing as contexts in which rejection and marginality often loom much larger than inclusion and acceptance.

As anthropologist Kath Weston's work reveals, many gays and lesbians experience ties based on "blood" as ephemeral and unreliable at the same time that they may find that bonds forged with friends and lovers—one's "chosen" family—are both more dependable and less apt to be conditional. But discovering that homosexuality can disrupt the workings of kinship doesn't mean, Weston reminds us, that "blood family" becomes irrelevant; indeed, despite gay people's often penetrating understanding of the uncertainties of kinship, they still refuse to dispense with it altogether. Even when Weston's narrators were well-acquainted with rejection at the hands of family members, they spoke with great emotion of their longing to revitalize these ties. And their metaphoric use of "family" to describe the closest nonkin ties argues for the continuing vigor of family as a set of meanings and expectations, if not an actual array of relationships and interactions.[13]

The commitment ceremonies and wedding narratives that constitute this chapter tell another story as well: that these rituals serve not only to symbolize couples' determination to define themselves as part of families but also to offer a setting in which the very idea of family is explored and sometimes reconfigured. To the extent that family members become key players in the ceremonies, couples can support their claims that these ceremonies are equivalent to weddings. But more broadly than that, commitment rituals often elaborate the formation of a new family that, perhaps paradoxically, enhances the old (conventional) one in that it promises it a future.

A key theme in these stories is embedded in the assumptions of naturalness and continuity that gay men and lesbians attribute to family. As do other (presumptively heterosexual) Americans, they construe kinship as the social expression of fundamental biological truths. In like fashion, adult desires—for committed couplehood, for children, for domestic harmony, or for exuberant sociability—are understood by these narrators as being the products of intrinsic propensities, whether these are interpreted as inherited or learned. This means that the urge to carve out a place in one's (biological) family doesn't need to be explained; it is simply an artifact of one's humanness, an expression of one's heritage, the outpouring of some essence that emerges from deep within one's character.

These ceremonies tell stories both of the triumph of family sentiment and of its fragility, but both kinds of stories draw on the shared theme of the importance of kinship bonds. Even when families disappoint, they are difficult to dismiss entirely; grievances over slights and rejection linger long after the occasions when they occurred. When family bonds prevail, even if indications of their stability are weak, couples revel in their acceptance, and celebrate their inclusion, even if peripheral, in their families. In these instances, "family" acts more as a set of meanings than an actual collectivity of persons; being comprehended within its boundaries releases gay and lesbian couples from the burdens of stigma, allowing them entrance into the restricted world of the ordinary.

5

COMMUNITIES INTERWOVEN

"We talked about having it both African and Jewish. We chose our colors, I think we chose our colors first." "Khadija Imani" explained the nine months of effort and planning that went into creating her wedding ceremony to "Shulamith Cohen," held in the suburban backyard of friends. Foremost in their minds was the importance of making clear their understanding of the cultural differences between them and the fact that their union would not disrupt their continuing allegiances to their ethnic communities—Jewish and African-American. "Our colors were black and white," they said. When I asked them if those colors had any particular significance, they both looked at me as though I was a bit slow. "Me and her," they both exclaimed at once, erupting into laughter.

Feeding each other fruit

While not all symbolic representations of couples' heritages are as straightforward, perhaps, as Shulamith and Khadija's, ethnicity, nationality, religion, and other dimensions of identity experienced as standing aside from or in addition to being lesbian or gay often have starring roles in the decor, liturgy, costumes, or food served at a wedding ceremony. Such ceremonies are not only vehicles for conveying a particular understanding of what it means to be gay and how gayness relates to citizenship in a wider sense, but also reveal couples' understandings of how multiple elements of belonging come to compose who they are and who they will be after their wedding ceremonies. At the same time, these symbolic maneuvers also allow couples to make statements about particular versions of being gay that they espouse; while some codes used in ceremonial contexts index gay or lesbian identity in general, others are used to break apart the unity of these same symbols, suggesting that primary loyalties may be to specific "communities" with which they identify.

The complex interplay of these diverse symbolic systems reveals two important elements of gay and lesbian experience and identity: first, that they are constantly undercut by and mixed with symbols drawn from other areas of life, and second, that "gay" and "lesbian" as labels are often not sufficiently particular to represent clearly the specific affiliations, loyalties, and points of reference that make up identity as lived on a daily basis. In particular, lesbians and gay men tend to represent their diverse affiliations in terms of membership in various "communities," conceptualizing identity as inclusion in an amorphous, but real, collectivity. This language resonates with the terminology of interest groups and entitlements that has become pervasive in the complex politics of multiculturalism and diversity.

Envisioning and Representing Community

In an era in which race and ethnicity are highly visible, politicized and problematized dimensions of identity, and in which battles over affirmative action, immigration, and entitlement threaten to tear apart the delicate fabric of public civility, gay and lesbian couples, no less than other Americans, tend to be conscious and self-conscious about "who they are" from the standpoint of ethnicity, race, class, and sometimes such other characteristics as political affiliation, involvement in a twelve-step organization, or commitment to a particular gay/lesbian subculture. That these designations are often confounded—whether mutually reinforcing or contradictory—reflects years of imprecise understandings of how such divisions leave their mark in American life.

While debates about how best to analyze the multiple levels of inequality that characterize the wider society resist easy resolution, it is clear that ethnic and racial allegiances are a central dimension of identity in the late twentieth century that affect gay men and lesbians just as they do other Americans. Even as "American" continues to be used unself-consciously to refer to Caucasians of Western European backgrounds who are not recent immigrants, ethnic identity has become elaborated among virtually any group that can make a claim to difference.[1] Anthropologist Micaela di Leonardo, for example, writes about the compelling language of "community" and how the Italian-Americans in California she studied used this terminology to situate their identities in the world. Community, she argues, is an ideological construction that generates a "nonmaterial, a conceptual, definition" of belonging.

> We are no longer talking about small settlements, about limited groups of people who see one another daily over a lifetime. We mean instead that *someone* perceives "togetherness" in a social network, or group of networks or even a social category, and thus labels the individuals in that network or category as a community. . . . This metaphorical use of community is now in common folk, scholarly, and especially political parlance: we hear of the Black, gay, women's or press community. . . . Labeling a human collectivity a community confers upon it a hoped-for alliance of interests, solidity, tradition.[2]

Sociologist Mary C. Waters, expanding on the notion of "symbolic ethnicity" earlier framed by Herbert Gans, speaks of the ways in which people claim ethnic labels, particularly so-called "white ethnics" whose notion of their heritage may be imprecise. Deploying seemingly superficial symbols such as ethnic food, music, and the observance of rituals thought to be traditional—the kind of apparent trivialization some sociologists have called "dime-store ethnicity"—seems to enhance feelings of connection with national origins, imbuing ordinary events with meaning and specialness. Waters argues that the choice to emphasize ethnic symbols paradoxically involves yearning for community while simultaneously allowing the individual to represent himself or herself as unique and individual, different from run-of-the-mill white people.[3]

In a somewhat different vein, anthropologist Yasuko Takezawa's work on Japanese-American ethnicity also addresses the flexibility ethnicity may display as its meanings and interpretations shift in various contexts and under changing historical conditions. Takezawa highlights the significance of the internment ordeal during World War II to the formation and continuity of a sensibility that marks Japanese-American identity. The internments, he demonstrates, were a collective trauma that elaborated and intensified notions of shared blood and descent, enhancing a sense of nationhood that would otherwise have been compromised by immigration to the United States. In like fashion, stigma and persecution have made key contributions to the shaping of a distinctive, though hardly uniform, gay and lesbian identity, a development that also may have coalesced, according to John D'Emilio, in the wake of World War II's organized discrimination against homosexuals in the armed forces.[4]

That being gay has assumed many of the attributes of ethnicity may easily be observed in a number of cultural developments. Richard K. Herrell, for instance, has pointed out that Gay Pride parades (his example is from Chicago) make use of many of the same kinds of ethnic markers that might be displayed at an Irish, Italian, or Puerto Rican parade. Herrell notes that, "Formally, all these parades are similar: they all have mostly self-organized contingents that walk or ride on floats down the street; signs and banners; singing and chanting; participants and watchers wearing distinctive clothing and carrying distinctive flags; musicians or speaker systems playing distinctive music."[5] Participants in these events claim a relationship to the city as a whole on the same basis as citizens of various ethnic populations, even as controversy as to the appropriate markers of gay identity is also represented. Both "assimilationist" models (marked, for instance, by marchers speaking for diversity and wholesomeness, e.g., members of gay/lesbian churches, gay professionals, gay parents) and "confrontationist" models (marked, typically, by drag, leather, and exaggerated versions of stigmatizing stereotypes) coexist or compete with one another for legitimacy in these contexts.

For gay people, then, the identity quest may entail distinguishing themselves not only as "gay" or "lesbian" but also in terms of ethnicity, national background, religious affiliation, social class, regional origins, or other attributes, sometimes supplemented by categorizations of specific kinds of gay, lesbian, or other sexual/gender identity. As even a cursory survey of gay/lesbian popular media will reveal, there is a large and constantly expanding roster of affiliations or sensibilities that offer diversified identities and communities to gay men and lesbians. Some refer to specific sexual preferences and practices, such as sadomasochism

(S/M) and leather; others have more to do with style and demeanor. Some examples are butch/femme (particularly for women), "bear" (particularly for men), twelve-stepper or recovery-movement member, and drag. The elaboration of discourses about bisexuality and transgender have added further inflections to gay/lesbian as core identities, and of course, all of the many possibilities are sifted through generational, class, race, and other filters.

Even as gayness has begun to assume some of the attributes usually associated with ethnicity, and as notions of "gay community" are enunciated largely in terms of models established earlier by nationalities vying for legitimacy in American life, recent cultural expression reveals a preoccupation with difference and specificity, manifested in many ways but especially in a flood of publications that define or elaborate other sorts of specific affiliations or loyalties.[6] As I have pointed out in an effort to consider how to define "lesbian cultures in America," the emphasis on unity and sisterhood that characterized the politicization of lesbianism in the context of Second Wave feminism long ago became more a matter of nostalgia than of reality. More recent writing has disputed the ahistorical and universalized images of lesbianism that were once so widely accepted, focusing instead on sources of difference and on the meaning and experience of lesbianism in various cultural contexts, particularly in different ethnic communities.[7]

Shane Phelan's discussion of efforts to treat sexuality as ethnicity traces such thinking to assumptions about sexuality being an essential attribute of each individual, authentic and stable over one's lifetime—often revealed in characterizations of people as "really" heterosexual or homosexual. But she suggests that a probably more apt parallel can be drawn between homosexuality and what Gloria Anzaldúa calls *mestizaje*, defined by a shifting existence in the region of borders, engendering exclusion and loss more than specific positive characteristics. In Anzaldúa's view, being a lesbian is akin to being a *mestiza*—one who has no race or nation but at the same time has access to all. Phelan elaborates, "As lesbians, we (both white lesbians and lesbians of color) are often denied by our families or our communities and cut off from major social institutions, but the fact of our birth and life within those communities and cultures is not so easily erased within us. We may be defined as other, but in fact we are always here, always present before those who would deny us. . . . Rather than being marginal, rather perhaps even than being liminal, lesbians are central to the societies that repudiate them. We are not accepted as lesbians, but our not being accepted does not entail that there is somewhere else we really belong."[8]

Nonetheless, many lesbians and gay men use the idea of "community" to visualize the networks of overlapping affiliations which they claim as components of their identities. Their image of community essentially substantiates ineffable bonds, conceptualizing them as visible, physical connections among people, as actual collectivities as well as more spiritual, less tangible likenesses.

In *American Gay*, Stephen Murray devotes considerable attention to the varied, and sometimes inconsistent, meanings of "community" that have been deployed in reference to homosexuality, whether used as a technical term by social scientists or as a folk category by gays, lesbians, or other defined populations. Looking back to studies of "traditional" rural peoples, Murray observes, we often think of "community" as referring to those residing within some spatially bounded geographical locale. Drawing on this conjunction between community and specific geographical locations, many scholars tend to be absolutist in their conceptions of community, requiring complete institutional diversity as the sine qua non of "community," a demand that disqualifies virtually any group unless it is associated with a geographically distinct territory, possesses a readily retrievable "collective history," and consists of more than what Robert Bellah and others somewhat disparagingly refer to as a "lifestyle enclave."[9]

But these geographically dependent definitions leave out of the picture many phenomena that participants perceive as "gay community." Thus, while it is true that homosexual populations are concentrated in particular, and often well-known, areas of large urban centers such as San Francisco's Castro district, persons who consider themselves members of the "gay community" do not necessarily reside in those neighborhoods. In some cases, territorial components other than residence may enter into definitions of community; Murray cites the concentration of distinctive institutions such as bars, bookstores, political organizations, and the elaboration and diversification of other sorts of commercial and voluntary institutions in particular areas as indicators of the existence of gay community as a geographical entity. Beyond this, however, Murray makes clear that community membership may entail more (or less) than association with a particular urban enclave. Notions of community may, rather, be revealed in subjective or native constructions of identity that defy or amplify simple geographical definitions. In the course of his effort to generate more objective and demographic definitions of gay community, Murray shows that views of what it takes to be a member of the gay, lesbian, or more recently, queer community overlap in varying ways with sexual, political, spiritual, and performance criteria, as they also intersect with other sources of identity or community identification (such as that provided by ethnicity or race).[10]

As we shall see in this chapter, gay and lesbian weddings and commitment ceremonies provide occasions on which ethnicity, nationality, community, and other indicators of identity beyond or within the boundaries of being gay or lesbian frequently take thematic center stage, sometimes with complicated and multilayered representations and sometimes with shorthand cues used to invoke an affiliation without dwelling on it extensively. The idioms within which community is enacted suggest a process of "imagining community" that recalls Benedict Anderson's understanding of collective identities as "cultural artefacts."[11] While couples may not feel it necessary to make these points on a regular basis in daily life, the merging of identities that is to some degree a theme of marriage seems to necessitate a parallel statement of individuality, particularly when couples come from distinct ethnic, national, or religious backgrounds. When family members or friends who represent these identities attend or participate in the ceremony, their presence reaffirms the couple's ethnic affiliations.

Black and White: A Color Scheme

Khadija and Shulamith's effort to make their wedding represent the coming together of two cultures only began with their color scheme of black and white. Both women had grown up in the same large Midwestern city at around the same time (they are thirty-nine and forty), but in vastly different milieus. Shulamith's family members are lower middle class,[12] religiously observant and Zionist Jews whose attitude toward Judaism verges, in her phrase, on being "separatist." In contrast, Khadija was raised in a working-class black community that viewed all white people, but especially Jews, with suspicion and hostility. Their coming together was not something either of them would have predicted, and in the early stages of their relationship they both resisted forming a serious commitment. Shulamith had just ended a long-term relationship and wasn't sure she wanted to be tied down, but probably more important, she was concerned about her long-standing attraction for non-Jewish women, something she and a Jewish friend (who was trying to understand a similar pattern in her own life) had spent a lot of time analyzing. Since her sister, also a lesbian, had a history of choosing only Jewish women as lovers, Shulamith was especially worried that her preference reflected some sort of personal emotional problem. She described her discussions with her friend:

> "What's this about? What goes on?" 'Cause our friends were always Jewish, but our lovers were never Jewish. Was it too close? Was it too similar? Was it too much of a mirror? Was there not enough spark? Was there not enough difference? Was it too family-familiar?

Khadija, on her part, had been struggling with some of the same issues and had come to the conclusion that she should consider only black women as potential partners. She explained her thinking on why a relationship with another black woman would have a better chance of being successful.

> There's a whole lot. There's automatic knowing of one another. Which is teaching in a mixed relationship. And it's automatic, not only knowing, but understanding. Automatic history with one another. You talk about something and it's been history although we've been raised in two different states. The same kind of food was set on the table. That kind of stuff. And [it's] also automatic you're on the same battleground together. The same struggles. You don't have to teach each other about one another's struggles and want the person to stand with you. You automatically have that same struggle together. And then in the lesbian community, it's not supported by black lesbians for black lesbians to be with white lesbians. And I missed that support of black women.

Since both women had been working through similar issues about ethnicity, neither was prepared to find herself seriously committed to this relationship. Their courtship was long and halting, and they hesitated for months before beginning a sexual relationship. But once they did sleep together, neither had any doubt that things had gotten serious. Shulamith explains, "So a month later we were in a committed relationship and a month after that we were engaged to be married." It was only some months later that they found a place to live together.

Everything in their wedding was intended to confront the issue of cultural difference. While some elements of the ceremony they designed offered a possibility for the reconciliation of their differences, both women wanted to make clear that their alliance would not constitute a merging or an erasure of history. At their rehearsal brunch, for example, held a week before the ceremony, the menu was intended to blend their two cultures. As Khadija explained, "We fixed black and Jewish food for the rehearsal. Fried chicken, bagels, and cream cheese. And we made that ourselves. We wanted to take everyone out to dinner, but that cost a lot of money, so we just fried it up and wiped it on ourselves! That was fun, and it was good. It tasted really good."

For the wedding, Khadija wore what she described as "an African wedding dress," white with gold embroidery, with a black-and-white kente cloth draped over her shoulder. With this, she wore a black hat trimmed in gold. Khadija wanted Shulamith to wear "a traditional Jewish wedding dress," but when Shulamith said there really wasn't any such thing as far as she knew, they settled on her finding a suitable dress in one or more of the theme colors. She finally bought a white dress and, after substituting a black rose for the pink one that originally decorated it, felt she had found something appropriate for an outdoor, afternoon affair that they intended to be dressy but not formal.

Other aspects of the ritual the two women created also reflected their desire to represent their two cultures both independently and in combination with one another. Most significant in this respect was their choice of officiant. As Khadija explained, they agreed that they wanted a lesbian who was both black and Jewish to act as "rabbi," though having an ordained rabbi was not important, particularly since, as Shulamith pointed out, "It wasn't a legal ceremony anyway." They undertook an extensive search for a suitable person and finally found a woman whom they both liked. "She was bi-racial and raised Jewish, with the Jewish religious traditions. And so she acted as our rabbi. . . . And we still have [something] like a kinship with that woman, and I feel like we'll always have that with her," Khadija said. Finding a Jewish woman who would serve "as rabbi" was complicated both by the personal specifications they had and by the fact that they had their ceremony on a Saturday, a day mandated as auspicious by Khadija's astrological calculations but not traditionally permissible for a Jewish wedding. In fact, the first woman they asked to officiate said that she couldn't participate in a wedding on the sabbath.

Khadija describes herself as a practitioner of "alternative religion," and some elements that were included in the ceremony she identified as coming from feminist spiritual sources. A "witch went around and cleared the space," for example, at the beginning of the wedding, and

Khadija used the Book of Runes as a source for their adaptation of the Seven Blessings (the *Sheva B'rachot*), the element of the Jewish wedding that puts marriage into the context of the seven days of Biblical creation.[13] She explained the process:

> It's something similar to tarot cards. But they're stones. Like you pick a particular stone, and you match it up with a book, and maybe it says, "partnership." So I took out things that were like "partnership," and "unity," and "marriage," and things that seemed like they were related to what we were creating. And took seven of those for the seven marriage blessings. And Shulamith was okay with about six of them. And then she made some alterations on one of those. So that's how we created the seven wedding blessings.

The ceremony was held in the suburban garden of a friend on an overcast autumn day in 1992. After two songs, one a Negro spiritual and the other in Hebrew, Khadija and Shulamith walked down the aisle, accompanied by a friend singing "You'll Never Walk Alone." The officiant lit a pair of candles, then softly recited the *Shehehiyanu*, a Hebrew prayer of thanksgiving. She then began the ceremony, introducing herself and explaining what would take place in the ritual.

> *My name is "Betsy Brown." I am privileged to have been chosen to assist Khadija and Shulamith in celebrating their commitment to one another. I am a black Jewish lesbian, and as such, I embody the three major traditions that converge in Khadija and Shulamith. Working with Shulamith and Khadija over the past few months, I have seen them create with love, humor, and respect a ceremony which truly reflects the nature of their relationship. Each partner has retained her individual spiritual beliefs, while also being committed to creating a space where a unified tradition born of this partnership can grow.*
>
> *We stand beneath the* chuppah. *The* chuppah *is a traditional Jewish symbol for openness. Shulamith and Khadija enter a union of openness. Their friends and family stand with the couple, the openness of the* chuppah *representing their welcome. Yet the* chuppah *also symbolizes that they are vulnerable to weather or catastrophe. The flimsiness of the* chuppah *reminds them that the only thing that is real about a home is the people in it who love and choose to be together, to be a family. The anchor that they will have will be holding on to each other's hand. The* chuppah *symbolizes a home of love, honesty, and community.*

The rabbi then asked (rhetorically) who would stand up in support of the union. A friend of each of the women, one Jewish and one African-American, spoke in turn from beneath the *chuppah*, making a short statement about her history of friendship with first Shulamith and then Khadija, and confirming her commitment to offer support and respect to the new union. After these two speakers had completed their comments, Shulamith's lesbian sister offered her congratulations, making clear that their kinship was especially precious and close because they had grown up together as lesbians. A fourth speaker addressed the two women as a couple, reiterating her support for their future relationship.

This brought the couple to the recitation of the Seven Blessings, which the rabbi explained had been devised by the two women, though she made no mention of their use of the Book of Runes for the text. The blessings she read were as follows:

> *The first blessing is Partnership. Partnership is a gift. You're both put on notice not to collapse yourselves into this union. True partnership is only achieved by separate and whole beings who retain their own uniqueness even as they unite. Remember to let the winds of heaven dance between you.*

> *The second blessing is Miracles. Miracles come from love and are created by love, and magnetized [sic] to you through love. When you want to give or receive love and miracles, all you have to do is intend to do so. Reach for the highest and biggest dreams. Create quality in your experience. Each one of you is a bundle of loving energy capable of creating anything you choose. Miracles come from your love if you're willing to open your heart, to love yourselves, each other, and others. Life will always be a miracle. The degree to which you are open and loving is the degree to which miracles will come your way.*

> *The third blessing is Trust. Trusting is opening your heart, believing in yourself and in the abundance of the universe. It is known that the universe is loving, friendly, and supports your higher good. Trust is knowing you're part of the process of creating and believing in your ability to draw to you what you want.*

> *The fourth blessing is Movement. Moving to a higher path, it's time to change the old and build the new.*

> *The fifth blessing is New Beginnings. A new beginning is akin to the moon, the intuitive part of our nature, with its urge toward harmonizing and ad-*

justing. In the sphere of personal relationships, which embodies the need to share, the yearning to be desired, it is a search after similarities.

The sixth blessing is Transformation. As you join in partnership and your lives continue to weave together, the fabric of your lives cannot help but be irrevocably changed. Your purpose in choosing each other as powerful women is to transform yourselves into your fullest potential selves. Your lifelong work will be finding the balance between keeping your separate identities and discovering your identity as a couple. Undertake to do it joyfully.

And the seventh blessing is Spirit. There's another realm of partnership that we're being called to consider. For the path of partnership can lead you to the realization of a greater union, a union with a higher self, the union with the divine. The ultimate gift is the realization of the divine in all things. God always enters into equal partnership.

This brought Khadija and Shulamith to their version of the circling traditional to Jewish weddings.[14] The rabbi explained that each would circle the other seven times and that the number seven signifies wholeness and completion. As each woman moved around the other, the rabbi read the famous passage from the Book of Ruth (1:16–17), where Ruth refuses to leave her mother-in-law Naomi.

Do not urge me to leave you, to turn back and not follow you. For wherever you go, I will go; wherever you lodge, I will lodge; your people shall be my people, and your God my God. Where you die, I will die, and there I will be buried. Thus and more may the Lord do to me if anything but death parts me from you.[15]

After the circling, another spiritual was sung while Khadija, Shulamith, and their witnesses signed the *ketubah*. The *ketubah* was then read aloud in Hebrew by Shulamith's sister and in English by the rabbi. While the language of the *ketubah* followed the typical wording of such documents closely, the statement closed with their promise "to establish a culturally diverse home together."[16]

At this point, the rabbi led the two women in their vows. "We are all teachers," she intoned, "and what we teach is what we need to learn, and so we teach it over and over again until we learn it. Shulamith, are you willing to be Khadija's teacher?"

Shulamith answered, "Yes, I am," slipping the ring on Khadija's finger.

"Khadija," continued the rabbi, "are you willing to be Shulamith's teacher?"

"Yes, I am," said Khadija, and she placed the ring on Shulamith's finger.

After another spiritual was sung, the ritual moved to a reconstruction of the African-American custom of jumping the broom. A friend wearing a colorful African dress and turban came up to the *chuppah* carrying two brooms tied together and decorated with crepe paper streamers. Taking the microphone, she spoke about having mixed feelings about the ritual. Of course, she was happy for Khadija and Shulamith and found the "Jewish ceremony" beautiful; on the other hand, she indicated that she felt that Khadija's African-American roots were somewhat subordinated by what she perceived as the predominantly Jewish character of the ritual.[17] She explained that jumping the broom originated among African-Americans and suggested that the broom could be said to symbolize cleaning out the house, that is, starting anew. When she prompted them, Khadija and Shulamith made three jumps over the broom, first over the ends of the broom wrapped in the colors that represented their own cultures, as the friend explained, and then over each other's cultures. The final jump represented, according to the friend, the way in which marital unity would smooth differences between them and between their cultures. The broom was then passed around the audience so that each guest could pull out a straw to keep.

The Hebrew song based on the Song of Songs ("Dodi li") followed the broom jumping, after which the rabbi held up a glass wrapped in a piece of black-and-white kente cloth. She placed it on the ground and Khadija smashed it, recalling the tradition of generations of Jewish grooms and evoking the characteristic cheers and applause from the audience.

Finding a balance between cultural amalgamation and separation in the wedding proved to be a tremendous challenge. When Shulamith and Khadija talked to me about the wedding some two years later, they were still concerned about lapses they felt had occurred that day and continued to worry that their message had not been adequately conveyed.

Incorporating African elements into the ceremony was particularly vexing because Khadija admitted some uncertainty about exactly what such elements should be. Drawing on their readings in African-American history, the two women decided that a broom-jumping ceremony would symbolize both their separate cultural backgrounds and the unity they felt they had achieved in their relationship. Slaves, they knew, could not legally marry, and instead devised the ritual of jumping the broom to formalize their unions. In the version Khadija and Shulamith planned, two brooms were tied together. The brooms were wrapped with blue and white crepe paper on one end, and with red, black, and green on the other, colors that represent their Jewish and African roots respectively.[18] Their original plan was for each of them to jump over the end of the broom with the colors representing her own culture, thus making clear her allegiance to her heritage, and then to jump over the other end, thus symbolizing the coming together of two cultures in their unified relationship. They also wanted to draw upon significant parallels they saw between the status of slaves and the civil condition of homosexuals, and intended to evoke that likeness as the main political message of their wedding.

> We wanted to bring that out at the wedding: Just as it was illegal for slaves to marry, it's illegal for lesbians to marry. So that was . . . an African part that we were bringing. . . . And we were to jump over our own culture so that we stay in our own cultures, and then jump over one another's cultures. There were two brooms tied together making one broom.

Shulamith and Khadija knew that some of their friends didn't really approve of what they were doing, specifically because their union was interracial. On the way to their rehearsal, a week before the ceremony, a black friend who had agreed to lead the part of the ritual in which the two women would jump the broom complained to Shulamith about the phenomenon of "sisters going with white women." Shulamith did not give this much thought at the time, being quite preoccupied with the arrangements for the wedding, but during the ceremony the friend's ambivalence revealed itself in her becoming flustered and skipping much of the text she was supposed to recite, omitting what they considered the most important explanatory material. Khadija and Shulamith blamed themselves for these missteps, feeling that they should have more sensitively gauged their friend's discomfort. But they also were distressed by the outcome, which they saw as having blurred a central message they had intended to convey in the ceremony.

The two cultures were also represented in the music played during the ceremony. A friend of Khadija's sang three gospel songs and a woman who often serves as a cantor and service leader at Congregation Sha'ar Zahav (San Francisco's predominantly gay/lesbian synagogue) sang two Hebrew songs, "Dodi Li" and "Eli, Eli," while accompanying herself on the guitar.[19] This performer substituted at the last minute for a friend who had planned to provide the Jewish musical component until a family emergency prevented her from attending. While Shulamith was glad the cantor participated because "it was important for me to have the [Jewish] music there," she was unhappy with the woman's performance, describing her voice as too well-trained and operatic-sounding, not like an "ordinary person."

Despite these complaints, the two women felt that the ceremony itself transcended the obstacles that almost undermined it. Shulamith describes her anxiety about the weather, which threatened rain. "It was overcast, which brought the temperature down. And then actually during the ceremony it started sprinkling very, very lightly. And then when Khadija broke the glass, the sun broke through. Right at that moment. It was so incredible. Just when she broke the glass, the sun burst through, and it cleared up, and the rest of the afternoon was beautiful." Shulamith considered the change in the weather an omen of a bright future for their relationship.[20]

Shulamith and Khadija had many levels of concerns about the appropriateness of their interracial relationship, mainly focused around issues of ethnic loyalty and commitment. Their ceremony was successful in their terms to the extent that it resolved these conflicts, problems that were further addressed by the support they received from both their families. Though only one relative from each side attended the ceremony (Shulamith's lesbian sister lives in the Bay Area and played a prominent role, and Khadija's niece traveled from the Midwest to participate), their families were friendly when they later visited them in the Midwestern city where they both reside. Despite the limited direct support from kin at the ceremony itself, both women's account of their visit to their relatives emphasized the more positive reactions and downplayed instances where support was unclear. They explained the failure of immediate relatives to attend as the result of financial problems, and each encouraged the other to make allowances for their relatives' limitations. Shulamith, for example, was initially distressed with her parents' wedding gift—their decision to cancel a debt Shulamith had incurred some years earlier.

> What didn't feel good was that it didn't feel like they were actually giving me anything. Like there was nothing that took effort on their part or energy. It was just something easy that they could just make go away, so it felt like more of a removal of something than an actual giv-

ing of something. So that felt hurtful. Khadija's viewpoint was that they were wiping a clean slate for us to come together. So that had a more positive feeling about it than my first reaction.

Khadija also emphasized the level of support she received from her family despite their absence from the ceremony itself. She had not been back to visit them for many years, and never had been candid enough about her lesbianism to bring a partner openly into her family's home.

> I had gone home with women before, but I would just introduce them as friends or whatever. But this was the first time that I've ever gone home as an "out" lesbian. And then bringing my lesbian partner with me. And then that she is a white woman. And then that she is a Jewish woman. [All that] was a lot to ask of my family. It was a lot.

To her delight and surprise, however, her family greeted Shulamith warmly and seemed to like her. This friendly response was similar to that she had received at Shulamith's parents' home across town, where, to the amazement of the entire family, Shulamith's usually undemonstrative father was almost effusive in welcoming Khadija to the family.

For both women, ties with their families of origin represent their most compelling, even if ambivalent, links to their ethnic origins, to their identities as members of embattled minorities. Although neither family responded with tremendous enthusiasm to Khadija and Shulamith's wedding, and neither family appeared to either fully accept or understand their daughter's homosexuality, the fundamental loyalties expected of kinship ties appeared to be intact, thus assuring both women that their union had not precipitated an enduring rift in their identities as Jewish and African-American. Khadija and Shulamith's wedding provided an opportunity for both women to proclaim their enduring loyalties to "who they were," ethnically speaking, which proved to be more problematic for both of them by complicating their well-established lesbian identities.

"Husband and Husband"

"Nasser Akbar" and "Paul Gustavson" were both thirty-four years old when they had their wedding, but apart from their age, little about their backgrounds is similar. Paul, a native of Minnesota, is a classical musician who travels all over the country to play in orchestras and ensembles. Nasser came to the United States from Bangladesh when he was a college

student and now works as a software engineer in Silicon Valley. Their
North Oakland home, which they share with roommates, is decorated
with posters that proclaim their progressive politics, described in conversation with them as "anti-imperialist." The community with which
they identify includes both men and women, gays and straights, and is
markedly international, multiracial, and multiethnic, as well as being actively committed to social change.

Nasser's interest in having a wedding was largely inspired by his growing resentment at his family's refusal to acknowledge the importance of
his relationship. Most of them took the news of his commitment to Paul
disdainfully, seeing it, he suspected, as a sexual dalliance without real
substance or significance.

> I was kind of sick of everybody validating my brothers' relationships
> because they're married, and my sister was getting married also. She
> got married just a couple of weeks before we did in June. And there
> was all this talk about her getting married and ... nobody validates our
> relationship. My family, particularly. And I ... decided well, we're just
> the same, and we can get married, too. So, there was a certain element
> of rebelliousness there.

Nasser's mother and father live in Bangladesh, where, according to
Nasser, same-sex "fooling around" is a fact of life, though one that typically coexists with heterosexual marriage. His mother's extreme reaction,
bordering on hysteria, to his coming out to her several years before the
ceremony was, he explained, not so much about homosexuality itself but
rather concern about his refusal to marry a woman, linked with anxiety
that he would embarrass her by telling family and friends that he was gay.
She worried about who would take care of him in his old age, doubting
that a relationship with another man would endure for more than a short
time, and fearing that without children he would one day be destitute.
Most tellingly, when he told her he would not consider giving up his relationship with Paul, she said, "Why don't you still get married?" Nasser
explained that in her view, "I could still get married and have Paul on the
side. That would have been fine, because that's the model that a lot of homosexual men [in Bangladesh] do." He notes with some amusement that
he *did* eventually get married, though his union with Paul was clearly not
what his mother had in mind.

In contrast, his father, who had traveled extensively outside Bangladesh, had what Nasser described as a more "rational" response. Speaking

in English when words like *gay* were required because there are no equivalent words in Bangla (Bengali), he asked about Nasser's relationship. "So
that means you're like husband and wife?" he asked. "No," Nasser replied,
"we're like husband and husband." Although his father did not launch
the sort of emotional outburst his mother had, he still told Nasser that he
considered the relationship to be "sick" and "perverted."

Paul's situation was quite different. His immediate family, a mother
and younger brother, were generally accepting of his being gay. He also
had a close relationship with a lesbian cousin and her partner and expected that they would be part of the ceremony. Only a year or two before, he had been best man at his brother's (heterosexual) wedding, and
though that experience brought him and his brother closer together, he
did not see that event as a ritual he wanted to emulate. "[It was] very traditional. Not religious terribly. It was in a church, but neither of them are
religious. . . . Your typical bland wedding. It was pleasant. Protestant.
Lutheran." His mother was not very enthusiastic about his brother's wedding either, objecting, according to Paul to, "the hollowness of certain ritual. She hated the pretense of it. And she hated the sense of obligation
that it left on so many people. So for her, that we would do it, she was perfectly fine with that. . . . Since it obviously wasn't going to be the orthodox, I don't think she was anticipating that it would be something un-
pleasant for her."

But the final impetus for the ceremony came from one of Nasser's
Bangladeshi friends.

> We are very close to a family from Bangladesh who live in the East Bay.
> A husband, wife, and two young daughters. So she and I have become
> particularly close over the last few years, and one time she was talking
> about, "You know it would be great to have a ceremony and we can do
> all these things." Bangladeshi wedding ceremonies are very elaborate
> and very extensive. They run for seven days, [with] seven events, and
> finally you take your wife away. . . . So she said, "You know, it would be
> so wonderful for you guys to do this." So that kind of gave [me] the idea
> of the ceremony itself. And I was also planning to take some time off to
> go to Bangladesh [by myself] and kind of felt that I would like to have
> more of a ceremony or kind of an official bond—not official—[but] a
> somewhat institutionalized bond, so to speak, with Paul before I go.

The two men knew that they wanted their wedding to bring together
aspects of both of their cultural backgrounds and to make clear state-

ments about their values. As Paul explained, "We didn't mind deriving from [a heterosexual wedding], but we didn't want it to ape a traditional straight wedding mindlessly. If we were going to borrow from [the] traditional wedding, we wanted the significance to be relevant to us." Not wanting to imitate heterosexual weddings, then, they hesitated about what to call the event. Their invitation highlighted this uncertainty. It featured a decorative ring circling their names that spelled out a range of possible terms, "ceremony of commitment, a public affirmation, a celebration of our union," and "marriage," though lower down on the page the actual wording of the invitation read: "Please join us for a celebration of our union . . ."

During the months of planning before the ceremony, Paul and Nasser devoted considerable time to poring over all sorts of books about weddings from diverse cultures, searching for customs to incorporate into their ceremony. They were careful to avoid invoking symbols that they understood as inappropriate for a same-sex couple, particularly those that are commonly interpreted as representing fertility, such as the custom of throwing rice or other grain at newlyweds. They also knew that they wanted to explicitly avoid describing their relationship as a withdrawal from their wider social environment, which they viewed as the classic feature of heterosexual marriage. As Nasser put it, "We didn't want to have our union separate us from the rest of the world. . . . [We wanted to say] that people who are there are part of this whole extended family, so to speak, and so we said our vows and made it clear that we are expressing our commitment to each other, but it's not that we are separating ourselves from the rest of the world, which more or less happens in a heterosexual wedding."

Their emphasis on their place in a collectivity that they defined as both personally and politically significant meant that it was important to both Nasser and Paul that the ceremony itself be collaborative and interactional in nature, rather than a ritual to be observed remotely from the sidelines. The ceremony was held in a picnic area in the East Bay hills, overlooking a panoramic view of Contra Costa County. The program proclaimed that the ceremony should not be considered "formal" and urged guests to "lie back and relax—get up and stretch—make yourself at home!" A picnic prepared by the two men with the assistance of several friends was served after the ceremony, and guests were invited to join Paul and Nasser afterwards for a party at the home of the Bangladeshi couple who had been so instrumental in making the ceremony a reality.

As they had intended, the ceremony deliberately combined elements drawn from both of their heritages, though the way in which they accomplished this privileged certain dimensions over others and also highlighted their shared identity as gay men. The Bangladeshi component emphasized the place of the culture in the wider spectrum of South Asia. While a number of South Asian customs were reproduced or configured for the ceremony, the Islamic elements that would be found in a wedding in Muslim Bangladesh were not included. But those features that signaled Nasser's South Asian origins were varied. The ceremony began with the reading in Bangla of a poem by Rabindranath Tagore, who Paul described as "the literary saint of Bangladesh." In the translation that appeared in the program, "Unending Love," the poem began,

> I seem to have loved you in numberless forms, numberless, times,
> In life after life, in age after age forever,
> My spell-bound heart has made and re-made the necklace of songs
> That you take as a gift, wear round your neck in your many forms
> In life after life, in age after age forever.[21]

The core of the ceremony consisted of a South Asian ritual known as *rakhi*, performed by Nasser's two Bangladeshi friends and a close woman friend of Paul's. Sometimes described as a South Asian version of handfasting (the European pagan custom that originally involved a spell being cast by the two people on each other), the ritual called for the joining of the couple's hands with colored ribbons, later removed without being untied.[22] The Bangladeshi friend who explained the custom indicated that there were diverse accounts of its origins and meanings, but that above all, it represented the two men's intent to declare their union but also to acknowledge that they are part of a larger community. Even as the symbolism of *rakhi* focuses on the couple's hands being bound together with ribbons and flowers, he explained, its larger meaning is the bond between themselves and the community; the ritual simultaneously allows the couple to declare their union while also acknowledging their membership in a wider collectivity.

At the conclusion of the *rakhi*, an ensemble of South Asian singers performed a Bangla song, also by Tagore. This evocation of Nasser's South Asian heritage was balanced with references to Paul's identity, represented in the ceremony primarily by the performance of a number of musical offerings by Dvořák, Britten, and Wilhelm Friedemann Bach, all played by musician friends. While the program identified each of these pieces, it provided the most detailed notes for the fanfare, taken from the "Serenade for Tenor Horn and Strings." Benjamin Britten had written the piece in 1942, the program explained, to be sung by his lover, Peter Pears. Paul felt it was important to insert gay references in the ceremony whenever possible, and chose the music with this in mind. Allusions to his Euro-American ethnicity were perhaps more subtlely inserted and often seemed to merge with his professional identity as a classical musician; the musical selections were all by European composers, for example.

Other features that suggested Paul's ethnicity were more structural than substantive. For example, the two men spoke reciprocal vows, which is characteristic of Christian weddings, as was the inclusion of a "sermon"—in this case a commentary on gay love by a friend of the two men. The program identified the time at the end of the ceremony for guests to offer their reflections as "Speak now or . . . ," an echo of the traditional request at the end of Christian wedding rituals.

Probably the most oblique expression of community identity was provided by the various comments and explanations that constituted significant portions of the wedding. As a fierce wind blew thick fog over the hillside, Nasser and Paul addressed the assembled guests on the subject of "Why this event?" They sat side by side and cross-legged facing the crowd, a sheer silk banner blowing in the wind over their heads. Paul began with an account of the process they went through in deciding how to label the event and their relationship. "Celebration of union" made the most sense, he explained, since their commitment to one another was already well established, and they wanted to make clear their understanding that their relationship was not just a "traditional marriage."

Both men became quite emotional as they told the story of their meeting and their discovery that they were in love and would be together "forever." From the beginning, their friends' support was vital, Paul continued, as tears streamed down his cheeks. He quoted Nasser as having commented on how wonderful it was that all their friends were helping them. "That's a big part of why we decided to do this today," Paul said. "It's to honor us, yes, but what we want to do is honor all of you who make *us* possible."

Their tone became lighter as they moved to the subject of their cultural differences and the challenges these differences have presented to them over the years as they have struggled "to meet each other halfway." Nasser reported his discovery that Paul was secretly taking lessons in Bangla, something he figured out when Paul began to say nonsensical things to him in the language. In the same vein, Paul described how the classical music he feels so passionately about had long mystified Nasser, who patiently attended concerts and operas with him in an effort to understand this alien art form. But while Paul was out of town performing, Nasser secretly signed up for a music appreciation course; when he began asking sophisticated technical questions about music theory, Paul figured out what he was doing.

Finally, each man said a few words about family. Becoming tearful again, Paul acknowledged the presence of his mother and brother, and also noted the influence of his lesbian cousin and her partner in presenting a model of a strong relationship. Nasser, now weeping as well, mentioned that his parents and siblings were not present, but that his cousin and cousin's wife were there in support of him. He then singled out several longtime friends who were there and who had supported him since he first came out. "These are my family," he told the gathering. He said that he was very touched that Paul's mother had come and still held out the hope that one day his own mother would be able to appreciate and support his relationship with Paul.

The sermon, entitled "For my gay brothers," put the ceremony in the context of gay pride and struggles to improve the status of lesbians and gay men. "Daniel," the friend who delivered these comments, is a gay Christian man admired by both Paul and Nasser for his eloquence and political astuteness. "The rules have been broken," he declared.

> The landscape is being made new. Love is love, no matter who and no matter where. There is no greater thing than love, no greater force in the universe. If human evolution is about acting with ever greater intelligence, to shape, to know, to live in and appreciate this world, then love must be the root of intelligence and becoming more intelligent must also really mean being able to act in love and to support the flourishing of love all around us. . . .
>
> It's tempting to think about what the world would be like if people were truly allowed to love all other people, if all men were truly allowed to love all other men, if all women were truly allowed to love other women. Would capitalism, could capitalism, a system based on competition and winners and losers and human life reckoned by the bottom line, be possible? Could war continue?

Turning to Nasser and Paul, Daniel continued,

> *Paul and Nasser, in taking this step, you strengthen all of our souls. You set back to right something that has been wrong, a tear in the human fabric you restore to wholeness. History has denied gay men, lesbians, and bisexuals the opportunity to bless and celebrate and witness and gain tax advantages* [laughter from the audience] *from our love for each other. Yet in terms of human evolution, of all our moving toward our ability to act, and think, and live, and love, all of human history has waited for this moment and the whole universe celebrates with you as you declare your love and commitment to union with each other.*

The sermon led directly into Nasser and Paul's vows. Nasser read his vows in Bangla, and Paul followed in English:

> *Today, before all of you gathered here, I declare my love for Nasser and my intention to live in union with him for the rest of my life. Nasser, I will put your welfare first, before my very own. I will share all my wealth and resources with you, your fortune and misfortune. I promise to give you my very best and I want you to demand that of me. I promise to you that this relationship, which is my anchor and my home, will not keep me away from the rest of the world. Instead, the love and hope that it inspires in me will enable me to be more a part of that world in which we live.*

In the middle of these vows, Paul's eyes filled with tears and by the time he had come to the end, he was openly weeping. The two men placed garlands of flowers over each other's heads and kissed. The crowd responded with cheers and applause. The couple then fed each other pieces of fruit and gave each other wine to drink from a pair of shiny metal goblets. Daniel returned, and spoke these words:

> *Paul and Nasser have decided that this union is the best thing that they can do for each other. It's founded on profound respect for one another and on the understanding that they are peers and equals in this life. Know that the world will ask you to deny each other many times. But for one of you to deny the other is to deny life and all that is eternal and worthy in this life.*
>
> *Friends, we're here today because Paul and Nasser have asked all of us to bear witness to their love and union. As in the rakhi ceremony, they have bonded with each other and with all of us. They ask our support. No matter how strong their love, they will need our help to sustain and encourage their bond and their love. Know this. Recognize it. Believe it. Do*

not take it for granted. This union is a celebration in the context of a community. It is an honor and a privilege for each of us to be here. With it [comes] a responsibility to support, defend, reflect, and keep the celebration of this love alive with them. This union is deeply important to them. Help them to carry it forward now and into the future.

With this, he invited anyone who wished to come forward to voice thoughts and feelings about the events of the day, underscoring the commitment of both men to make their union public in the context of something they conceived of as community, a collectivity that has a right to offer opinions as to the significance of the proceedings. The guests who took advantage of the opportunity to comment were quite varied. The first, Nasser's college roommate, who was Jewish and heterosexual, spoke of feeling that he and Nasser were like brothers. He remarked that while much of the world denies the validity of same-sex love, "there is a world that celebrates your relationship and this is that world," gesturing toward the assembled guests. He ended his comments by chanting the Jewish prayer of thanksgiving, the *Shehehiyanu*, in Hebrew, English, and finally in Bangla.

Among the others who came forward were a straight Bangladeshi man, a straight couple who brought their baby with them and who spoke of how this ceremony recalled their own wedding six years earlier. A lesbian coworker of Nasser's spoke of how his presence enhanced her days in their workplace, and a heterosexual woman shared her grandmother's advice on how to keep a relationship strong, "Never go to bed on a fight."

Paul and Nasser's wedding embodied their notion of "community" as a broadly inclusive collectivity with shared values and political principles. In constituting the "public" that would witness and validate their bonds, the two men invited men and women, gays and straights, South Asians, Euro-Americans, and a number of people of other ethnic or racial backgrounds. While they first imagined that their wedding would bring together close friends and relatives, those whom they judged most important in their lives, many other people whom they knew less well, if at all, asked to be included. These "friends of friends," all gay or lesbian, must have been "striving to have the affirmation," Paul said later. "They were just very excited about supporting gay ceremonies," Nasser added. Not only did they present their relationship to the community for support and approval, but the community joined them and eagerly took up their cause.

The ceremony sparked intense emotion among the participants, with many guests moved to tears at various points. The fact that Paul's mother and brother were both in attendance particularly impressed many of the gay men and lesbians who were present, and quite a number of them rushed up to them to tell them how glad they were that they were there. (Paul's brother's comment to his wife when he arrived back home was, "Well, it was just like a wedding, except they congratulated *me* for coming.") Some gay couples, particularly several of the mixed-race same-sex couples, said afterwards that the ceremony inspired them to consider solemnizing their own unions.

At least as directly as the content of specific texts, the structure of the ceremony itself told the two men's story. They carefully incorporated elements that invoked each of the identities they viewed as essential to the sort of statement they wanted to make about themselves and thus juxtaposed evocations of South Asia, gay/lesbian rights, classical music, and anti-imperialist politics in rapid succession. The ceremony not only expressed their ideas about how to define "community" but stimulated others to conceive of themselves as somehow sharing Paul and Nasser's lives.

In their wedding, the two men intended both to acknowledge and to vanquish the enormous differences they perceived between their cultural backgrounds. At the same time that differences were marked—Paul's ignorance of Nasser's native language and Nasser's innocence of Western classical music—the accounts the men gave of their growing intimacy emphasized the efforts each was willing to make to overcome their unfamiliarity with the other's culture. Tellingly, the attempts each made to learn more about the other—the classes they each took—spoke to virtually identical understandings both of the problem and of the most logical way to resolve it.

Representing Multiple Allegiances: The "Bear Tip"

"Travis Johnson" and "Manuel Vargas" are avid square dancers who spend several evenings each week at events sponsored by Bay Area gay square dance organizations. Both thirty-four years old, they live in a spacious flat near San Francisco's Castro District that is crammed with audio and video equipment, CDs, and books. Travis, whose origins are in the Pacific Northwest, is a carpenter who works for a local nonprofit organization that provides housing for AIDS patients; Manuel, born in Puerto Rico of Spanish descent, is a physician, specializing in AIDS and

HIV. At the time I first met with them, in April 1995, they were planning a "ring exchange" ceremony that would be the first phase of a pair of rituals they envisioned as marking the establishment of their relationship.

Both men identify as "bears," referring to a gay male sensibility that emphasizes the large and hairy male body as a symbol of self. Bears typically dress casually, in jeans, T-shirts, and flannel, and proudly display both facial and body hair, frequently going shirtless at dances and other events. Many are proudly overweight and craft their images as the antithesis of the sleek "clone" or the sculpted (and typically hairless or shaved) bodybuilder, disdaining the interest in fashion and style stereotypically associated with gay men. The image of the bear has two facets. On the one hand, physical symbols of burly masculinity, naturalness, and the outdoors are central to the bear's presentation of self; on the other hand, bears draw on the image of the teddy bear, soft, cuddly, and perhaps a bit vulnerable in conceptualizing their identities.[23]

When Travis and Manuel talk about being bears, they refer frequently to their involvement in a wider network they call "the bear community." Along with the other sources of identity they explicitly reference, primarily "the square dance community" and the "leather community," they use their membership in the bear community throughout conversations to explain who they are, who they regard as the members of their support system, and what their relationship signifies in the larger social landscape. "Bears," Travis explains, are men "who identify as males." This means that a bear event, such as the "bear tip" or bear-centered square dance, "ends up being very male, usually shirtless and fairly high energy." Manuel adds with a laugh that these men are "usually furry, usually bearded, usually not very skinny."[24]

When I press them for a definition of "bear," Manuel says, "Basically, if you consider yourself a bear, then you're a bear." But Travis elaborates.

> We can define how *we* define "bear," but this is one of those "explain god" sort of questions. . . . Facial hair in some form is generally considered a must. . . . [But] that's even in contention. There are people who say you *must* have a beard. But roughly it's some sort of facial hair and body hair is a plus. . . . Being chunky or hefty or just plain large is one of the definitions. The person who founded the Bear Hugs, which is a bear sex party, wrote a thing in one of the newsletters that I really liked which said that the Bear Hugs was started by a group of men who didn't fit into any of the community definitions. They weren't the "A"

gays. They weren't the pretty boys on Castro. They weren't enough of something to fit into the leather community. Someone suggested they just simply didn't fit into chaps! But they were a group of men who decided to celebrate who and how they were, however that might be. And that philosophy certainly seems to be present in the larger bear community. While the elements we described certainly are rampant, it doesn't seem to be an exclusionary group.

Manuel continued:

> Usually the most important thing is that it's somebody who is happy with who they are and accept themselves as who they are. So they don't have to shave in order to look like something else. They don't have to lose twenty pounds to look like somebody else. They don't have to dress a certain way to look like somebody else. So it's usually somebody who's more comfortable with themselves and their sexuality.

Travis and Manuel met through their mutual involvement in a gay square dance class. Travis joined the class shortly after his lover died of AIDS when a friend who belonged to the square dance club "dragged" him out to keep him from staying home to grieve alone. At around the same time, Manuel had ended a long-term relationship that had soured and came to the class hoping to find a healthy way to get exercise and relax after his demanding workdays. Neither was seeking long-term involvement as a specific goal, though both had always hoped eventually to "settle down" and both valued what Manuel describes as "a heterosexual marriage with a man."

Their romantic involvement began about six months after they first met when both men attended the national gay square dance convention. After another six months, they decided to move in together and at that time began discussing having a ring ceremony at the next square dance convention, held in Chicago over the 1995 Memorial Day weekend. They see this ceremony as marking the movement of their relationship to a new level of seriousness. As Travis explained when the ceremony was in the planning stages, "It'll be almost one year . . . and it seems like the right thing to do significantly, the next step . . . [after] the courtship process, if you will. Making a decision to move in together. Going through all the stresses involved in merging households."

When they moved to a new flat together, Travis moved out of the home he had shared with his previous lover, "Matthew," who had died there, as he explained, in his arms. Although he and Matthew never had a ceremony, they had registered as domestic partners because Travis wanted "some tangible commitment": "And that sort of insignificant piece of paper is very important to me now. And the fact that that relationship was in some ways unfulfilled or compressed makes [it] . . . seem important that we do the markers."

Over a period of only seven years, Travis was in two relationships with men who died of AIDS. He describes those relationships, particularly the more recent one, with Matthew, as having been lived in "dog's years" because a lifetime of experience was compressed into a short, but intense, period of time. Now that he is with Manuel, and since they are both in good health, Travis says, "There is a reasonable expectation that we will have some number of years together."

> ELLEN: You're both negative?
>
> TRAVIS: No, we're both positive. But both of my previous partners had become ill quite quickly.
>
> MANUEL: And there have been no indications that either one of us is going to get it.
>
> ELLEN: So you've been positive but healthy.
>
> TRAVIS: Right. So it is roulette. There's no guarantee. But there is at least some reasonable . . . expectation that we'll have something between zero and ten years.

In this context, their exchange of rings conveys a number of levels of meaning. For Travis in particular, it offers a chance to savor the possibility that this relationship will endure for a reasonably long period of time. For Manuel, who was raised in Puerto Rico in a family with strong Spanish roots, it also resonates with his notion of what is standard in his culture.

> For me, rings [are] not necessarily the ultimate symbolic commitment, but it's a serious symbol of commitment and it's an official symbol that can be shown to the world and that is there to be shown and demonstrated that I have a significant other that I care enough about to be carrying this, that I'm committed to enough that there's this ring. And in Hispanic culture, particularly traditional Spain, there is a lot of tradition of getting engaged and having a ring ceremony at that point. And then get married.

Manuel also felt that being public about a relationship was absolutely vital, along with being monogamous and making a commitment to stability. He explained:

> My expectations are, number one, to acknowledge us publicly as a couple. If people don't like it, tough. . . . It's definitely not going to be hidden, it's going to be public. And there's a point to where it could become flaunting and then that probably I would not feel comfortable with. But definitely not something that's going to be so private in the middle of a forest that if a tree fell down, did it really fall down, and did anybody really hear it make any noise. No, not that type of thing. I want to celebrate ourselves as a couple and I want to do that with our friends, the people who support us being in a relationship. Support us being a couple. The people who helped us become a couple. The people who share our lives with us. And those are the people that we are going to celebrate with.

But a vital part of the ceremony Travis and Manuel planned was its location at the national square dance convention. The convention was held at a large downtown Chicago hotel in tandem with the International Mr. Leather (IML) and national bear conventions at adjoining hotels, bringing some five thousand gay men to a small circle of overlapping events for an intense three-day period.

Travis and Manuel's ceremony was held during the "bear tip" at the square dance convention, an event that drew a large number of bears, most clad in variations of bear insignia: jeans or cutoffs, T-shirts and tank tops (or shirtless), motorcycle, engineer, or cowboy boots. (*Tip* is a square-dance term that refers to the event framed at the beginning of a dance by the process of squaring up and at the end by dispersal. It is used in this context to define a square-dance occasion that draws a particular group of participants.) Travis and Manuel wore jeans, boots, and shirts with complementary patterns; both shirts had a barbed-wire motif, but one was black on white and the other white on black, chosen so that they would match, but not be identical. Travis explained:

> We did the mixing of the metaphors of it being IML and bear weekend and the bear tip. It was an interesting metaphor as the mix of the three communities that we comfortably belong and run around in. The leather community, the bear community, and the square dance community. Who all happened to be having conventions that weekend! And we did a pretty clear conglomeration in our costuming. We wore

the suspenders which come directly from El Camino Reelers, which is the square dance club [we belong to]. . . . We were wearing our leather boots, a bit of leather, and then the matching barbed-wire western shirts. . . . And the boots that [Manuel] had are very high engineer boots, which are not the best for square dancing but clearly a leather fetish item. I was wearing my leather motorcycle boots.

The other members of their square were drawn from those who participated with them in the previous year's memorial square dance, which was danced in memory of all the friends and lovers the men had lost to AIDS. This had been an intensely emotional experience, which ended with all the members of the square weeping and embracing each other for ten or fifteen minutes after the dance was over. "We were the square in the middle of the floor sobbing and hugging with everyone dancing around us," Travis told me, remembering the previous year's convention and the bond that remained among themselves and the six other men. Their participation in that convention also marked the start of their relationship, so an evocation of one of its especially meaningful events enhanced the "anniversary" aspect of the ring exchange.

They began the ring exchange as their square was forming. They were not together at the beginning, but followed the caller's instructions to the center of the square. Once there, they read their vows to each other and exchanged rings while the rest of the square continued dancing around them. Travis began:

> *Manuel Pablo Vargas, with this ring, before our peers and chosen family, I, Travis Michael Johnson, promise to stay by your side, to share and grow, argue and disagree, and always work together to make life better.*
>
> *I promise to stand with you in times of sickness and in health, happiness, and despair. Times of plenty and of struggle.*
>
> *I will always be faithful to our love and to you. Whether right beside me or separated by time or distance, you will have my heart always.*
>
> *I love you, Manuel, my lover, my spouse, my friend, Baby-Daddy Sir-Boy, Husband.*[25]

Manuel then read his vows:

> *I, Manuel, choose to celebrate my love for you, Travis, and with this ring, I vow to be here for you, to value your thoughts and feelings, to be honest with you, to maintain our balance, to respect you as my best friend and to love you as my spouse.*

Pon tu mano sobre mi mano,
Y a tu lado todo el mundo correré.
Ven conmigo, cierra los ojos,
Y en silencio, sin palabras,
Yo mil cosas te diré . . .
Acompáñame![26]

At the end of the dance, now a couple, they returned to one side of the square together. After the "bear tip" was over, Travis, Manuel, and about thirty of their friends moved to one of the hotel's cocktail lounges, where a champagne and cake reception had been set up. At the reception, they repeated their vows so that everyone would be able to hear them, and Travis read a poem he had composed to express his feelings about the relationship. The poem drew on square-dance allusions and in-jokes to enunciate the qualities Travis sees as essential to a successful relationship—the ability to be flexible but also to be committed to one's "real home," even while having occasional sexual connections with other men. Square dances frequently require dancers to move around the square, partnering various members of the square before returning to the starting point, "home."

Our relationship is like dancing.
If we remember where we started, listen, try hard
and have help from everyone we meet
we'll end up together at home.
We won't always be together,
with luck we get to swing at least three others.
If we remember who's our partner and where home is,
We always have somewhere to fall back to.

When things break down
we know it's safe at home together.
We just wait till the next chance and try it again.
When there is a recurring problem,
We work-shop it till we get it right.

If we learn both parts and don't get stuck in one role,
we have more fun,
understand better and
it's easier to dance with others.
With practice and time it gets easier
and we move on to the next level.

No matter how good we get, breaking down
and starting again is part of the dance.
Learning good recovery skills makes it easier to keep up.
With good Basic skills we could end up in c4 heaven.[27]

As Manuel and Travis explained, one of the features that distinguish-es gay and straight square dancing is the ability of many gay and lesbian dancers to play both "male" and "female" (or in gender-neutral language, "lead" and "follow") roles. For heterosexuals, switching roles carries im-plications of cross-dressing and sexual ambiguity, particularly for those square-dance enthusiasts who dress in stereotypical western costumes that include jeans, cowboy boots, bandannas, and cowboy hats for men and full skirts with petticoats for women. For gay men and lesbians, the two roles have a more focused meaning in the context of the dance; while they may be derived from other aspects of personal presentation—as for couples who view themselves as butch/femme (for lesbians) or butch/nelly (for men)—they are, strictly speaking, "roles" rather than "identities." There are no strict limits at a gay/lesbian square dance on who may lead and who may follow, and the more accomplished dancers take pride in their ability to do both.

After the ceremony, a group of friends took the two men out to din-ner and they continued celebrating until they finally returned to their room and both promptly fell asleep. Travis describes their exhaustion with some amusement, emphasizing that from everything he's heard "from straight friends . . . [this] is a fairly typical wedding night." Here the wedding narrative shifts from an evocation of the various specialized gay sensibilities the two men share to a reminder that they are also part of the wider population of newly married couples. While the wedding marked the celebration of the romantic, erotic, and specifically gay ele-ments of their relationship, it also allowed them to make claims on im-ages associated with marriage more broadly construed. From this point of view, a marital commitment need not always be sexual; the everyday experience of falling asleep and not having sex speaks to the naturalness of the relationship and its embeddedness in the domain of domesticity.

This desire to clarify their association with the world beyond the square dancing, leather, and bear communities led Manuel and Travis to decide to plan a second ceremony for later on. They explained that they would "do one stage which is at [the] square dancing [convention], which is basically like our engagement, which would be the ring exchange and some vows. And then do more of a celebration-party at a later date . . . where we share with all the people here and get a chance to let some of the people know in case they would want to come, they would at least have some notice." Those who would be invited to the second ceremony, which as of this writing had not yet occurred, included friends not involved in the square dance scene or who were not able to attend the convention in Chicago, straight friends from both San Francisco and other places where they had lived, and a small number of relatives.

Besides the desire Travis and Manuel expressed to have people other than the members of their overlapping gay communities witness their commitment, both men indicated that the second ceremony would have a more explicitly religious or spiritual significance. Travis grew up in a Pentecostal milieu and has had an intermittent involvement with the predominantly gay (and Pentecostally influenced) Metropolitan Community Church (MCC). Manuel has maintained his Roman Catholic roots through ongoing participation in Dignity, an organization for gay and lesbian Catholics. He regularly attends Dignity's weekly mass, held at a local Presbyterian church.[28] While they have not yet begun to work out the details of this future ceremony, both men agree that the most important component will be spiritual, and that either a Catholic brother or an MCC minister will probably officiate in an outdoor location like Golden Gate Park or possibly their backyard. When I asked whether they were considering outdoor settings because churches might not be available, Manuel said, "We could get the church, but I don't think that's the main part of it. At least for me, the spiritual part doesn't depend on the building. It depends on the intentions and the actual liturgy of the ceremony."

Travis long ago gave up his direct relationship with Pentecostal religion, even though he enjoyed going to services when he lived with his aunt, a Pentecostal minister.

> Unfortunately, at some point, I started paying attention to what they were really saying, specifically what they were saying about *me*, and decided that that wasn't for me, and moved out and sort of continued pursuing my life here in San Francisco. . . . But I still have some very spiritual connections to all that. I clearly see the appeal in the spiritual side of it, and I agree that the square dance [ceremony] was really very us-centered. Even to the point where we were doing our ceremony while the world danced around us. And it would be very nice to

bring our family community together here at home. And my aunt will probably attend. I'm quite sure my father would not.

Travis goes on to explain his father's unwillingness to know any details of his life as a gay man, which includes his total ignorance of Travis's two long-term relationships, both of which ended in death from AIDS. But he has warm feelings for his aunt, who despite her "rabid Christianity" cares about him and his partners, and he fully expects her to overcome her religious reservations about homosexuality and play a role in the ceremony. When I asked Travis what was important to him about making sure that there was a "spiritual dimension" in the ceremony, he laughingly admonished me for asking such difficult questions.

> I'm not really sure. It gets into the what-is-god question, almost. That is, I'm not really sure, but I also believe it's not all accidental. And . . . I'm also a twelve-step person, so speaking in those terms, it is nice to recognize that there is a higher power and that this stuff doesn't happen by accident. Things are gifts. And it's nice to recognize that in a public way. And to get some sort of universal blessing, to be New Age about it.

Travis and Manuel view the utility of achieving public recognition of their relationship in terms of two interpersonal contexts: the gay world—specifically, the overlapping communities of bears, square dancers, and leather men—and their "family community," defined as those relatives who support their relationship along with nongay friends. They conceptualize both of these milieus as "communities" in which they have a claim to membership.

Gay and Lesbian Weddings as Symbols of Community

The three ceremonies discussed in this chapter illustrate the complexities involved when actors use the symbolic properties of weddings to address the multiple sources of identity and affiliation that characterize them as individuals and as couples. For one thing, these rituals can facilitate efforts to mediate between conflicting premises of community membership by making clear that the individual components of the new unit being established—the married couple—still regard themselves as being fully connected with the communities that give them individual identity. At the same time, though, that these rituals reaffirm community membership, they also elaborate and celebrate the integrity of couple-hood, promoting the unity of the couple as a bulwark against forces that may work against them—whether these forces be the life-threatening impact of the AIDS epidemic, the less lethal but still powerful effects of heterosexual cultural dominance, or the more general influence of soci-etal trends toward privatization.

Thus, Khadija and Shulamith assert that no matter how committed they are to their relationship, their personal identities remain grounded in the African-American and Jewish communities, respectively. Getting married, in this idiom, represents an agreement to supplement individ-ual identities with a spirit of exchange. Though neither woman believes her community membership will be other than what it has always been after the wedding, the implicit agreement here is to allow their loyalties to overlap. While both women would probably acknowledge the exis-tence of something called the "lesbian" or the "gay community," their marriage presents an instance in which it is their ethnic identities, de-fined as community affiliation, that become salient. Their lesbian or gay identities are in some sense taken-for-granted, particularly in contrast to their problematic and embattled ethnic selves.

Nasser and Paul's ceremony seemed to aim at enunciating their dif-ferences and marking the significance of their Euro-American and South Asian origins. But while the structure of the wedding made explicit ref-erence to these traditions, the content dealt much more directly with their mutual commitment to a community with which they both identi-fied—Bay Area gay and lesbian progressives and their allies. In contrast to Shulamith and Khadija, Nasser and Paul's differing ethnic back-grounds were understood as given and thus required little elaboration. The ceremony merged Euro-American structure with markedly South Asian content and thus blurred, rather than sharpened, their differences.

On the other hand, getting married can also provide the foundation for assertion of a shared community membership that challenges more monolithic constructions of "gay" or "lesbian." For couples like Travis and Manuel, this symbolic maneuver operates not by contesting the unity their marriage offers them but by elaborating allegiances that com-plicate the relationship between identity and community, and in fact, undermine the specialness of such domains as kinship and ethnicity by turning them into categories of community. This reading of community highlights the elective element Kath Weston describes so powerfully in *Families We Choose*; constituting one's friends as a kind of kin makes the point that blood relationships are no less chosen or ephemeral than friendship ties, and that bonds between friends may have the attributes of permanence and unconditional loyalty presumed to be definitional for kinship ties alone.[29]

Lesbian and gay weddings can provide an arena for exploring and defining the multiple images of community that make up celebrants' ideas about who they are as individuals and as couples. The variety of idioms they utilize toward this end underscores both the instability and variability of the concept of community as it emerges in the lives of gay men and lesbians. While for some, the community of reference is "gay" or "lesbian" or both, others may elaborate the variants of those labels with which they identify. In still other instances, race, nationality, religion, profession, or political values may take center stage as both the textual content and the structure of ceremonies remind us of who this couple is and what it means for them to solemnize their union. And since ritual communication is a two-way street, the message intended by the couple and that received by the audience may differ or even shift over the course of the ceremony.

6

THE REAL THING

"I'm sure you're aware that some people in the gay community aren't comfortable with the idea of commitment ceremonies or weddings. You know, they think people who have them are mimicking a straight institution and that we should define our own culture rather than trying to imitate heterosexuals." Whenever I brought this subject up, couples nodded knowingly. Some of them told me about gay friends who were less than enthusiastic about, or even openly hostile to, their wedding plans; others described situations where straight people seemed to see their ceremonies as an invasion of sacred heterosexual ground. "So

Pronouncing vows of commitment

what do you say to people when this comes up, or what do you think you'll say if you hear someone say something like this?" In posing this question, I was really asking people to tell me about the authenticity of their weddings, and perhaps beyond that, to help me understand to what extent gay men and lesbians conceived of gay and straight cultures as opposing forces.

"Who says getting married is only for heterosexuals?" Couples expressed some variant of this response in virtually every interview. "Is it copying heterosexuals to want some of the good things that straight society offers?" some said. "Isn't love what it's all about?" said others. Still others reasoned, "If God has brought us together, then we are only fulfilling His will in making our union public." Couples who had had or were planning commitment ceremonies and weddings understood their impulses as marks of their common humanity with heterosexual couples; the impulses that make weddings meaningful, according to this reasoning, are felt no less by same-sex than by opposite-sex couples. The notion that their celebrations were authentic rested on the concepts of God, love, and humanity to which these gay men and lesbians subscribed.

God, Love, and Humanity

In *The Real Thing*, the cultural historian Miles Orvell chronicles the struggle between what he calls a "culture of imitation" characteristic of nineteenth-century American culture and a "culture of authenticity" that emerged in response to the dominance of the machine in the twentieth century. According to Orvell, the preoccupation with authenticity was particularly pronounced in the direction taken by advertising during the century, particularly as photographic images, promising a kind of "verification of fact," became ubiquitous. Authenticity, in this reading, is synonymous with desirability. Jackson Lears, another cultural historian, argues that as the culture of mass production, profligate abundance, and advertising came to seem ever more joyless, American culture became increasingly focused on achieving redemption from the deadening sameness of modern life.[1]

These directions are not inconsistent with the expression of another signature American trait—individualism.[2] From this standpoint, authenticity resides in the revelation of that inimitable entity, the self, and being true to oneself is fundamental to establishing claims to integrity and moral stature. The notion that each of us has a true self that will one day demand release, that secrecy and concealment are affronts to virtue, and that even those whose characters appear to be most thoroughly compromised have true selves that are worthy, is deeply engrained in American culture.[3]

In the years since Stonewall, these constructions of authenticity have assumed a particularly central role in the evolution of the gay/lesbian ritual of "coming out." Coming out narratives are animated by a conviction that one's real self emerges when one reveals one's homosexuality to friends and family, and even to oneself. As Bonnie Zimmerman has noted, the theme of the coming out story in lesbian fiction is the discovery of one's true self, often envisioned as a homecoming. In such accounts, coming out—discovering and making public one's lesbian or gay identity—tends to be imagined almost as an autonomous force, something like gravity that cannot be suppressed indefinitely. This view of authenticity predictably models being "in the closet," or hiding one's homosexuality, as the virtual repudiation of one's personhood, certain to be dehumanizing, demoralizing, and hazardous to one's psychological health.[4]

How can one be assured of the authenticity of anything in a world that offers the temptations of artifice and delusion at every turn? Many of the narratives I gathered drew on couples' accounts of emotional intensity as evidence of the artlessness of their experience. Assuming that the real self is lodged within, straining to reveal itself, powerful feelings are taken as indicators of truth and reality, an assumption enormously aided by the rise of popular psychotherapeutic models of individual happiness.[5] In coming out narratives, for instance, the sensation of being "at home" typically attests to the authenticity of the revelation, as personal conviction endows experience with an authority that cannot be contradicted by anyone who, in essence, "wasn't there." Testimonies of personal experience also stand at the heart of Second Wave feminist politics; personal narratives convey a sort of "truth" that is absolute because of the uniqueness of individual lives even as their "truth" is also attested to by the discovery that these occurrences seem to be both culturally structured and pervasive.[6]

Another solution can be located in one's relationship with the divine. To experience a personal revelation of truth, to achieve a state of intense spiritual awareness, to perceive oneself as being in communication with God—any such event may signal the discovery of some sort of fundamental truth, particularly in the Protestant reading of spirituality that permeates mainstream American culture. If one cannot imagine another way to be, if the feelings of comfort and security associated with a particular relationship are emotionally fulfilling, one may experience a growing conviction that one has achieved a condition that God mandated or intended. To repudiate that condition, either by concealing it or refusing to honor it, would amount to an abdication of faith. If we are all human, then our earthly condition must be a reflection of the image of God in which we were created.

Other derivations of authenticity can be located in the construction American culture puts on the concept of "love." In his groundbreaking study of American kinship, anthropologist David Schneider identified the basic cultural elements that give the kinship system coherence and meaning. The meaning of kin ties may be understood in terms of two basic components—the *order of nature* and the *order of law*—out of which all kinship relations are established and defined. According to this system, there are two ways of defining relatives—"by blood" and "by marriage"—and though only the former of these is thought to be constituted in a natural substance, both are seen as real and bounded by codes of conduct. Because blood ties have a material basis, Schneider's reading presumes that they are taken to be permanent and hence involuntary; marriage (or by extension, any other tie, such as friendship, defined by a legal or social arrangement) can be terminated and is, therefore, inherently voluntary and potentially impermanent.[7] Both are, however, signaled by love—*cognatic* love in the case of parent and child and *conjugal* love for spouses. These two types of love are enacted significantly in sexual intercourse and the kiss, both of which Schneider explicates as symbols of a process whereby opposites are unified in the biogenetic events of reproduction.[8]

Love, then, in the Schneiderian understanding of American kinship, is compelling in its realness. Though love arises between individuals not united by a natural substance (blood), sexual intercourse imbues that bond with other natural substances, or failing that, with a seemingly irresistible physicality. Insofar as love is perceived as a powerful and mysterious force, it intrinsically possesses authenticity. Furthermore, as sociologist Anthony Giddens reminds us, the experience of romantic love tends to be idealized in Western cultures, conceptualized as a transcendent state that marks the completion of a quest for one's intended other.[9] Falling in love seems to transform a fantasy of wholeness into reality, and as it fulfills a dream that all are assumed to share, its attainment tends to resist interrogation.

For gay and lesbian couples, a ceremonial and public avowal of "being in love" may dramatize an implicit opposition between "true" and "romantic love," a contrast that has its roots in Victorian discourse. As sociologist Steven Seidman has argued, true love has been imagined as idealistic, spiritual, and altruistic, the antithesis of romantic love's foundation in sensuality, egoism, and deception.[10] Since (particularly male) homosexuality conventionally conjures up images of promiscuity, a couple that declares their true love for one another refuses, in effect, to be defined by prevailing representations. Insofar as "love" has been most elaborated in American culture as a feminine characteristic,[11] closely allied with the attachment to others expected in women, its elaboration in same-sex weddings further confounds tendencies to view gay men (and lesbians, perhaps to a lesser extent) as more concerned with individual gratification than with relationships and expressive emotionality.

The recognition of others also can validate a claim to authenticity, for how could the community, particularly representatives of the heterosexual majority, be wrong? Couples speak frequently of the importance of having witnesses to their commitment, of the significance of the community's presence at the event that seals their union. The community's approval has the power, in some of these accounts, to vanquish the hostility of the wider society toward gay and lesbian love. In these cases, the community, because of its commitment to the couple and its recognition of them as among its constituent units, has greater authority than the unenlightened homophobic public. Such community validation is even more effective when the relevant "community" spans the boundaries of gay and straight, male and female, friend and relative, young and old. Efforts to assure inclusiveness and diversity among wedding guests, then, counter accusations of bias or favoritism: if a group of heterosexuals (or others who are otherwise different from the couple) recognize the significance of these events, their validity must be beyond dispute.

The authenticity of gay and lesbian weddings can also be confirmed by the perception that they are voluntary, rather than the product of social pressure and convention. Over and over, couples laughed as they reminded me that they could hardly be accused of getting married to please their parents or get a lot of gifts, while others occasionally joked about "having" to get married to legitimate their offspring. Voluntary behavior is seen, in this construction, as springing from the heart, as being pure and uncontaminated by the desire to gain some benefit from a course of action. In a world thought to be corrupted by the pursuit of profit and advantage, true love shines as a beacon of authenticity, as something trustworthy, innocent, and beyond disbelief.

As is often true for heterosexual weddings as well, self-conscious orig-inality in ritual form can be invoked to demonstrate how thoroughly a couple has repudiated convention. To the extent that couples strive to avoid cliché or predictable representations in their ceremonies, they may attempt to signal their inventiveness and to demonstrate the individual-ity of the occasion, often composing their own texts as a way to avoid using prepackaged sentiments. Even when the product of their creative efforts may draw on familiar sources or bear an eerie resemblance to boilerplate matrimonial language, the couple may be satisfied that by un-dertaking to write their own service or to draft their own vows they have succeeded in creating a ritual that speaks to the uniqueness and legiti-macy of their relationship.

Paradoxically, perhaps, authenticity can also be demonstrated not only by originality but by a lack of originality—that is, by reliance on tra-ditional sources for the substance of a ceremony. As we saw in chapter 3, some gay and lesbian couples who stage commitment rituals construe their task as one that locates them within an existing history or tradition. Establishing a claim to authenticity may then depend on the couple's success in making their ritual a convincing example of its genre. In these cases, the assertion that the ceremony in question is *really* a wedding is strengthened to the extent that it does not depart from whatever charac-teristics are understood to be essential for a ritual to be so defined.

All these sources of validation and recognition can be solidified through the bestowal of gifts. While it is unlikely that receiving presents is the primary inspiration of any gay or lesbian (or heterosexual) couple planning a ceremony, gifts, particularly those traditionally associated with weddings, such as china, silver, crystal, and household goods, au-thoritatively signal the establishment of a sanctioned domestic unit—a family. When such gifts are family heirlooms, moreover, or are given by blood relatives, or when relatives contribute to the cost of the ceremony, they indicate that the same-sex couple has been integrated, symbolically at least, into the constellation of kin. In much the same way, being called upon later to host family holiday celebrations may intensify claims to being part of the wider world of relatives.

"Just an Ordinary Jewish Wedding"

On a chilly January day in 1994, my partner and I made our way to the first lesbian wedding I had been invited to since beginning this research.

At the bottom of the invitation was a single word—"formal"—that indicated the sort of affair this would be. I knew that "Rachel Goldberg" and "Nancy Weinstein," whom I had earlier interviewed as they finalized their plans for the ceremony, had planned a ceremony that would conform in every detail to the requirements of traditional Jewish weddings.[12]

The location of the wedding was an elegant downtown San Francisco hotel, mainly decorated in pale colors with touches of marble and chrome at every turn. A large sign in the lobby directed us to an escalator leading to the second floor where the Weinstein-Goldberg wedding would be held. As we arrived, we were greeted by a woman in a tuxedo who invited us to sign the guest book and directed us to an area where drinks and hors d'ouevres were being served. Other guests were arriving as we did, many dressed in party dresses of either the slinky or frilly variety while others sported tuxes or other sleek tailored clothing. Hair was freshly moussed, nails newly manicured and glossily polished. Many of the guests carried brightly wrapped gifts which they deposited on a table to one side of the entrance. While the majority of those arriving appeared to be lesbians with a smaller number of gay men among them, there were also a number of heterosexual couples present, some of whom had distinct New York accents that I knew might make them friends or relatives of Nancy, a New York native.

After we and the other guests had nibbled on hors d'oeuvres and sipped drinks for about an hour, one of the tuxedoed attendants directed us toward the other end of the large room, set up with chairs on either side of an aisle that led to a *chuppah*. The *chuppah* was supported by four potted plants and flanked by large flower arrangements; to one side of it two musicians played background music. The rabbi was the first to arrive, walking briskly up the aisle and setting up his materials under the *chuppah*. Shortly afterwards, as the crowd of some fifty guests craned their necks for a better view, the procession began. First down the aisle was Rachel, looking sleek in her tuxedo. Next came two women, one in a tuxedo and the other wearing a long pink gown and carrying a bouquet. They were followed by a woman in a glittery off-the-shoulder dress, also carrying flowers. Then a flower girl, who looked to be about five, appeared, tossing rose petals in all directions. Finally, Nancy, the bride, came down the aisle, on the arm of another tuxedo-clad woman. She wore a long white dress with a train, a bridal veil, dainty white silk shoes, and carried a trailing bouquet.

The rabbi then began to lead Nancy and Rachel through what I recognized as a traditional Jewish ceremony. They first walked around each other seven times, creating a complicated pattern of alternating circles. This was followed by the blessing of the wine, before which the rabbi explained that the cup from which they were drinking was a family heirloom, the very same cup that had been used at Rachel's grandmother's wedding. The next step, the exchange of rings, was followed by the couple repeating traditional vows in Hebrew and then in English. The rabbi commented on the event, speaking about the couple and the beginning of their life together, emphasizing what he saw as the complementary nature of their personalities and the ways in which their union would create a kind of wholeness. He then read the *ketubah*, the marriage contract, in Hebrew and English, explaining that this custom was rooted in ancient Jewish traditions. After the *ketubah*, the rabbi chanted in Hebrew and repeated in English the Seven Blessings, which likened marriage to the seven days of Biblical creation. Finally, he led the couple to the breaking of the glass, which he interpreted as representing their ability to carry on through the hard times that they will undoubtedly face during their marriage. The sound of breaking glass was greeted by cries of "Mazel Tov!" (congratulations) and enthusiastic applause.[13]

The wedding party then moved to another room in the hotel where tables had been set up for a sit-down dinner. Placecards directed each guest to a table with six or seven others, and the wedding party was seated at a long "head table" at the front of the room. The band played on one end of the room; toasts to the newly married couple were offered, mainly from the other occupants of the head table; the couple and many of the guests danced the hora and various ballroom dances; and both of the newlyweds, seated on chairs, were lifted high over the heads of the guests and bounced around to the klezmer tunes of traditional Eastern European Jewish folk music. After dinner, the ornate three-tier white wedding cake was cut, and the couple fed each other pieces of cake, taking care to smear each other's faces with icing. Later in the party, Nancy threw her bouquet and Rachel tossed a garter to the eager crowd.

As we prepared to leave, we went up to the head table to thank Nancy and Rachel and to compliment them on having put on a beautiful wedding. They appreciated our comments but responded to our compliment by pointing out that this was "just an ordinary Jewish wedding."

In many ways, the wedding I just described *was* ordinary. It included the principal ritual elements of a traditional Jewish wedding (as performed in the Conservative tradition) and most of the informal features associated with such ceremonies among American Jews of Eastern European extraction. It also incorporated a number of customs more American than Jewish, such as speaking individual vows and throwing the bouquet and garter. The text of the ceremony dwelt on the importance of the couple establishing a "Jewish home." It defined marriage and family as the fundamental creative forces in the Jewish community, and presented lifelong conjugal commitment as the heart of meaningful social existence.

But this was a wedding that joined two women. And while the rabbi's comments emphasized gendered complementarity he perceived between their characters—he described Nancy, the "bride," as "soft and compassionate," and Rachel, the "groom" (or as she later characterized herself to me, "the groomette"), as "strong in her convictions"—the vows the couple had written for themselves focused on their "sameness" as two women and the mutual understanding this would foster in their life together.

In earlier conversations, Rachel and Nancy expressed their desire to publicly affirm their commitment to many of the goals expected of couples embarking on marriage: they wanted to have children in a family context and they wanted their relationship to be recognized by family and friends. But although, and perhaps because, their marriage could not be legally sanctioned by the state, they also wanted something else: to have their religion support it and thus to be legitimized by the Jewish community. Nancy explained to me how the public nature of the event was important to her. "It makes our relationship valid. It's before God and everybody saying we pledge to be together for the rest of our lives." Rachel felt it would be particularly important to be married by a rabbi who shared her conservative Jewish values. "I just wanted it to *mean* something. You know, it doesn't mean anything when it's not recognized by the religion." And they explicitly wanted to express their appreciation and support for the traditional nuclear family as an institution. Nancy plans to get pregnant by donor insemination but said that Rachel "feels that we should be married before I even get pregnant." Rachel explained her strong views on the family and premarital pregnancy as follows:

> You see, a lot of people see being gay as this really weird thing. And for me, I've always been gay. I mean, I was gay when I was a kid. I've just always been gay and for me, it's just a part of me and more and more evidence is that it's biological and genetic. And I feel like just because I'm gay, that doesn't mean that all the other things that govern the world that I live in and the values that I have and the values that I grew

up with and the society that we live in all of a sudden go out the window, just because my . . . interest is in women.

Rachel's understanding of "the progression of things" is that first parents should date, then have a wedding and get married, and then have children. "I just sort of always carried that idea [that] things should go along in a certain way. And I don't see just because I'm gay why that should be any different."

From this perspective, Rachel and Nancy understood their wedding as something that would have been "ordinary" except for the fact, almost a technicality in their reckoning, that the state restricts legal marriage to heterosexual couples. They followed traditional Jewish custom to the letter, rejecting all suggestions by the rabbi for even slightly innovative readings, and explained emphatically that this ritual was a *wedding*, not a "commitment ceremony," which they described as a countercultural concoction not recognized by the Conservative movement in Judaism. Thus while their union cannot now be sanctioned by the state, it is, in their view, legitimated by institutional Judaism. They point out that Conservative Judaism strongly opposes marriages between Jews and non-Jews, but that their wedding united two Jewish women committed to creating a "Jewish home." While the Conservative movement does not condone same-sex unions, their interpretation is that it has not gotten around to explicitly forbidding such rituals when they are called "weddings," as opposed to "commitment ceremonies." Rachel and Nancy are careful to explain that their ceremony had all the elements of the traditional wedding and thus could not be construed to be an unacceptable "commitment ceremony." Reinforcing this statement, Nancy began to hyphenate her name as Weinstein-Goldberg following the wedding, though Rachel maintained her old surname, claiming that her professional activities as an attorney would not permit her to change her name.

While the couple, however, viewed their wedding as "ordinary" and a mark, on the one hand, of their solidity as citizens and as Jews, and on the other hand, of their repudiation of the association between being "gay" and being "queer" (in the sense of aggressively transgressive), the rabbi saw their desire to publicly celebrate their relationship as a courageous rebellion against the injustice done to them both by mainstream Judaism and by civil society. In his comments during the ceremony, the rabbi, a heterosexual Conservative Jew, remarked that they were bravely demanding the right to have their marriage sanctified by Jewish law and tradition despite the fact that "not all of Jewish society," as he put it, was ready to support a marriage of two women. He was impressed by what he saw as "their courage," and by the fact that they did not face any of the pressures to marry that heterosexual couples respond to. Because their decision to marry within Jewish tradition was freely chosen, in his view their commitment was all the more significant and worthy of support. A later conversation with the rabbi confirmed my suspicion that Conservative Judaism does, in fact, oppose same-sex marriages as a matter of policy, though sanctions imposed on rabbis who perform such ceremonies are only informal. (In contrast, rabbis who perform or even attend interfaith weddings risk expulsion from the Conservative rabbinate.)

Rachel and Nancy's ceremony constituted a multilayered demonstration of authenticity. They understood that most people did not accept the union of two women as a real marriage, but went about organizing an event that would make that exclusion moot and would assert their right to a place in the domain of "weddings" and "marriage." The symbolic authority of the rabbi and their strict adherence to the traditions associated with the Jewish wedding allowed them to claim the blessing of God and the Jewish people. At the same time, their replication of virtually every feature of a Jewish wedding—from their clothing to the organization of the reception—strengthened the legitimacy of their argument that they were, in fact, a married couple and the creators of a Jewish home. Their interpretation of Jewish law and the nature of the Jewish community as primarily preoccupied with the replication of Jewish domestic units made their inclusion as a Jewish family axiomatic.

Ironically, the rabbi's interpretation of the event classified it as an instance of resistance to the rigidity of the Jewish rejection of same-sex unions. Because he felt strongly that it was wrong to chastise homosexuals for profligate sexuality while also denying them the means to sanctify their relationships, he viewed his own participation as a matter of conscience. Nevertheless, he was somewhat anxious that the fact that he had officiated at a same-sex ceremony could cause him some professional embarrassment were it to become well known. And he was perplexed, as well, by some of the symbolic maneuvers undertaken by Nancy and Rachel, specifically their choice of seemingly gendered clothing to mark their status in the ceremony. Since they were two women, he reasoned, it seemed odd that they didn't both wear dresses.

The rabbi's notion of the authenticity of the event, then, was rooted in virtually opposite attributes from those Nancy and Rachel cited to demonstrate its validity. For the rabbi to assure himself of the rightness of performing the ceremony as an act of conscience, he had to contrast it with a traditional Jewish wedding and to accentuate the distinction between a (heterosexual) wedding and a (same-sex) commitment ceremony. This objective contrasted dramatically with Rachel and Nancy's goal of validating their ceremony as *the same as* a Jewish wedding—an *ordinary* Jewish wedding.

"God Is the Common Thread"

"Peter Berger" and "John Cisneros" had a lot to say about God when we met over coffee and cookies about five months after their fall 1993 wedding. John, thirty-two, now works as a software consultant, while Peter, thirty-seven, who has held a variety of jobs in food-specialty and catering businesses for some years, is trying to get a baked-goods business established. Both men spent years as initiates in Roman Catholic seminaries before their plans for the priesthood were derailed by their coming to terms with being gay. John left his California seminary when he realized that he could no longer deny his desire to be in a committed relationship with another man. Peter was expelled from the seminary he attended in Massachusetts after he was told that he "wouldn't fit in"; he has always suspected that the real reason was that he was discovered to be gay.

Although the two men share both Roman Catholic upbringings and the seminary experience, they feel that what they really have in common is a commitment to a particular sort of "faith life," which John explains as referring to how "we think about God, our relationships with God, how we relate to other people, how we interact with people, our morals, our ethics, what's important to us, [and] being centered." Peter elaborates on their vision of faith life with illustrations from their ceremony.

> I'm remembering the blessing that [John's] mother gave us. Part of the service was a variation on the Prayers of the Faithful. In the Roman Catholic mass today there is a part of a liturgy called the Prayers of the Faithful. And how we incorporated that into our service is that our friends were invited to offer their blessings, hopes for us. . . . [John's] mother's blessing was one of the most moving blessings, and she was choked up during it, as were many people, and it had to do with the presence of a third person in the relationship being God. So her blessing for us was love and joy, but also to never forget

that there is a third person involved in that relationship. For me, I think for us, God is the common thread in our lives. And our relationship only makes sense in the context of community, in the context of family, in the context of God.

John goes on to explain their relationship as being a "covenant" in the sense that the Catholic marriage sacrament "is supposed to reflect a reality of God and God's relationship with the couple, the community, the world." This understanding of marriage shaped the discussion the men had prior to their ceremony when they confronted the dilemma of whether they should call the event a "marriage" or a "commitment service."

> [In] our discussions we fleshed out the fact that what we are about in our commitment *is* a marriage in the sense of that sacrament in that our love can reflect the reality of God just like a heterosexual couple's can. So in the Catholic sense of sacrament, our relationship, our marriage is that.

John and Peter became acquainted through their mutual involvement in a Catholic parish located in the heart of San Francisco's Castro district. People who knew them both had been trying to introduce them for some time, and they finally did so at a coffee hour following mass one Sunday.[14] Once they began dating, their relationship evolved over a matter of months as they discovered the depth of their shared beliefs and values and began to acknowledge that they both had long dreamed of forming a committed relationship and marking that commitment with a service. The intensity of their faith in God and their firm conviction that God is, in fact, a "third person" in their relationship, authenticate both their union and their desire to make their relationship public; beyond how being visible as a couple may benefit them personally, Peter and John are eager to serve as "role models" for younger gay men looking for images of stability, commitment, and pride.

Despite their grounding in the traditions and beliefs of the Catholic Church, however, Peter and John had no choice but to accept, with great sadness, the fact that the Church has yet to extend recognition to gay unions. But according to their reading of Roman Catholic tradition, marriage is a sacrament which a couple extends to each other and which the priest merely witnesses as a representative of the "community." This understanding of marriage as a "communal event" not requiring priestly intervention meant that John and Peter's commitment service would still be legitimate and authentic despite its being performed outside and without the sanction of the Church. Both men's accounts emphasized their reliance on the structure of the Catholic mass as the blueprint for their ceremony, even as the Church's rejection of them as a gay couple forced them to stage their service outside the boundaries of an institution to which they retained an intense commitment. They acknowledged that these circumstances meant that a number of specific details diverged from the structure and content of the mass—its location in a suburban garden rather than inside a church, their use of secular, as well as devotional, music, and readings not drawn from biblical sources, the absence of consecrated bread and wine, and the inclusion of "community blessings"—but insisted that overall the ceremony would be readily recognizable as a mass by anyone familiar with Roman Catholic tradition.

> There's an opening song, which we had, and then there's a gathering prayer, then we had what we called "liturgy of the words." We had two readings and then a song was sung in between. Then what was different [from a mass] in ours, we had the blessing of the community, [in] which the idea was that it's the community's affirmation of what we're doing, . . . then the exchange of rings and vows, and then a response, and then prayers over bread and wine.

The two men read their vows, which they had written together, in unison:

> We are talking now
> about promises, about commitment.
> Now is the time to celebrate our life together.
> This is our marriage.
>
> John, you are the joy of my life.
> Peter, you are the joy of my life.
> In the presence of God and our family,
> I declare that I will love and treasure you,
> with all my heart and mind.
>
> I will be honest and faithful with you.
> I will share my heart with you.
>
> I will walk with you.
> And when you cannot walk, I will carry you.

I will endure whatever comes.
I will be your home.

"Wherever you go I shall go.
Wherever you live, I shall live.
Your people shall be my people.
And your God, shall be my God."[15]

I entrust my life to you.
You are my companion, my love.
This is my covenant with you
in these days of my life.

Since the ceremony not only took place outside a church but marked the union of two men, something not accepted by the Church, the prayers over bread and wine could not constitute communion. John likened the ritual, instead, to another Catholic rite called *agape:* "It's not consecrated, but it's a communal event where people are sharing and nourishing and giving sustenance to each other."

> Our bread and wine, because we're not Catholic priests . . . wasn't con-
> secrated bread and wine. So the whole notion [of] that act, that ex-
> change of bread and wine . . . is that we nourish each other, and this
> exchange of wine and bread is a symbol of the nourishment that we
> give each other.

The theme of nourishment presented itself again elsewhere in the ceremony. The opening reading, for example, was a poem called "Be-ginning Again"[16] which imagines love as sharing bread and thereby pro-viding sustenance for one another. And the prayers for bread and wine, adapted from John 2:1–11, also placed love in the context of sharing, this time invoking "community" as the ultimate sanction for the ritual. First John read:

In many traditions the sharing of bread and wine
symbolizes what bonds and sustains the community.
What we are about makes sense only in the contest of
community. We offer this blessing in thanksgiving
for your love and support of us.

Loving and gracious God,
over and over again
you show us how much you love us.

> You blessed our ancestors with a promise of fidelity and love for
>   all generations.
>
> Sacred stories from our traditions
> remind us of this covenant
> and of your constant care
> and concern for us.
>
> God of power and mercy,
> In your generosity
> you have given us this good earth,
> the stars above, and Heaven beyond.

Peter continued:

> You call us to partake in the banquet of life,
> to laugh and dance,
> to eat rich foods, and drink choice wines
> —to celebrate your spirit and kindness.
> You have blessed us with many gifts and we thank you.
>
> God of peace and justice,
> Your joy is with us always.
> As we call you companion and friend,
> You call us to companionship with each other.
> Today as we celebrate our union, we thank you for this gift.
> And we ask you for your blessing.
>
> Gracious God,
> as we celebrate your glory among us,
> we ask you to bless this gathering,
> together with our family and friends,
> who are not with us today.
>
> Bless this bread and wine that we enjoy
> from your bounty and make us always mindful
> of the needs of all who are poor—
> who are hungry, who are lonely, who weep.
> May their presence help us to grow in love for one another.
>
> Amen.

The importance of gaining the support and blessing of the community assumed heightened importance as the participation of Peter's fam-

ily, in particular, became increasingly problematic in the months approaching the wedding. Until he wrote to his mother to invite her to the service, Peter had never explicitly come out to any member of his family. He had hoped that his mother was aware of his homosexuality, but she claimed never to have known, and in fact, refused to acknowledge her invitation directly, only writing to say that she didn't expect to be in California in September.

Peter has since tried to engage her in more extensive discussion, but his efforts have not succeeded and his relationship with her has become strained. His siblings were just as uncomfortable with the prospect of a gay wedding as his mother; none of them was willing to come to the ceremony. Even more painful, one brother who was planning to marry a few months later wrote asking Peter not to attend his wedding because his presence would cause the family embarrassment. These rejections were offset somewhat by the participation of one of Peter's aunts and three of his cousins, all of whom had to fly in from other parts of the country. These relatives had all guessed long before that Peter was gay, and his aunt confided to him that his paternal grandmother, now deceased, had also come to the same conclusion many years earlier. "I feel really consoled that my grandmother knew," he told me. "I was born on her birthday and we were always very close. So it felt reassuring to me to know that she had seen that."

John's family was considerably more at ease with the occasion, and his mother, in particular, played a central role in the ceremony by offering one of the community blessings. John had come out to his parents years before, when he was still in the seminary, so they had had considerably longer to come to terms with his homosexuality, despite their distress at the time they first learned of it. They now regularly include John and Peter as a couple at family occasions like Thanksgiving, and even John's father, who has shown the most discomfort with having a gay family member (and who declined the invitation to the wedding), has begun to show what John describes as "progress."

The ceremony was held in the garden of friends, a heterosexual couple, whose wedding in the same location Peter had attended a couple of years earlier. The sixty or so guests represented both gay and straight people from "all walks of life," as John explained. "Some from church. Others not from church. Friends came from out of town. By far, I think the majority of people who were there were friends from church, because our closest friends are people who we know from church. But we had people who don't go to church." Many of the guests were asked to participate by reading or singing, and a gay male couple, who not long before had celebrated a commitment service of their own, served as "facilitators." The ceremony was followed by a party.

John and Peter's wedding exemplifies the ways in which religious beliefs may be drawn upon in helping a gay couple to conceptualize what it means for them to marry. It also foregrounds a number of other issues which prove to be central for many gay and lesbian couples in the process of planning and experiencing a commitment ritual.

On one level, the question of legitimacy and authenticity looms large throughout Peter and John's account of their ceremony and particularly with respect to their solution of the theological dilemmas it posed for them. As committed Roman Catholics who share a deep belief that a relationship with God permeates every aspect of their lives and who are active participants in their local parish, Peter and John's fundamental spiritual focus is the Catholic Church. Their sense of injury and banishment from the Church is acute and is highlighted at every turn by their preoccupation with how their service compares to a mass and their concern with demonstrating its moral equivalence to that standard. Despite the numerous points of departure from the content and structure of a mass, both men emphasize the similarities between the service and a mass. Moreover, they explain the notion of sacrament in a way that further legitimates their union as a "real" marriage, in a sense *more* authentic than mechanical Catholic observances because they have taken care to adhere to the spiritual foundations of the Church. Peter ties the exclusion from the institutional church to his isolation from his family, and particularly his mother:

> Yes, I'm sad that we could not be married in the Church. Saying that, I remember, going back to the early days of the Church, the *people* are the Church. . . . Where the people are gathered, that is where the Church is. I'm sorry that we could not be welcomed in the building of the church. The bigger sadness is that my mother was not there.

John and Peter see the Catholic Church as becoming more open to gay men and lesbians, even as its official stance remains resolutely hostile to homosexuality, while lesbians, and perhaps even more, gay men, have come increasingly to see themselves as deserving and capable of the kind of stable relationships they are committed to. They understand their role as a kind of *prophecy*. John puts it this way:

A prophet [is] one who stands on the outside of a group of people and is basically heralding or speaking words that the majority of the people don't want to hear. So [we are] prophets in the sense that we're a public couple, and hopefully our lives would reflect things and model things that are very, very good, but there's probably the majority of the people in society who are going to say to us, "You're not good. You're bad." And want to shut us up. Just like typically in Scripture, that's what they want to do with prophets. Prophets are the ones who are coming in and saying, "This is what the reality is. And this is what you need to look at." And everybody else trying to shut them up. In that sense, we're prophets because what we hope is that our lives will say something. We're realizing that we're probably going to be ridiculed. We're probably going to be spit upon, rocks thrown, whatever, figuratively. People aren't going to like what we have to say. But we're here. And that notion of prophecy is very important to us.

John and Peter also take pains to place their notion of "community" at the heart of the ceremony, using the presence and approval of community as a kind of authority to counteract the degree to which the service might be seen as a deviation from Christian ideals. The notion that community is diverse is characteristic of most gay and lesbian weddings; as couples make claims to legitimacy that crosses boundaries, they effectively deny the power of those boundaries to limit the terms of their identity. This becomes a much more central issue, perhaps, when members of biological families refuse or restrict their involvement; in this case, the hostility of Peter's relatives was to some extent offset by the comparative acceptance offered by John's mother and siblings. Invoking ancient words, such as the many quotations John and Peter selected from the Old and New Testaments, further makes the point that their claims are no newfangled political whim but rather at the heart of Christian moral consciousness.

We don't do this apart from our community. Why we had the public celebration and why we invited our friends is because they're part of it. Again, we said it before, our relationship doesn't make sense outside of the context of community, and in fact, if we didn't have a community, I doubt very much that our relationship could sustain itself. Because our relationship cannot exclude community and other people. We have to have a support system.

In like fashion, the two men explain that they are strongly considering parenthood for the future, though they are not yet sure whether it would be best to approach that goal through adoption or artificial insemination with a surrogate mother. They mention that a line in the traditional Catholic marriage service asks the couple whether they are willing to welcome children into their lives. While this question was long assumed only to apply to heterosexual couples, John and Peter argue that a strictly biological interpretation of that question no longer makes sense in the context of a Catholicism that has come to accept a broader construction of "procreation" as including adoption, "the capacity to love and nurture," and other behaviors that can be viewed as "life-giving." In other words, their desire to raise children together is further evidence of the authenticity of their claims to be legitimately married within the Roman Catholic tradition. These claims are further upheld by instances of family support for their union, such as the attendance of John's family and his mother's blessing. But they also draw evidence of some level of family support from instances that might be said to indicate approval obliquely, if at all, such as Peter's discovery that his grandmother had apparently tacitly accepted his homosexuality. This knowledge is particularly meaningful to him because he was close to his grandmother and because they shared the same birthday, an allusion, it would seem, to deep spiritual communion between them.

These claims are further authenticated by the emphasis they placed, as Peter and John describe it, on "simplicity" in every aspect of the ceremony. They used everyday household articles as the ritual objects in the ceremony, made most of the food themselves (or with the help of several friends), gave each other no wedding gifts apart from their rings, and followed the sharing of bread and wine with the singing of a song by Aaron Copland, "Simple Gifts." In avoiding what Peter rejected as "conspicuous consumption," they reaffirmed the centrality of fundamental spiritual commitments in their ceremony, and asserted that their service was as worthy of recognition as any staged by a heterosexual couple.

John and Peter see themselves as part of the Catholic Church; at the same time that they have endured repeated rejections at the hands of organized Catholicism, they steadfastly interpret such hostility as peripheral to the real spirit of the Church. They are extremely active members of their local parish and are well known as a couple within the parish community. But their pastor not only did not accept their invitation to the service, he failed to respond in any way to their invitation, even avoiding them when they called him on the phone to find out whether he would attend. Since the ceremony, he has made no mention of it even though they have interacted with him many times. But they see no need to involve themselves in a "special interest group" like Dignity because they believe that their parish is, as Peter puts it, "very welcoming of gay men and lesbians, and for me, I keep the focus on the local community, the local church, as opposed to the larger Church." Dignity, in this view, is the last resort for Catholics who have no way to participate in the Church, and as long as their parish allows the participation of gay men and lesbians, even as it refuses to fully recognize them, they have no need to seek a spiritual life elsewhere.

In the Shadow of David and Jonathan

Hear these words from the eighteenth chapter of the first book of Samuel (vv. 1–4):

"When David had finished speaking to Saul, the soul of Jonathan was bound to the soul of David, and Jonathan loved him as his own soul. Saul took him that day and would not let him return to his father's house. Then Jonathan made a covenant with David, because he loved him as his own soul. Jonathan stripped himself of the robe that he was wearing, and gave it to David, and his armor, and even his sword and his bow and his belt."

These were the words a San Francisco Baptist minister used to begin his meditation at the 1995 wedding of "Ken Taylor" and "Greg Bowers." The guests gathered in the shadowy chapel of the hundred-year-old landmark Swedenborgian Church, an outstanding example of the arts-and-crafts style of the late nineteenth and early twentieth centuries, set behind a high garden wall in San Francisco's Pacific Heights and rented for the occasion. Inside the chapel, a fire crackled in the huge fireplace spanning its rear wall. The ceiling was supported by bark-covered madrone trunks; the congregation took their seats on woven-rush chairs. Candles illuminated the intimate space.

Ken and Greg both hail from the Midwest, Ken from Oklahoma and Greg from Kansas. Now in their early thirties, they share a large hilltop home in one of San Francisco's working-class neighborhoods with their two dogs. Ken works for a federal agency and travels frequently around the western states; Greg is a computer consultant employed by a large software company. Both grew up in blue-collar families. Their wedding coincided with the second anniversary of their relationship.

Though they had extensive discussions before making a final decision on what kind of ceremony to have, Ken, a lifelong Baptist, spoke eloquently about the particular importance he felt having a church wedding would have for him. Since moving to San Francisco, Ken has been an active member of a Baptist congregation located near the Castro district. While the membership of the congregation is diverse, it has a substantial number of gay congregants. The congregation some years ago took the radical (for Southern Baptists) step of designating itself as "open and affirming" of same-sex relationships, an action that eventually led to its expulsion from the denomination and its subsequent decision to affiliate with the American Baptist Church, a more liberal denomination. Ken takes his religion seriously.

> It's always been a big part of my life. It's helped me get through some very difficult situations. I feel I have a relationship with Christ personally. I've always grown up with that. And even growing up gay, and growing up in a Baptist church in Oklahoma *and* being gay—there were obviously some issues to deal with there—[but] I've always felt, I still felt very grounded whether I was having problems at home, a relationship, or work or whatever. It keeps me centered and keeps me focused. It's always been a part of my life.

Both men liked the young minister who recently had become the pastor of Ken's church, so once they decided that they wanted to have a public ceremony, they asked him to officiate. Ken explained why it was important to him to have a ceremony that would involve other people.

> It meant a public display of what Greg means to me, what we mean to each other. And it also means—and I don't know the right phrase—I don't want to say "elevate" a gay relationship to a heterosexual ceremony, because that gives the connotation that we're *below*. I wanted to try to maybe just take the next step as far as community is concerned. That we can do this. I mean, most people like myself have been resigned to just accepting [that we could never have a wedding]. Like Greg was thinking that he was never going to have one.

While having a church wedding was only one of the things Ken and Greg both thought they would be denied because they were gay, it loomed large in both men's thinking. As their discussion of the ceremony unfolded, it became clear that having a wedding had something to do with rejecting the outsider status they had once assumed to be an inalterable fact of homosexuality. Greg described his thinking on the subject.

> Even when I was coming out, I thought, "This is awful. I'm gay and I can never get married, and I can never be in a relationship like that." And then as I started becoming more comfortable with being gay, and was out, and had friends and the community, and it just became my lifestyle, and my life, that's the way I was. . . . I knew that I would like to be in a long-term relationship, but as far as getting married, I never really considered that. So then when he asked me to marry him, it was like, wow, okay.

Ken explained why having a wedding was important to him.

> For me, in a selfish way, I didn't want to deny me and Greg the tradition of going through a ceremony just because we're gay. I guess I had pretty much written off [when I was] younger that because I'm gay, I'll never have a wedding. And so I decided, well, why not? I love this man. Why can't we? It went from there.

Deciding was also the most visible sign of a growing commitment to being out for both men. Around the time they began planning the ceremony, Ken launched a gradual, but determined, process of coming out at work, a process he described as positive and affirming. He became close friends with a woman coworker who had recently become engaged and her excitement about her wedding stimulated him to share his dreams with her. He confided in her and sought advice as he planned a romantic trip to Hawaii during which he would formally propose to Greg, and after Greg had accepted, began to share information with her about weddings in general and both of their specific plans.

> I came out to her before I proposed to Greg. . . . She was excited about getting engaged. . . . And I was thinking, "Well, why can't I be just as excited as she is?" And we're close. So I came out. And she was thrilled. And I told her what I was going to do. And she was even more thrilled. She gave me a hug. And it was like no problem at all. . . . And every time we get together we talk about wedding stuff.

Having other people there was a vital ingredient as far as Ken was concerned. In emphasizing the role of community in the wedding, he speaks both of the value of intangible resources like love and community, and about a way to intensify bonds with chosen family.

> One of the things that I've learned is that sometimes the important things in life aren't things that you can kind of touch and feel and buy. But it's friends and family, family meaning not just blood. And having the support of your friends and family around in what you do and enjoying life and getting the most out of it. Then having those people around at one of the most important events of your life is important. And that was part of my thought process. Because I don't really see it as a *public* ceremony. I see it as a private ceremony with eighty of our closest friends.

The pastor's comments assured the couple that there is a precedent for their love in Scripture, a precedent that means that God understands and supports their union.

> *It is clear from this scripture that a love relationship occurred between David and Jonathan. A beautiful love relationship that was honored by God. Marriages, by and large, were for convenience, for reproduction and for eschewing* [sic] *favor with another family. But in the case of David and Jonathan, we have love. Pure and simple love. A love that never ended and that grew in devotion over the years. I dare say that their love was among the purest in the Bible. When Jonathan died, David wept over his grave and said, as recorded in 2 Samuel 1:26: "I am distressed for you, my brother Jonathan; greatly loved were you to me; your love to me was wonderful, passing the love of women."*

Ken and Greg's ceremony was perhaps not very different from the sort of ceremony any other couple from a mainstream Protestant church might have expected to have in 1995.[17] A tuxedo-clad usher showed guests into the church. Two candles were lit at the start of the ceremony to represent the two separate entities who would be united. The couple made their entrance with the accompaniment of an organ fanfare. Coming into the chapel down the two side aisles, they met at the altar and stood before the black-robed minister. They were led through "vows of intention," that spoke of their intent to face the future together. After the Scripture reading and the minister's homily, the couple faced each other to pronounce their "vows of commitment." They exchanged rings, which the minister explained as "circles symbolic of eternity," made of precious metal "symbolic of pure love." Each swore to the other, "I choose you to be my spouse, today and everyday." While a vocalist sang "Love Changes Everything," the couple knelt and prayed, the minister's hands on their shoulders. They completed the ritual by using the two candles to light a single "unity candle," representing their change of status. The minister declared them "joined together forever."

What made this ceremony different, of course, is that Ken and Greg are both men, and while they perceive themselves to be part of God's kingdom and entitled to be united in marriage, their ceremony also took note of the levels at which they departed from or were excluded from tradition. The program, for example, named the two best men (together called the "unity party"), the minister, usher, vocalist, and organist, but also indicated that Greg's mother was "in attendance." I overheard the guests seated behind me exclaiming about how "wonderful" it was that she had come.

But these moments of difference were effaced by the many ways in which Ken and Greg adhered to convention. After the ceremony, we moved to the adjoining parish house for a reception. Piano music was played as the guests filed in from the courtyard. Two professional portraits of the couple adorned the entrance area; in one they wore T-shirts while in the other they were discreetly undressed. Gifts were piled in the far corner of one room. As we entered, we encountered a massive table displaying appetizers, while next to it bartenders dispensed wine, champagne, and mineral water. After greeting the grooms, guests mingled in two reception rooms; later, we moved into another room to serve ourselves dinner from a second elaborately arranged buffet. The wedding cake, multitiered and white, with a distinctive asymmetrical design, was available for inspection on a central table.

Greg and Ken's wedding confirmed the validity of their relationship on a number of levels. To the extent that the ceremony and reception adhered to the familiar forms of other (heterosexual) weddings of their experience, it was clear to them that the occasion was as real as any other wedding. The acceptance they received from numbers of nongay people enhanced this perception, as did the support they received from gay friends, viewed as "chosen family" in this context. Each of these sources of confirmation, however, paled next to the biblical recognition the minister provided. By interpreting the story of David and Jonathan as evidence of transcendent acceptance of homosexuality, and perhaps as even the model for marriage in general, the minister attested to the legitimacy of their claims. As long as David and Jonathan's love remains as an example of same-sex devotion, no one can dare to question the authenticity of Greg and Ken's love or their marriage.

At the same time, however, that both men emphasized the ways in which their ceremony followed the forms customary for such occasions in the Baptist church, they insisted that they were not "mimicking" heterosexual weddings, and, moreover, that their wedding was purely their own creation. Prior to the wedding they explained it this way.

> KEN: I don't feel that we're mimicking because . . . Well, I'll answer it this way. Susan and I, the straight woman at work, have had conversations about [our weddings] . . . and she's made comments to me on more than one occasion about how much more enjoyable it would be for her if she weren't bound by so many traditions. She *has* to do this. She *has* to do that. . . . And I'm sitting there enjoying the freedom of doing what we want to do. Do we want to have a best man? Do we want to have a best man and a best woman? What you'll see on May the 5th is a ceremony that reflects truly the ceremony of Greg and I. It will be simple. It will be quick. It will be meaningful. Spiritual.
>
> GREG: It won't be just like this staged production that's already been worked out by tradition, where you have to have so many bridesmaids and so many groomsmen.
>
> KEN: I don't feel like we're mimicking. . . . We're talking about having equal rights. The same rights. Well, one of the benefits of being equals in society is going through commitment ceremonies and doing responsible things. And to me, this is another responsible thing to do.

"So did you feel there was something you wanted people to know by the end of your ceremony?" I asked Ken and Greg when I visited them some weeks after the wedding. Greg hesitated and then said, "Maybe if anything, just that gay couples can get married."

But Ken had more to say,

> Another message that I wanted to try to convey is that we can be spiritual and be Christ-like and have some spiritual relationship, whatever it is that you choose to have. Don't be relegated to the outer limits of society and feel that you can't. And one of our friends called and his message was short, simple, but powerful, that, "Greg and Ken, I was really impressed with your ceremony. That's not what I expected. I'm

glad it was that way." Something of that nature. His comment was telling. It's that most people who go to gay ceremonies don't really expect it to be meaningful.

Painful rejection from their families, nevertheless, made it more difficult for Ken and Greg to hold on to the feeling that their ceremony represented a real wedding. For Greg, whose family ties have long been attenuated, the rejection he experienced was not unexpected, though he still grieves over his mother's insensitivity during her visit. To Greg's amazement, one of the first things his mother did when she arrived at their home the day before the wedding was to report to him, "Well, your brother thinks you're both going to hell." Nevertheless, she seemed to enjoy the wedding, and even told Greg that she was so moved by the ceremony that she cried. But both before and after, Greg feels that she acted as though nothing special was happening. "She was having a great time and she told me, 'Oh, I'm so proud. And so happy.' And she was crying. And the next day, it was like it didn't even happen. Almost. And then I haven't heard anything about the whole event from any of my family since then."

ELLEN: So how do you interpret that? What do you think that means?
GREG: I don't know. I question why she came out. Did she feel obligated because she went to my brothers' and my sister's weddings? I don't know. 'Cause I even said, "If you're not comfortable, everyone there pretty much is going to be gay." And she said, "Oh, no." She works in a hospital so she works with gay men in the hospital. So she's not unaccustomed to being around gays, lesbians. I really don't know how to interpret her behavior, lack of, or whatever. The whole time she was here we never discussed what we were doing or why. It was just almost like we were spending the day getting ready for a party, that kind of thing. . . . It sounds materialistic again, but it's like the gift thing. I bet my brother, when he got married both times, they got gifts both times. And my sister when she got married both times got gifts. And my other brother. All my brothers and sister have been married twice, and I'm sure that they all got gifts both times. And I didn't get anything, and I paid for her ticket to come out here.

Ken's family's response was, if possible, even more painful. Though they have never approved of his homosexuality, Ken felt that he was always particularly close to his family and he fully expected that his parents would both come to the wedding. His attempts to work out a way to subsidize his mother's airfare didn't work out and, in the end, neither of his parents were present, a fact that was made more painful by Greg's mother's attendance, after Greg paid for her ticket. Nor did they send a gift, or refer to the wedding in any other way in subsequent communications. Ken talked at length about his feelings.

> Another disappointing factor is my family was the type that I thought they would just surprise me. That they would just show up and surprise me. And I was looking for them the whole night. Even up to the time that the reception was over. I thought maybe they're going to show up and surprise me. So I was setting myself up for disappointment, anyway.

He has told his sister how badly he feels, "I don't mean to make it sound materialistic, but she sent us a gift. And she's the only one in my family that did. So I'm not equating gifts with emotion, but I guess it was her way of acknowledging." His anger and sadness have been transformed into what he calls, "putting my family in its proper place," a process by which he reminds himself that his relationship with Greg is the most important thing and that he should never expect his family ties to be stronger than that or more reliable. He has not spoken to his mother at all and sent her only a perfunctory greeting for Mother's Day, a marked departure from his usual, more effusive style. In telling the story, he can't help comparing his mother's behavior to some of his less affluent friends who gave small, but thoughtful, gifts.

> It's not the gift. It's not the value of the gift. . . . The fact is that there was some thought behind it. And it was just a way of supporting. It's not that here's something expensive. My mom is broke too. But the card that she sent us, sent me, before said, "Good luck to you." And it was, "Dear Ken." I don't think she has that much malice to do it intentionally. I'm at a loss now. She just doesn't get it.

The spiritual intensity of Ken and Greg's wedding helped to offset the feelings of illegitimacy their families' behavior engendered. By picking a Baptist preacher to officiate, Ken explained, "We didn't want it just to be a get-together and a party. We wanted to elevate to the point where heterosexuals can't exclusively have this religious experience." Because this was a gay wedding, moreover, they had no choice but to create something that would truly be meaningful to both of them. As Ken explained:

> The only thing really is the fact that we didn't have much of a precedent and we could just go with what we wanted and what we felt and things that were meaningful to us. We could pick and choose and we didn't have to worry about offending family, didn't have to worry about offending other people. I can't imagine being straight and going through what straight people go through, the fact that you've got two sets of families and really the principles involved are secondary. The event is for everybody else. And that's so backwards than what it should be. I consider myself doubly blessed, being gay and going through a gay wedding.

The friendly treatment they received from the store where they registered, the flood of gifts that arrived before and after the wedding, the elegant reception, the positive responses of their friends, the congratulatory aftermath both men experienced at their jobs, the intense emotions of the ceremony itself—all these reassured them that their message, "that gay couples can get married" got through. But for Ken, whose religious commitment largely shaped the ceremony, it was more than that.

> It was a spiritual experience. . . . Nothing can really compare to me standing there. I've described it before as kind of stepping outside the moment, where I'm standing there and I'm realizing that I have my partner to my left, [who] will be there for life. I've got my best man to my right who is a person who is very dear to me, my best friend, my confidant, other than Greg. My pastor right in front of me, guiding me. God above me. And everybody that's supporting me behind me. It was one of those incredible moments where—not to sound touchy-feely—but everything just seemed right. It was one of those moments where it just was right. And I just told myself, I'm going to remember this moment. I'm going to just soak it up.

The Family China

"Karen Newton" and "Andrea Katz" had a lot of support from family and friends as they prepared for their wedding. Both attorneys in their early thirties, the two women had been together since meeting at the Gay Pride parade some two years before. About six months into the relationship, they became "engaged," though they had not yet moved in together and felt it was too early to begin planning the actual ceremony. But they designed rings and had them made by a San Francisco jeweler, explaining to him that these were their engagement rings and that they would later need wedding rings to match them. When I met with them several months before the ceremony, Karen explained the process.

> It's yellow gold and white gold and sapphire and amethyst. Because . . . I wanted yellow gold and a sapphire and she wanted silver and an amethyst. And we ended up designing something that combined the two. . . . And for our wedding bands, we had a very thin simple gold band designed to go with this. And mine is yellow gold, and hers is white gold. . . . [They] are identical. So it's kind of like this is the merging of the two identities and then there's the individual identities, too.

As they described the planning of the Jewish ceremony that they eventually had on the terrace of a landmark restaurant in San Francisco, they agreed that almost everyone they had dealt with had been pleasant and supportive. From the jeweler who made their rings, to the event planner at the restaurant, to the furniture salesperson who sold them their new couch, they reported that everyone has acted like there was nothing out of the ordinary about two women having a wedding. While they attribute some of this "tolerance" to living in the San Francisco Bay area, where they expect that people are used to unconventional relationships, they also believe that their own self-acceptance has a lot to do with their experience.

> KAREN: We don't walk in there kind of uncomfortably going, "Gee, what are they going to think of us being lesbians?" We just are very unself-conscious about that with ourselves. And I think that that sends out a cue to other people, "Oh, these are just two normal everyday people coming in to . . ."
>
> ANDREA: "Spend their money."

In other words, they believe that their own sense of legitimacy creates an atmosphere which reduces the amount of discrimination they might otherwise encounter. They are both out at their jobs and to their families, and with the exception of Karen's father, who has asked her not to tell her stepsisters (his children from a second marriage) about her lesbianism, all the relatives seem to be comfortable, or to have become comfortable over time, with their relationship. Andrea describes her family as being particularly impressed with Karen because "she's a Jewish lawyer who makes a lot of money." But once they began planning the wedding, her mother, who earlier had been somewhat secretive about her daughter being gay, shared the news with all her friends and relatives. Andrea's parents have lived in the same working-class Jewish neighborhood in a large Midwestern city all their lives, and their relationships with friends and family nearby run deep. For years, her mother has been attending weddings and showers for her friends' children, secretly worrying that her own children would never bring her the *naches* (Yiddish for "gratification") of being the mother of the bride. So once Andrea told her about the wedding plans, her mother began to tell everyone about the coming event.

> She thought, "Damn it, you know. My kid's getting married and I want the same thing." So she took the initiative on her own. . . . She took it upon herself because she was . . . just very proud and very happy.. . . [She thought,] "I want people to know my kid's getting married, and I want to share that. And I want people to participate the same way I've participated in their kids' ceremonies."

Andrea's mother's enthusiasm resulted in her giving the two women a list of thirty-seven relatives and friends she thought they should invite to the wedding. When her mother's girlfriends decided to throw a shower for Andrea and Karen in absentia, she received another call from her mother. "She called . . . and said, 'The girls want to know if you guys need comforters or a microwave or what is it you need for your pre-wedding gift?' And you know, they'll want to know what china we want."

Early in the planning process, Karen and Andrea decided to register for gifts at two San Francisco stores, Macy's and Gump's (an elegant store specializing in china, silver, crystal and other home furnishings). Andrea laughs as she describes the transformation in her consciousness of herself as a lesbian that contributed to making this decision.

> In my younger more radical-dyke feminist days, [I] would just have plowed into Macy's and Gump's [to] get china and break it. And now it's turned around that I actually wanted to do this, facetiously, but part of it is I want it to be recognized as a real relationship. So I want to go to Macy's and Gump's and register. And I want china. . . . I've been to several weddings and certainly I know that in the cultural mi-

lieu I grew up in and that my mother still participates in strongly . . . you go to showers and you get gifts. And people register. And I'm just fascinated by the idea that we can go to five stores and just, you know, do wish lists and then just send this out across the country, and we'll get 25 percent. Things that we will use. It's not like little *chatchkes* [Yiddish for "trinkets"] that are going to be wasted. But actually things we'd use. And there is also the recognition element, that again, this is like everybody else does it. And I want that. In some ways it's the campiness of it, of just like having that experience, of computerizing across the country and telling people, "We want the towels with the red stripes, not the blue ones."

Both women also associate owning china, silver, and crystal—"nice things"—with establishing themselves as a family. They intend to have children together, recently purchased a house, and host many holiday dinners and other festive occasions in their dining room. Karen muses, "I just think it would be really nice to be able to set up a household with the kinds of nice things that, you know, I'd like to pass on to my kids." Andrea adds that her mother has offered to give her the family china, a gift that has led her to speculate on why having these things is important to her.

It's where the china and the crystal and the silver come in. . . . And I definitely want china for that reason. . . . My mom's china, which is very, very dear to her, as much as she says, "I hate what you kids did to it," that china shows the wear and tear of Thanksgiving dinners and seders and Rosh Hashanah dinners and Sunday nights with grandma and grandpa and everybody over. It's a real *feeling!* We will get pieces of that china . . . and I want that. And . . . there's a certain formality that I want to be able to have. I don't know that I would associate it with necessarily Shabbat or Jewish holidays, but certainly for Thanksgiving dinner, I want to do that.

Karen adds, "Well, we do Thanksgiving. We do Passover. . . . We *are* the family center here."

For Karen and Andrea, evidence that becoming a married couple will allow them to make claims on being a family is authoritatively conveyed through the symbolic medium of wedding gifts. On one level, registering at department stores and being the beneficiaries of the structured largesse of wedding showers attests to the legitimacy of their assertion that their relationship is for real, as worthy of support as any heterosexual marriage. On another level, possessing these household goods, both the new items they have chosen and the family china, will offer a constant reaffirmation of their status in the years to come. The family china, the formal silver and crystal, and the other accouterments of middle-class domesticity symbolize family, encoding stability, tradition, and the fulfillment of intergenerational continuity. They are marks of authenticity.

Asserting Authenticity

What are we to make of couples' assertions that there is nothing really unusual about a same-sex wedding? On one level, the claim appears to be a straightforward demand for equity and civil rights. That is, if society has a benefit to confer on couples, in this case recognition and validation of their unions, then denying that benefit to anyone is inequitable, as unfair as any form of economic or social discrimination.

But on another level, the argument behind these statements is somewhat different: that the approval extended to straight marriages is justified by the love that is their foundation. Since same-sex relationships have the same basis—*love*—and perhaps, because they resist convention, even reveal it in a purer form, they must be entitled to the same symbols of validation. Gay and lesbian commitment rituals, then, become forums for demonstrating the authenticity of couples' claims to moral equivalency with heterosexual marriage. A variety of symbolic means may be mobilized toward this end: the re-creation of liturgical forms associated with weddings, the elaboration of symbols that evoke love in its purest and most selfless contours, the participation and approval of biological kin, the bestowal of gifts that validate the couple's domestic aspirations.

Couples' symbolic maneuvers are most convoluted when they require confrontation with religious denominations that are hostile to homosexuality, such as the Roman Catholic or Southern Baptist Church or the Conservative wing of Judaism, but they may also contribute to strategies lesbian and gay couples devise for seeking the support of more liberal religious institutions. Explicitly deploying religious symbols or seeking religious endorsement may, on the one hand, reveal spiritual loyalty to a particular institution or, on the other, may be used to confirm claims to naturalness and normality, to define gay/lesbian marriage as conduct that need not be questioned. These symbols locate the commitment that is the focus of the celebration in a historical and community context and thereby inform the audience and the participants that gay/lesbian marriage is not really anything astonishing or a departure from tradition, that it is, rather, natural and congruent with the past.

Ironically, some of these strategies have the effect of declaring lesbian and gay commitment rituals, and the relationships they reinforce, to be even *more* authentic than heterosexual weddings because of their departure from convention. Couples report comments from friends and relatives about their weddings that highlight their emotional impact. Both couples' accounts and my own observations indicate that weeping is common at these ceremonies and that guests, whether homosexual or heterosexual, frequently describe these weddings as the most affecting and powerful they have ever attended. Whether it is the juxtaposition of symbols of convention with images of deviance that produces these effects or the way in which the ceremonies demonstrate the triumph of love over adversity is difficult to determine; suffice it to say that the perhaps expected perception of inauthenticity or ridicule rarely surfaces. In some cases, this even amounts to heterosexual participants' attributing greater authenticity to a gay union than they find in conventional marriage. One couple I interviewed, for example, reported that a straight woman friend who attended their wedding left her husband only weeks later, overwhelmed by the feeling that her marriage was mere convention while what she had witnessed at the gay men's ceremony spoke to "true love."

The intensity of claims to authenticity in gay and lesbian weddings calls into serious question the accusation by some skeptics in the gay community that efforts to integrate relationships into mainstream cultural forms constitutes the adoption of an assimilationist social program. These claims instead assert that the language of accommodation is irrelevant to the symbolic integrity of same-sex weddings. In these schemes, implications that couples who marry are cowardly or allegations that they have been entrapped by "heterosexual" cultural conventions are simply beside the point.[18] Couples repeatedly disputed the notion that marriage or wedding ceremonies *really* belong only to the straight world. They claimed, instead, that they had a moral right to legitimate their relationships and that they were merely making their claim explicit. By taking this stance, they effectively argued that by having a ceremony they were doing no more than restoring the world to the condition in which it should have been all along rather than attempting to reconfigure the very terms under which marriage could occur.

7

MAKING A STATEMENT

"Duane Thomas" and "Mike Rubin's" wedding was definitely not a routine event. In the spring of 1991, Mike and Duane, who a few months earlier had participated proudly in San Francisco's inaugural domestic partnership registration, put on a ceremony guaranteed to be remembered by everyone who attended. While the ritual followed the outlines of a traditional Jewish wedding in most respects, its catering and costuming were organized around an elaborate country-western theme. The vows the two men made to each other were spoken with the utmost solemnity, bringing tears to the eyes of many of the as-

History and resistance: Tallith and western wear

sembled friends and relatives. But campy humor was also at the heart of the event, permeating even its most serious moments with a mockingly ironic commentary on conventional weddings.

As a self-consciously subversive occasion, Mike and Duane's wedding reveals ways in which traditional cultural forms can be manipulated to constitute a kind of resistance to heteronormativity. From this perspective, it follows a tradition that historians of lesbian and gay activism have traced to the earliest documented manifestations of gay community awareness, examples that had faded from public awareness until resurrected by movement-inspired historians. In their detailed analysis of Buffalo's working-class lesbian bar culture in the 1930s, 1940s, and 1950s, for example, Elizabeth Kennedy and Madeline Davis argue that the gendered butch/femme culture that flourished in the period they studied offered the foundation for a kind of "pre-political movement." The forms of resistance Kennedy and Davis see in Buffalo's lesbian bar culture exemplify the notion of "everyday resistance" developed by political theorist James Scott in *Weapons of the Weak*. "Everyday forms of resistance make no headlines," Scott reminds us, pointing out that these forms tend to be overlooked both by conservative elites and by scholars of the right and left.[1]

Though the women who frequented Buffalo's rough lesbian bars and fought—through acts of "everyday resistance"—to protect their space against incursions by hostile outsiders might not have articulated a view of themselves as insurrectionary, their struggle laid the groundwork for the formation of a more explicit lesbian culture of resistance in the context of the 1970s feminist movement.[2] Exploring some of the same questions in his study of gay New York between 1890 and 1940, historian George Chauncey documents a range of gay institutions that promoted rather direct confrontation with the surrounding mainstream culture and suggests that the existence of these precursors of gay liberation made that later movement possible.[3]

These historical examples point to ways in which resistance need not be purposeful, self-conscious, or explicit to contribute to the subversion of a system of domination. It is this view of resistance as an attribute that can be read into behavior retrospectively that makes possible an understanding of "queer" identity as an intrinsically subversive configuration, whether it takes the form of implicit or "pre-political" resistance or emerges in more explicit, deliberate strategies of destabilization.

Being queer, from this point of view, is all about making people—gay or straight—squirm. While the homophile movement of the 1950s and 1960s focused on seeking a modicum of tolerance and human dignity for homosexual men and women, and the gay rights movement of the 1970s and 1980s largely was concerned with demanding equal civil rights for gays and lesbians, queerness—less a movement than a sensibility—seems to be about rejecting assimilation, subverting not only heterosexist conventions but lesbian and gay traditions as well.[4] "The new generation," explain Allan Bérubé and Jeffrey Escoffier in an issue of *Out/Look* devoted to an examination of Queer Nation, "calls itself *queer*, not *lesbian, gay, and bisexual.* . . .*Queer* is meant to be confrontational—opposed to gay assimilationists and straight oppressors while inclusive of people who have been marginalized by anyone in power. Queer Nationals are undertaking an awesome task. They are trying to combine contradictory impulses to bring together people who have been made to feel perverse, queer, odd, outcast, different, and deviant, and to affirm sameness by defining a common identity on the fringes." As historian Lisa Duggan puts it, the notion of a "queer community" is shaped "only by a shared dissent from the dominant organization of sex and gender."[5]

Certainly many kinds of queer cultural projects meet the expectations of resistance that the theory would seem to demand: the increasing inclusion of bisexual, transgendered, or other unorthodox sexual identities within a widening definition of "queer"; the intellectual efforts called "queering" that inspire new readings of old works and new bases for criticism and evaluation; the efforts to sabotage conventional approaches to life or art that depend on notions of the binary, whether in reference to sexuality or gender. Artistic production that mixes genres, political demonstrations that infuse the "personal" into the formerly "public" domain, and perhaps, most of all, manipulations of style that speak of incongruity, confusion, and blurred categories at all levels—all these forms play with our expectations and undermine our notions of the orderly and predictable.[6]

Queer cultural ventures are fundamentally exhibitionist, seeking public attention by using performance to confront conventional values and aesthetics, to generate a politics that is "in your face" and outrageous. The commonplace trappings of matrimony, and especially the lavish spending encouraged by advertisers and commercial interests, are particularly amenable to the kind of parody basic to queer performative strategies, as Lauren Berlant and Elizabeth Freeman assert in their reflections on "queer nationality."[7] Costumes, music, food and drink (particularly the multitiered wedding cake and the champagne tulip or flute), and the rest of the celebratory extravagances encouraged by consumerist forces are readily understood by Americans from virtually all cultural backgrounds, particularly insofar as they are played out in media representations (which are much more likely to be the subject of "queering" than ordinary experience). Most people have either attended weddings as participants or as guests, or are at least familiar, because of the ubiquity of popular portrayals of weddings, with their classic features. And because weddings can be such emotionally momentous occasions, many people have strong feelings—either positive or negative—about them.

To tap into the imagery and symbolism of the wedding, then, is to unleash a flood of highly charged meanings, to draw on the power of memory in ways that may not always be easily anticipated or controlled. Some of these images attach to generic symbols of "American" weddings, while others are more clearly associated with specific religious, ethnic, or class traditions. How powerful any particular challenge to or parody of symbols is likely to be varies, of course, with the contexts associated with them and the degree to which they are evocative of emotionally significant experiences. Lesbian and gay weddings can offer occasions for deploying both outspoken and tacit protests against heterosexism, their subversive powers both intentional and seemingly accidental.

"Because We're Queer"

Mike and Duane articulated their decision to seek public recognition for their union as part of a wider political struggle, one that has gained urgency as the AIDS epidemic has become a more insistent presence in their lives. Duane explained why he felt it was important to have a ceremony.

> For me, it was a lot of the psychological implications for myself. It's a world that doesn't recognize me as sometimes a human being but more frequently as a couple or anything. Now on forms at work and all of that, when they ask "married, single," I don't check any of them. I write in "domestic partner." And I just kind of feel like the world doesn't recognize me but maybe if *I* recognize me I'll be better off.

Mike, who also claims to have always wanted to marry when he found the right (in his words "healthy") relationship, sees the wedding even more explicitly in political terms.

Well, I'm a little bit more in the militant kind of place. And especially these last ten years with the epidemic has really made me much more politically conscious and socially conscious. . . . I'm at a place in my life where there is no room to not be who I am. . . . And I consider myself married. I'm proud of it. I'm proud of being a gay man. . . . And you know, for me it is a celebration of our relationship, a celebration of our love. There's no reason to do it behind closed doors or to keep it a secret.

But Mike and Duane also felt strongly that they had to have a "theme wedding" because they wanted the ceremony "to really reflect us." Mike explained that, "We didn't want things that were [about] fertility or child-raising, because we have no interest in that. . . . We wanted things that represented *us*." When I asked them why it was important to have a theme wedding, Duane gleefully exclaimed, "Because we're *queer!*"

As Esther Newton's 1993 book, *Cherry Grove, Fire Island*, documents in particularly rich detail, theme parties have a long and central history in gay male culture as venues for camp representation. Newton recounts stories "Grovers" told her about lavish gatherings with such themes as babies, high heels, Hollywood, the Bible, opera, and heavenly bodies, many of which later became part of community folklore. The themes carried through in costumes, invitations, and decorations, and sometimes were the basis for contests that celebrated the originality and ingenuity of responses to a particular motif. Religious themes and those featuring dramatic female roles were particular favorites, as were motifs that required multiple players (e.g., a group of bearers carrying in a mysterious, heavily-veiled "lady"). Theme parties were frequently staged as fund-raisers for charity and to celebrate important events such as anniversaries, birthdays, and mortgage burnings. Cherry Grove theme parties tended to be large events, inclusive of most of the community and often having the aura of a Hollywood premier with nonparticipants lining up to watch the costumed queens as they arrived.[8]

In view of the emphasis Mike and Duane placed on situating their wedding in this venerable gay tradition, their most difficult decision, as they told me their story, was not *whether* to have the wedding, but what *theme* to select. The problem was resolved on a trip to Reno when they saw "these absolutely fabulous vests" in a country-western store and settled on a country-western theme. This meant that their attire (including the vests), attire recommended for the guests, invitations, decor, food, and music, all followed a cowboy theme, easing the process of planning the event, and, incidentally, allowing for significant economies, as Mike detailed the planning process they went through:

> I mean, what kind of food would you have at a country-western thing? Oh, turkey, corn bread, ham, baked beans, cole slaw. And everything started making sense. And we thought, well, not only can we get dressed up, why don't we ask everybody to get dressed up? And then we thought, everybody has blue jeans or a pair of cowboy boots or a bandanna you can throw around your neck, or something like that. And then we'll dance, we'll two-step and we'll line dance. And everything started to fall into place.

Mike is Jewish, but it was Duane, whose background is Baptist, who first suggested including some elements of the traditional Jewish wedding ceremony. Having seen *Fiddler on the Roof*, he knew that the wedding canopy, the *chuppah*, could be an evocative image. The two men did some research on Jewish weddings, both reading a popular book on the subject, and discovered, as Mike explained:

> A *chuppah* is supposed to represent your home. And it's supposed to open on all four sides to allow visitors to come from all directions to come to your home. So we thought, "Oh, that's kind of fabulous. Now that we know what it means, that's really kind of a neat thing." And it said in the book something like it can be made out of cloth. And I thought, "Cloth! I still have my *bar mitzvah tallis* [prayer shawl] that my grandfather gave me. Wouldn't that be wonderful if we used that?" So it was able to tie in my past and tie in what it represented to us.

But Duane and Mike didn't feel that simply reproducing a traditional Jewish wedding would fully serve their needs. For one thing, the person they had chosen to officiate was a close friend, "Mary," an Episcopal priest. Mary was excited about their decision to use the Jewish liturgy as the framework for the ceremony, did some research, and made a number of suggestions about adapting particular elements to make them fit the two men's requirements.

> We did seven . . . blessings. And [the book] had traditional seven blessings. But [Mary] said, "Well, why don't we take that idea and then change it so that it works for you guys?" So we chose seven very, very close people in our life. And we asked them to bless us in a very specific way.

Mike and Duane opened their ceremony with welcoming remarks in which they articulated their understanding of the occasion as a gathering of "family" in the most meaningful sense of the word, an event that would express the love their family feels for them and that they feel for their family. Before the wedding, they had chosen seven friends and relatives whom they considered to be particularly close and asked each of them to prepare a personal blessing to read in the ceremony. The blessings were all inserted within a formulaic wording beginning with "May the glory of your love bless you with [*insert blessing*] all the seasons of your life." For example, the first person offered the following blessing:

> *May the glory of your love bless you with health and well-being all the seasons of your life.*

This blessing was followed by six more:

> *May the glory of your love bless you with a home of happiness and real comfort all the seasons of your life.*
> *May the glory of your love bless you with wealth and riches all the seasons of your life.*
> *May the glory of your love bless you with forgiveness and generosity of spirit all the seasons of your life.*
> *May the glory of your love bless you with patience and understanding all the seasons of your life.*
> *May the glory of your love bless you with humor and joy all the seasons of your life.*
> *May the glory of your love bless you with a home of security and peace all the seasons of your life.*

While Mike and Duane omitted some traditional elements (specifically the *ketubah* or traditional marriage contract) because of cost, their only serious and conscious deviation from Jewish wedding ritual (besides having an Episcopal priest perform the ceremony) was their incorporation of the kaddish, the mourner's prayer, into the ceremony. Mike's mother, who has always been supportive about his being gay, was truly shocked when he announced at a family dinner that they were going to include this prayer in their wedding. Duane describes the scene:

> I picture her dropping her fork. And your sister and she both going "What?" You know, it's like Mike and I said, "We're going to sacrifice a chicken at our wedding, too." I mean, I thought it was like we had said

something really *shocking*. And to her it really *was* shocking. That at a joyous occasion you bring up a mourner's prayer.

Mike added, "But yet, how many friends have we lost? That was part of what was going on with us."

That losses from AIDS continue to be central to the way Mike and Duane think about the community event that their wedding became was clear on the evening I visited their home. After discussing the wedding for about an hour, we moved into the bedroom to watch the wedding video on their VCR. As the camera panned the crowd of two hundred gathered in a South of Market loft, Mike pointed out those guests who had passed away since the ceremony—more than twenty men. AIDS is a daily presence in Mike and Duane's lives; Mike is HIV positive, though so far asymptomatic, and works full time for a local AIDS service organization. Their decision to marry and to celebrate their marriage with a wedding was made with the knowledge that the years they will have together may be limited. The epidemic is central to the way Mike and Duane understand the meaning of being gay; desperate circumstances mean that no single gay relationship is a private matter alone.

At the same time, however, neither Duane nor Mike conceives of their relationship solely in the context of gay community and confrontational outness. Their ceremony, then, permits them to articulate their queerness at the same time that it enables them to make a claim on the historical depth that Jewish tradition represents. The values this tradition allows them to elaborate, significantly, are those that also enhance their communal responsibility—openness and hospitality. They are most particularly realized in the transformation of the Seven Blessings the two men devised; seven friends offer blessings for particular areas of their lives in place of the traditional text. So while the ceremony follows the structure of a Jewish wedding in its basic shape, the message that prevails celebrates the gay community and underlines the men's commitment to strengthen it. Finally, Mike and Duane celebrate and elaborate difference, organizing their ceremony in a way that, they proudly claim, "could *never* happen at a straight wedding."

Mike and Duane's wedding seems to subvert the expectations of traditional weddings at every turn. It was crafted as a celebration of queerness, and while it draws on the Jewish tradition for its basic form, these traditions are deployed in a way that references a camp sensibility. The *chuppah*, for example, has already proven its theatrical merits in *Fiddler on the Roof*.

At the same time, however, the sentimental enunciation of love and commitment remains at the heart of the ritual, expanding the meaning of the Jewish liturgical elements to make a claim for inclusion beyond the boundaries of gay community. Mike and Duane use Jewish tradition to soften the subversion of their theme wedding, interweaving camp and convention to create a cultural product that defies easy categorization.

Defeating Death

In recent years, gay men's ceremonies of commitment have seemed to flourish almost in direct proportion to the massive impact of the AIDS epidemic on the community. Not a few of the men I interviewed were HIV positive, and some of those who described their weddings to me early in the study had died by the time I began writing. Unavoidably, as the study progressed, my attendance at ceremonies expanded from weddings and receptions to memorial services. It can be said without fear of exaggeration that a consciousness of mortality suffuses every action of men who are HIV positive and has pervasive effects on men who are negative as well.[9] The number of deaths since the early 1980s when the disease was first identified has been staggering, and even a cursory glance at obituaries not only in the gay press but in mainstream publications confirms that mortality from AIDS continues to be high among gay men.

As the enormous literature spawned by the epidemic amply demonstrates, the AIDS crisis has led to an intensified concern with spiritual questions, stimulating new forms of personal exploration while also leading some gay men and lesbians to increasing involvement with existing religious and therapeutic traditions. Gay involvement in both gay-centered and mainstream religious institutions has increased, along with growth in a variety of New Age movements and therapeutic modalities. New books dealing with religious issues in relation to homosexuality are extremely popular, and that is particularly the case for works that deal with some aspect of same-sex marriage.[10] Gay community newspapers are filled with advertisements and announcements for support groups, workshops, and retreats, as time that was once spent (at least by some gay men) at pleasure-oriented bars and baths is now taken up with community service, twelve-step and recovery groups, and political activism.[11] Durable relationships and domesticity have a higher profile than ever before among gay men, and while it would be naive to conclude that this represents an absolute shift of direction from the past, such concerns have clearly become more salient since the advent of the epidemic in the early 1980s. In part, the political centrality of the same-sex marriage issue emerges from this transformation; certainly, as I outlined in chapter 1, the cultural reflections of a new sensibility are pervasive.[12] As weddings have become a more prominent cultural feature in the gay community, it seems that they have offered an idiom for conceptualizing loss and reducing its impact. The numbers of ceremonies among gay men, several gay clergy told me, have increased dramatically with the spread of the epidemic, while the interest in commitment rituals among women seems to have remained at about the same level.

These shifting sensibilities are most dramatically represented in the language of the many AIDS obituaries placed in gay community publications. The deceased are frequently described as having "gone to a better place," being "at peace," or joining lovers who died earlier. Surviving partners may speak in these death notices of their conviction that they eventually will be reunited with their loved ones. Enduring ties to those who have passed away are evoked at memorial services and through such material reminders as panels in the now gigantic AIDS quilt, plaques, place names, and other gestures aimed at honoring the deceased and assuring that they will be remembered.

Some ritual responses to death and dying intersect with the proliferation of weddings and commitment ceremonies, sometimes finding expression in a sort of hybrid ceremony that might be called a "deathbed wedding." In these situations, one or both of the men are close to death. The ceremony is performed either in their home or in a hospital room, usually with only a very small number of close friends or relatives in attendance. Even more than other gay commitment rituals, the meanings of these occasions are layered, both invoking the future, as do other weddings, and honoring the past. When Rev. Jim Mitulski, pastor of the predominantly gay San Francisco Metropolitan Community Church, told me about the large number of such ceremonies he had found himself doing beginning in the early 1990s, he was clearly perplexed.

> What does this mean? It means something that they'd always meant to get around to but hadn't. It means closure. But that's not what weddings are conventionally. It means comfort to both [men] that somehow death isn't ending this, and it makes the person who's dying feel better. And I think the person who's not dying feels better, somehow.... I can't figure out what they are even. They're weddings and funerals together.

Because the last couple I've had, the people in the room say, "Just say something about what this relationship means to you and why you're here." It's like a memorial service, almost. Sort of. They're sad, but they're beautiful.

These ceremonies are, in a way, about reincarnation, about denying that the deceased will no longer be present, Mitulski argues, illustrating his understanding of the ways in which Christianity can meet needs that reveal implicit beliefs very far from Christian doctrine. Over the years of the AIDS epidemic, in particular, he has watched the language of his congregants shift from typical liberal Christian beliefs to something much more mystical and magical.

Christianity does not believe in reincarnation.... On paper, marriage is for life, but not for eternity. And when you die, marriage is not a dimension of the life to come, if you will. This is of course what the church teaches. What do people believe? Everything on the map.... There's kind of a spiritualist dimension, in a phenomenological sense, around a kind of religion where the afterlife, seances, all that stuff [are important]. That's never been orthodox Christianity.... People didn't grow up with that is what I'm saying. And it's fascinating to see it. I mean people [now] talk a lot in our church about *angels* and things like that. This is a liberal congregation, and that's not part of the rhetoric of liberal Christianity, certainly. And I've been a minister in the gay community now for ten years, pre-AIDS, mostly. [In the past] you never talked about heaven. You never talked about angels. Angels are people who've died and who are still here.... I hear a lot of this vocabulary about feeling the presence of angels. That's the word. Angels. I mean, angels are medieval Catholicism. They're not contemporary Christianity. But people are finding meaning in these things that even ten years ago you never heard about.

For some men, knowing that their lives together may not be long forces them to feel that public acknowledgment of their relationship is an urgent necessity. One couple, both now deceased, told me of how important it felt to have a ceremony as they struggled to make a life together in the shadow of AIDS. At the time that I first met "Barry Geller" and "Matt Swanson," they were still excited about the wedding they'd had only a few months earlier at a downtown San Francisco hotel. Their ecumenical ceremony had been performed by the pastor of Matt's church, one of the local MCC congregations, and by Barry's uncle, a Reform rabbi from Southern California. Barry was still working full time, but Matt had had to go on disability a few months before the ceremony and had become largely dependent on Barry financially.

Despite the warm support he received from his uncle, Barry's immediate family has been very uncomfortable with his being gay and was shocked by his plans to get married to another man. Barry went to visit his father and stepmother a few months before the ceremony to let them know about his plans and to try to answer whatever questions they might have.

> Their reaction was that it is a mockery of the institution of marriage. And I said, "Well, what is marriage? And what is a family?" He says, "To us, marriage is where two people get married in order to raise a family." I said, "Excuse me, but you two did not get married in order to raise a family." He says, "Well, it's different for us." I said, "Why is it different?" He said, "Because we're older." I said, "So we're both dying." Because we both have HIV and it's progressing. I said, "What's the difference?" And he said, "Well, it's just different."

Except for the cost of the flowers which Matt covered out of his disability income, and the flower arranging, which Matt did with his mother's assistance, Barry paid for the entire ceremony—including rental of space at the hotel, a buffet dinner, champagne and wedding cake for ninety guests, a guitarist who played during the reception, and a one-week honeymoon to Disney World and Cape Canaveral, Florida. He had always been careful about finances, and in the past made careful plans for retirement, prudently living within his income and never accumulating debt. Barry told me that he doubted he would have been prepared to spend the money it cost to put on their wedding had they not both had AIDS. But if his relationship with Matt was to get the recognition he felt it deserved while they were both alive, he was going to have to do something out of the ordinary.

Manuel Vargas and Travis Johnson (see chapter 5) were conscious of how being HIV positive affected their decisions at many levels. Travis had survived two other lovers who had died of AIDS, and though both men were still healthy at the time I met with them, they used the metaphor of "dog years" to express the telescoped way they have experienced time in the context of the epidemic. Travis found comfort in the fact that he and his previous lover had registered as domestic partners; the certificate is now one of his cherished possessions. Formalizing his bond with Manuel, both at the somewhat campy ring exchange they staged at the national gay square dance convention and in a more religious ceremony they hoped to have in the future, offered a way to establish the permanence of what they shared, to inscribe their relationship in public memory, much as a couple might carve their initials inside a heart on a park bench or tree.

The desire to defeat death through ritual is not only an issue for gay men. In *Cancer in Two Voices*, Barbara Rosenblum and Sandra Butler chronicle their time together while Barbara suffered from what was eventually terminal breast cancer. One year after the diagnosis, the two women staged a "rebirth party" to celebrate the first year of Barbara's survival. That celebration, Sandy writes,

> [was] designed to hold back the disease process, to affirm and insist upon life. I fear that without the documentation ritual provides, our lives together will be washed away like an elegantly constructed sand castle in the wake of this determined wave of cancer. We need to exhort the heavens, "*L'Chaim*. To life." We need to begin again.[13]

A year later, as Barbara's condition continued to worsen, they decided to have a commitment ritual. Barbara writes of her feelings as they planned the ceremony:

> As I hold my breath until the liver procedure later this month, Sandy and I prepare for a ceremony of commitment, one she has wanted for years. I had hesitated, felt ambivalent, not comfortable with rituals. But each time Sandy and I have attended one, I have found myself unexpectedly moved, stirred by this creation of form, this reshaping of experience to envelop loved ones. Now with the gravity of my liver metastases, we both feel ready to create a ritual that will honor us, the life we have created together, and the community that rings and nourishes us. The time has come.[14]

Sandy describes the process of planning the ceremony while they continued to pursue various medical options:

> Planning the ceremony of commitment has become an oasis of calm in the midst of this devastating medical news. In less than a week, our friends will gather to witness our love, to honor Barbara's courage in this time of shrinking possibilities, to dignify her insistence on a conscious death. I need the comfort of ceremony, the visibility of ritual, a

way to honor who we are and what we have created in our lives as a couple. To insist upon being seen—something that as a lesbian couple we have never taken for granted. To stand proudly and name our relationship, what we have meant to each other, and the ways in which our lives brought people together.

After affirming their love for each other and speaking of all that it had meant to both of them over the years, Barbara turned to the friends assembled in their living room and said:

> We face our future together with each one of you in this room. It is now the time of the biggest fight—*of* my life, *for* my life. You are my allies against despair and discouragement, against pain from disease. I will rely on all of you to be midwives in my passage and I consider myself blessed by your presence in my life.

Their friends offered prayers and blessings, encircling the couple as they came to the exchange of rings. As Barbara placed the ring on Sandy's finger, she said, "This ring represents the unbroken circle of life and the completeness of our bond." At the end of the ceremony, klezmer music, "old and familiar from Barbara's childhood," was played. In a dance recalling generations of Eastern European Jewish weddings, each guest held a handkerchief that joined her with the person beside her. "Thus connected," Sandy writes, "we moved through each room of the house, dancing, filling the house with the energy, with the enthusiasm, with the holiness of this day."[15]

Barbara and Sandy had carefully planned this ritual of commitment (like the "rebirth ceremony" staged the previous year) as a deliberate effort to use spiritual resources to interrupt the disease process. Breast cancer made them highly self-conscious about their bond to one another, their ties to the wider community, and their place in history. The rituals they organized, the book they wrote together, and the film that documented their relationship during Barbara's last three years of life all constituted a refusal to let death have the last word.[16]

Unexpected Resistance

The effects of rituals are not always what couples expect. Some described the ways in which preparing for their weddings had compelled them to be more public about being gay than they feel would ordinarily have been comfortable for them. Shopping for caterers, cakes, photographers, locations for their ceremonies, and perhaps most pointedly, rings, forced them to be visible. One lesbian couple recalled their trips to jewelry stores as awkward ventures, since asking to see matching rings forced them to come out to salespeople. The clerks, of course, wanted to make a sale, and were courteous, "but it was just one of those, 'Okay, here we go. (Deep breath.) We want hers and hers wedding rings. What do you have?'"

Another couple, though, remarked that even buying matching wedding rings wasn't necessarily interpreted as a sign that they were a couple. At the store where they finally selected their rings, the salesperson persisted in writing up an order for one ring even after both women had tried on the display model. Throughout the interaction, the couple had spoken of the purchase as "ours" and had chosen the ring "we liked." After they reminded the clerk that they were ordering two rings, identical but to be made in different sizes, she became quite flustered, still claiming not to understand until they carefully explained that they were getting married to each other.

For some, expressions of resistance may emerge in the aftermath of a wedding, testimony to the perhaps unanticipated consequences of the ritual. For Margaret Barnes and Lisa Howard, whose restrained and tasteful ceremony was consciously designed not to suggest confrontation or conflict with mainstream sensibilities (see chapter 4), getting married spawned dramatic changes in how they viewed themselves in relation to the wider community. Because they were concerned about the potentially awkward situations they would face if they were questioned by coworkers about their spouses, Margaret and Lisa chose rings that neither matched nor, to their eyes, would be readily identified as "wedding rings." Prior to the ceremony, they explained that while they wanted to celebrate their nearly ten-year-old relationship and provide a context for their families and friends to get acquainted, they were not eager to do battle with mainstream society. Fearing that the proprietors of the elegant Victorian inn where they wanted to hold the wedding might refuse to cater a lesbian ceremony, they described their occasion as a "family reunion," only revealing the truth to the establishment's event planner after their deposit check had cleared the bank. While there would be no way to hold the ceremony without its actual focus being obvious, they had no desire to use their negotiations with the facility as an excuse for an "in-your-face" sort of confrontation.

About a month after their ceremony, I settled into a lounge chair in Margaret and Lisa's garden. Over iced tea and cookies, they showed me their photo album, and with much laughter, recounted various odd happenings from the wedding weekend. Beyond the humor, however, their description was intense; they perceived the ceremony as having deepened their relationship in ways they had not anticipated. An even more unexpected outcome was their decision to come out at work and to become much more public than they ever had about being gay. When Margaret returned to work after her week off, she responded to her colleagues' casual questions about her vacation by announcing that she and her partner of ten years had gotten married. The responses she received seemed to be warm, for the most part, but she said that even if they weren't, she now felt it was her responsibility to let her coworkers see that gay life is not represented only by the Sisters of Perpetual Indulgence.[17] The wedding led her to see her relationship as the core of her life in a way that meant that disguising it would be betrayal.

A few months after this meeting, I spoke with Margaret on the phone and she described an adventure she and Lisa had had at an elegant Peninsula restaurant with close friends, a straight married couple. The couple, whom they know from business school, count their anniversary from the same time that Margaret and Lisa do, and the two couples have celebrated the date together for many years. This year, for their joint tenth anniversary, they went out to dinner. During the dinner, the waiters overheard talk of an "anniversary," and when they served dessert, they decorated a small cake with a candle and presented it, with much ceremony, to the man and woman. At that point, the straight couple said, "But what about them?" pointing to Lisa and Margaret. When the confused waiter said, "But they're not married," Margaret and Lisa immediately answered, "Yes, we are," holding out their left hands and displaying the very nonmatching rings they had chosen so that they would not resemble wedding rings. A second cake arrived in minutes.

Ken Taylor and Greg Bowers (see chapter 6) confronted some of the same issues in the months following their wedding. Because his employer has a policy of not discriminating on the basis of sexual orientation, Ken has mounted an effort to secure domestic-partner health benefits for Greg (who works freelance and thus has had difficulty locating adequate health insurance coverage), arguing that the nondiscrimination policy is meaningless if same-sex partners are not able to obtain the same benefits as heterosexual couples. While he doesn't see himself in any way as being an "activist," Ken does think that these efforts may have some significance over time.

> I feel that my responsibility is more along the lines of what I'm doing at work. It's like a one-man battle. And that's one brick out of the wall. That's my brick. And I guess the message would be that together, collectively, we're removing one more [brick] of our own little wall that our community has decided to put up. And that is that we want to separate ourselves from the mainstream. And I'm saying "no." We live in a society together and we love each other and this is one of the benefits of being in love, that you can show that to your friends in a ceremony.

Ken's notion of the battle he has to wage involves saying "no" both to those heterosexuals who would exclude his relationship with Greg from equal treatment and to those in the gay community who advocate a strategy of separation from the wider society. He wants recognition for his relationship from the mainstream, particularly if that will assure him and Greg economic equity, but he also wants the gay community to acknowledge the validity of their choice to solemnize their union in a particularly Christian context.

Ken began these efforts months before the wedding, taking a first step in the process he describes as his coming out at work. But now that the wedding has occurred, Ken is out as never before, a dramatic change for a man who described himself as having spent much of his life doing whatever was necessary to avoid offending those who might object to his homosexuality. For years he had taken pains to substitute "she" for "he" when sharing personal stories at work, and had assumed that he simply had to accommodate others' desire not to be confronted with the fact that he was gay. His experience with the wedding has changed that.

Ken started the process by coming out to a straight female coworker with whom he was already friendly when she got engaged and began talking about plans for her wedding. Once he had shared the news that he, too, was getting ready to get married, the two of them spent hours exchanging wedding-related information. (For example, it was this coworker, Susan, who told Ken about the church where he and Greg eventually had their ceremony.) After the event, Ken's coworkers gradually noticed his new wedding ring, and stories circulated around the office.

I used the wedding as a way to tell people when they discovered that I was gay, and married, that I'm not going to be an in-your-face sort of person. If they want to talk about it, then I'm just as normal as anybody else. I'm not going to be one of those who comes up and says "I'm gay. You'd better accept me for who I am." I want the message to be, "Oh, okay." And that's it. And so far that's been the reaction.

Ken's hope, that his being gay would eventually become a "nonissue" at work, was realized on a business trip a few weeks after the wedding. He went out to dinner with a group of his coworkers, some of whom he didn't know very well. To his surprise,

> someone offered me a toast, wishing me well, and congratulations on the wedding. It was the very first time ever that it was really open, the fact that Ken is gay and we're acknowledging it, and we're discussing it. And I just said, "Well, I really appreciate it. You don't know how much that means to me."

While Greg's ties with his family had long been attenuated, Ken perceived himself as close to his parents and siblings and, despite their discomfort with his homosexuality, expected support from them at important moments in his life. He was still very upset some six weeks after the ceremony as he reported their apparent disinterest in the entire event and their failure either to attend or to send a gift—or even to show any interest in hearing about the wedding. He had offered to subsidize his mother's airfare from Oklahoma, but they were not able to work out suitable arrangements. Then, to make matters worse, Greg's mother suddenly accepted his offer to pay her expenses and came out for the ceremony, making Ken's mother's absence all the more painful.

> The way I describe it is nothing has really changed. My perception has just changed. I have put my family in its proper place. I guess in my previous relationship, I put them even before my relationship. And now, it's in its proper place.
>
> ELLEN: So when you say you put your family in its proper place, what do you mean by that?
>
> KEN: I guess that came out more harsh than it really is. What I mean [is that] my priority, you know, spiritually, [is] God, Greg, friends and family. And down below you've got things like job and other commitments and responsibilities. But before, I would put family above in my list of priorities. I just kind of realized that Greg is

more important and they need to accept me on my terms. And I'm tired of being the son who pleases everyone. And I was always that way. And if I'm not going to please them, that's okay. We haven't had any harsh words, nor will we.

Ken's experience of having his relationship with Greg validated and supported at the wedding, then, has strengthened his resolve to view his homosexuality as something positive and to demand that his family honor that view.

My gay lifestyle has always been a point of contention since they found out about it. And it's almost like, "Well, your brother's had an alcohol problem, your sister's had this problem with sleeping around, and you're gay." You always [get] lumped into some problem category. Well, you know what? I don't buy into that. Especially since May the 5th, actually not that day, but especially symbolically May the 5th, I am *proud* of being gay. I would *rather* be gay.

Alternatives to Weddings

Of course, wedding-like commitment ceremonies are not for everyone. Many couples feel strongly that drawing on rituals they associate with wedding ceremonies carries implications of convention that they are unwilling to accept. At the same time, however, they may still find themselves becoming ever more outraged by the lack of recognition their relationships receive, particularly when they are denied any of the vast array of financial supports routinely available to heterosexual married couples. Such situations as the serious illness or death of a partner, or the failure of family members of one person to acknowledge the importance of their spouse, may offer especially pointed reminders of the invisibility of same-sex relationships both in the legal system and in the imagination of most heterosexuals.

Larry Brinkin and Wood Massi had been together about six years when the question of marriage came up. Both men, in their late forties when I interviewed them, describe themselves as former hippies, and both have long histories of political activism. Each had spent many years living in communal households and neither held monogamy in particularly high esteem. They spoke wistfully of the sexual adventures they enjoyed in the 1970s, and Larry spoke, as well, of his strong need to spend a significant amount of time in solitude. So when Wood popped the question in 1989, actually asking Larry, "Will you marry me?" Larry wasn't immediately comfortable with the idea. He explained that he'd always felt rather negative about the institution of marriage, but that a proposal from Wood, with whom he was—and is—intensely in love, wasn't something he could ignore. At first, Wood said he wanted to have a ceremony and invite all their friends, but Larry vetoed that suggestion. When I asked why he didn't want to do that, he said:

> I'm not totally sure, but I didn't really want to ape what heterosexuals do. I just thought it was this heterosexual thing. And it sort of annoyed me. Weddings have always annoyed me, mostly because I wasn't allowed to participate. You know, I wasn't allowed to have one of my own. In fact, I have a policy that I *never* go to heterosexual marriages, ever. I won't. I refuse. I used to. I went to some of my siblings', the first ones', when I was younger, I went to some of those. I decided this probably in the early seventies, because I'd already been to a few. But once gay liberation happened and I thought about it, I decided I would never go to one again until gay people or same-sex couples could get married legally. And that's still my policy. And it's been hard because when it's my sibling or my dear friend, I really want to do it, and it's nothing against them personally. But I just refuse to do it. I wish all lesbians and gay men would refuse. Although I don't hold it against them. So that was part of it, that I had this resentment about marriage in general.

On the other hand, Larry realized that having some sort of ritual of commitment privately was something he wanted to do with Wood.

> I had such mixed feelings about the whole thing. It was very romantic and wonderful, and flattering, and sweet, on the one hand, and on the other hand, it was like what am I getting myself into? What is this? Even the language. I really have trouble with the language "Will you marry me?" I mean, I didn't even know how to respond to that. Because to me, marriage is a legal term. And I still have this resentment. But I just tried to give it the meaning that he intended, and that I understand, meaning "a commitment." And that I could say yes to. . . . But I was interested in talking about our commitment to each other, and exchanging vows. That appealed to me.

Once it was clear that Larry was comfortable having a private ritual,

Wood was easily able to compromise. The "bottom line" for him was having *some* sort of ritual, or as he put it, "to have something special happen." "The compromise," Larry explained, "was that though they weren't present for the exchanging of the vows, the following week or something we had a party to celebrate our commitment. And everybody came to that." Wood added, "With a cake and photographs." "Everybody" included a large group of friends. Though both men invited their families, Larry's couldn't come because of the expense of traveling from the various other states where they live, and Wood's objected strenuously to the idea that two men could get married. Wood's father, who still lives in the area of the Deep South where Wood was raised, is both politically conservative and a fundamentalist Christian. Though his father has never been comfortable with Wood's homosexuality, announcing that he and Larry were "getting married" produced an explosion. Larry described the intense reaction Wood's father had to the news of the "wedding."

> [Wood] said, "Larry and I are going to get married." My theory is it's simply that language. 'Cause he wrote back and he said, "Well, who's going to wear the gown?" You know, "get married" to him was like walking down the aisle. And that's what he pictured. He didn't picture what it actually meant. That's my theory. I think if Wood had said, "We're going to be committed to each other and exchange vows on the beach," he still would have been upset, but not quite as upset as "we're going to get married."

ELLEN: So was there a religious objection?

WOOD: That was it. And see, I have a different take on the word *marriage*. I feel that the gay and lesbian community should appropriate that word. That we shouldn't just let heterosexuals be married. That's what people think of when they think of family and commitment, they think of marriage. And that's what we have, is a marriage, in operational terms. So that's why I want to call it being married, and I don't care that heterosexuals have had that word all the time.

The commitment ritual itself took place at the men's favorite beach south of San Francisco. They arrived late in the day, when almost no one was there, and read their prepared vows to each other. Each man had written his vows on his own, and neither knew what the other was going to say until that day.

Wood's vows to Larry were as follows:

My darling Larry, I vow to you today, and for the rest of my life:

To love you as completely as I can, no matter what happens to either one of us, and no matter who or what we may become.

To take care of you when you need it; and to ask for and accept your care when I need it.

To allow you, as much as I can, access to my inner reality, to the hopes, the dreams, the fears, and the doubts that motivate my life.

To gently seek access to your inner reality.

To truly listen to you and to know what is happening to you, in you, and with you.

To try to understand and respect your values.

To be actively responsive to your needs, feelings, and beliefs.

To speak honestly and deeply with you, telling you as clearly and explicitly as I can what I am asking and what I am offering.

To confront conflict between us directly.

To meld with you, but also to maintain my own independence.

To let you be free; to leave you alone when you need it.

To respect your privacy.

To help you grow and change.

To give you permission.

To acknowledge and accept our differences, our limits, and our incapabilities.

To try to understand what is really going on between us with regard to equality and mutuality, not expecting perfect balance in all things.

To try, to the absolute limits of my capabilities, to comfort, care for, support, honor, and love you for the rest of my life.

These things I also ask of you.

Larry composed his vows to Wood in the form of a letter:

Dear Wood:

I love you. I have had six years to be with you, think about you, talk with you, sleep with you, make love with you, argue with you, be loved by you, worry about you, be delighted by you, be in awe of you, and love you. Now I am ready to tell you of my feelings for you and my commitment to you.

I feel huge waves of love and friendship and respect for you. You're my lover, my partner, my pal. If I continue to feel about you the way I feel today, there is no doubt in my mind I would want to be with you always. I feel lucky to have found you, and I feel lucky that you love me and like me and want to be with me. I love your brilliance; you are one of the smartest people I have ever known, and your intellect stimulates me, keeps me awake and interested. Your knowledge and understanding of music and art and thought have broadened mine immeasurably.

I love your beautiful body. It exactly expresses who you are and what you feel. Making love with you is delicious and fun and passionate and sexy and new.

Most of all I have come to love your passion for liberty and rights and freedom. Your politics also reflect exactly who you are, and you have managed amazingly to make the leap from an upbringing steeped in racism and reactionary thought to a commitment and an understanding of what is wrong in the world and what a right world would look like. That love of a fair, loving world and that hatred of injustice and bigotry is the essence of my bond with you.

What I am committing to you today is my pledge to try to be the best possible friend I can be to you, and the best possible lover. There is nothing more important I can give you, and there is nothing harder for me to give, than honesty. I have lied a lot in my life. The lies have often been in the form of swallowing my real feelings and attempting to invent feelings I think I should have. I am going to try hard with you to express what is really happening inside me, and invite you to do the same.

I will try to communicate not only honestly, but thoughtfully and clearly. I will try to speak not only with clarity, but from the heart. I will try to be a terrific listener, really listening to what you are expressing and not just preparing my rebuttal in my mind as you speak.

I will do my best to strive for as much intimacy as possible. I truly want to share with you—I want to share our money and resources and responsibility for each other and our thoughts and feelings and our bodies and fears and laughs and our joys and depressions.

I want to now pledge to you the deepest, most important thing I have, and that is my sense of self. I can tell you truly that our relationship could seriously falter and maybe even end if I fail to pay attention to my needs. Though I love you very deeply and feel committed to you, I also love myself and know from 43 years of experience what my needs are. I must have solitude and time with myself regularly and meaningfully. That includes time to stare at the wall, masturbate, go to movies, read, listen to music, cry, think. I promise you that I will work very hard to work with you to make sure that happens, and to also make sure it happens for you when you need the same solitude.

> *I also pledge to honor the long-time friendships I have with others; to not abandon them because of "coupleism," and to make sure that I honor your long-time friendships, too.*
>
> *Finally, or maybe hopefully not finally (since I hope we will always build on our commitment), I pledge to be creative in our relationship. I don't want to mimic the old, stale model of marriage. I want for us to forge some new territory, to take chances and do things in remarkable new ways, to try to figure out together ways to solve our problems such that we continue to grow and expand the rest of our lives. I'm not interested in being a couple of boring couch potatoes. I want us to remember we are hippies, regardless of how we dress or how old we are. I will do my best to assure that we never forget the values we developed through the years, values learned from love and drugs and sex and reading and the arts and the spirits of the living things that came before us. Those values are the tools to keep us young and new and creative. If we are successful as a couple, our love will reach out to our family of friends and to the struggles for freedom that will engage our energy.*
>
> *I'll do my best.*

Throughout the proceedings, they told me, they had a single witness, but one whose presence Larry found particularly significant.

> It was a seagull. It was amazing. We were sort of sitting right by the cliff looking at the ocean. And the seagull came right up very near us, stood there the entire time and just looked at us. It was just amazing to me. And we hadn't broken out the food yet, so there was no food that was obvious. Just watched us the whole time. And my best friend in the world, Charlie, had died in May. This was October. And I don't know, I had this feeling that it was sort of an embodiment of Charlie, who would have been with us or part of our thing because he was my best friend. So that was really wonderful. I loved that seagull being there. It was just fabulous. So we exchanged these vows and we discussed what they meant. And we kissed.

Wood and Larry's exchange of vows placed their commitment to one another squarely in the context of a wider understanding they shared about the political significance of being gay and its relationship to struggles for social change and justice. Both men take pride in their involvement in the cultural and sexual experimentation of the 1960s and 1970s; both came to San Francisco in the 1960s and took part in the antiwar and gay liberation movements. Both identified as hippies and lived in communal households. And while they recognized that the years had changed some things in their lives, such as the AIDS epidemic making Wood fearful of sexual adventures and their becoming more settled in their careers, they insisted that their relationship be dedicated to the maintenance of the spirit of challenging authority that had shaped it from the beginning.

Larry remarked that his hesitancy about entering into a marriage also stemmed from his mistrust of mainstream institutions of all sorts.

> That too was part of my ambivalence. Not just that marriage is heterosexual but that it's sort of bourgeois. Everybody ending up in couples. 'Cause I was used to living collectively. . . . In fact, when there were couples in the commune, they often got criticized if they were too couple-istic, if they kept to themselves too much and weren't communal enough.

But while he doesn't believe in monogamy "in principle," in practice he and Wood have been monogamous since they began to live together in 1989. He attributes this lapse in principle both to trying to do what Wood wants and more basic problems of time and energy. "I don't have time to not be monogamous! It's too much trouble!" he laughed. He sees his job, enforcing antidiscrimination policies for the city, as continuous with his activism even if he gets paid for it and wears a tie to work. "It's just this old thing about 'Look at me, I'm in this house. I'm with this man. In a marriage.' What's happened to me? How have I failed?"

In contrast, Wood, who works as an administrator at a local college, is shocked to see himself in the role of a middle-aged professional and worries that perhaps he's no longer as radical as he ought to be. But he is sure that his domestic arrangement with Larry is anything but bourgeois.

> But my personal life with Larry I'm perfectly satisfied with. And it doesn't seem retrograde to me at all. In fact, it seems like a celebration to me because it's two gay men doing what they always said we couldn't do. We're not supposed to be able to have long-term relationships. We're not supposed to be able to get along with each other. We're supposed to just fly from one person to another. So to me, just maintaining the relationship is a politically radical act. Which is sufficient in itself.

Larry and Wood are both concerned about maintaining continuity between their earlier lives as hippies and radicals and their current situations. But their definitions of how best to resist the attractions of middle-aged and middle-class existence, how to stay true to their principles and preserve their identities are strikingly different. Larry's work is the thread that connects the politics of his past and present, but domesticity threatens to engulf him in bourgeois complacency. Wood, on the other hand, is perplexed to find himself occupying a position of authority in his work, and thereby to be identified with the powers that be. But he sees marriage not as an imitation of tired old heterosexual norms but as a successful challenge to a culture that defines gay men as incapable of commitment. Being married to a man, then, is simply not comparable to being married to a woman, for Wood.

Larry and Wood's different perspectives, however, on how to maintain congruity between their politics and personal lives coalesce in their support for domestic partnership registration as a legal response to the privileges accorded heterosexual married couples. In 1981 Larry's then-lover died, propelling him into a historic lawsuit against his employer at the time, Southern Pacific Railroad, after they denied him bereavement leave. He sued under provisions of the Fair Employment and Housing Act, which includes marital status as a protected category. Represented by the American Civil Liberties Union (ACLU), Larry argued that denying him bereavement leave upon the death of his domestic partner constituted discrimination based on marital status, on sexual orientation (under a local San Francisco ordinance), and that it violated the right to privacy as defined by the California Constitution. Though he produced copious evidence of the seriousness of his eleven-year relationship, including information about their shared bank accounts and car ownership, and the fact that they were both helping to raise a child who lived in their communal household, the company claimed that there was no evidence that the two men had a "bona fide relationship." He lost the case both in San Francisco Superior Court and on appeal, with the court finding that there was no way to prove the existence of the relationship, particularly when there was evidence that they had not been monogamous.[18]

> The opposition attorneys, the company attorneys, had me go through every single year of our relationship and say how many other sexual partners I had had. . . . There was an article in the Duluth newspaper that I got ahold of about the case. And the headline was . . . something like "Man with 57 Husbands Demands Bereavement Leave."

This experience convinced Larry that some sort of domestic partnership registration was needed. After City Supervisor Harry Britt's unsuccessful attempt to institute such a system in the early 1980s (his bill was vetoed by Mayor Dianne Feinstein), Larry became active in the lengthy campaign to establish the system that finally came into existence in 1991, after a bitter political battle involving three separate ballot initiatives over a three-year period.

> I became very interested in domestic partners from then on. Even though I myself was ambivalent about the whole thing, . . . I realized that not being able to be married is a huge form of discrimination not only because of the ritual aspect and the recognition by government, which people want, but also the benefits that accrue to you by getting married, like bereavement [leave]. Or health benefits. Or all the other things. There's a myriad of things. So when it came time to do all these political campaigns, it wasn't just political, it was from my personal experience, because I knew what it felt like. And also, had we had a domestic partners registration system at the time, I would have won my lawsuit, I'm convinced. Because they kept saying, "Well, how do we know? How do we know? There's no marriage license." We had put on the stand the benefits administrator for Southern Pacific and asked him whether anyone ever in the history of Southern Pacific benefit programs had ever been asked for a marriage license. And he said no. So obviously, there was a double standard. But I still would have won if I'd had that. And now, there are a lot of domestic partnership benefit programs, and most of them require this certificate.

Wood and Larry were among the 251 couples who registered as domestic partners on February 14, 1991. After each couple registered, they descended the grand staircase as their names were read to the crowd of well-wishers assembled in the rotunda of San Francisco's ornate City Hall. Although they had never doubted that they would be part of the festive event that marked the first day of registration, they were both astonished by how emotionally powerful the experience turned out to be. Larry still gets excited when he describes what it was like.

> I was so incredibly moved by it, I was amazed. I was really taken by surprise, I have to say. Well, I mean, there we were with lots of photographers and people that we knew all around us. And it just felt great to do this with *government*. You know, the government of my city, where

I pay taxes and live and vote and work and activate, recognized our relationship by giving us this piece of paper. It felt great. It felt great also because of the emotional commitment I felt. It was real. It was another exchanging of promises, and these were practical things that we had to really think about because it requires that you be responsible for each other financially. And so we talked about that, and what that meant. And it was great. It made me cry. It was really very moving. Going up to the clerk and kissing. It was wonderful.

Larry and Wood balanced complicated political stances in arriving at the decision to have a private commitment ceremony and to register for domestic partnership. While they reject anything reminiscent of heterosexual marriage as the model they want to adopt, and while they fervently demand the right of same-sex couples to marry, they have carefully constructed alternative ways of formalizing their union so that they need not define themselves as having capitulated to bourgeois values. At the same time that they argue that they should by rights have access to the same privileges opposite-sex couples have extended to them when they marry, their commitment to maintain a radical challenge to conventional proprieties can be preserved only with continuing ambivalence toward the state's role in fostering particular kinds of domestic arrangements. Emotional intensity, the authenticity of which cannot be questioned, and a commitment to opposing bigotry and pursuing justice make their relationship worthy of protection at the same time that they wish it to stand as a challenge to the institution of marriage.

An Anniversary Party

Ambivalence about associating their relationship with some of the meanings conventionally connected to "marriage" can lead to ritual solutions different from those devised by Larry and Wood. But when couples construct ceremonies as alternatives to weddings, they may find themselves struggling between the desire to omit elements that might evoke the spirit of a wedding too explicitly (particularly those associated with institutionalized religion), while also using terms like *wedding* and *marriage* to explain what kinds of rituals they are creating. Many of these ceremonies intentionally involve other people in an occasion that gives heightened public existence to a relationship, often ratifying arrangements that may have existed for many years.

On a Saturday evening in November 1993, "Cathy Polanski" and "Sylvia Diamond" hosted more than one hundred guests at a large "anniversary party" at their Greenwich Village apartment. The handprinted and photocopied invitation they mailed out billed the event not only as a celebration of their twenty years together but also as the seventeenth anniversary of their close friends "Ruth Dunlop" and "Molly White," and featured a photo of the four women enclosed in a Cupid's heart. Besides the details about time and location, the invitations said: "Affirmation and witnessing of our marriages, 9 p.m. Other couples are invited to join."

Cathy and Sylvia frame their relationship within their long shared histories of political activism, what Sylvia calls their "accidentally parallel lives." They met at a Gay Pride march in 1973, when both were active in lesbian feminist liberation. Both are the children of leftist parents, were involved in the civil rights movement during the 1960s (they eventually figured out that they had both participated in the same Freedom Ride in 1963, though they don't remember meeting at that time), and were brought up in the New York area with minimal exposure to religion. Although they are now busy professionals (Cathy, forty-six at the time of the ceremony, is a physician; Sylvia, fifty-one, is an accountant), they continue to place their political principles at the center of their sense of self, and strongly identify the struggle for gay rights as a matter of fundamental justice closely related to a host of other struggles.

Their decision to have a "wedding" was prompted not by a desire to acquire any specific institutional benefits of marriage, but from dismay at the inequities they see same-sex couples continuing to endure. Earlier in 1993, Cathy and Sylvia were among those New York couples who registered as domestic partners on the first day that the city offered this new benefit. Although neither expected to receive any direct benefits (and, in fact, they were not completely sure of what specific benefits might be gained from the status), they felt that the act of registering enabled them to take an important political stand. Cathy explained:

> What it meant to us was to go public in New York City. I mean, we've always been out. We were both activists before we came out. But it just seemed to be right and fitting that when this was offered to us that we put it on record even if to guard against future deprivations of gay rights. You know, even to go on record as saying it's important that there be domestic partnership. Here we are and we stand for it.

The actual experience of registering proved an exercise in inequality.

Sylvia pointed out that domestic partnership registration is done in a shabby office right next door to another shabby office where heterosexual couples apply for marriage licenses. But while Municipal Building employees make a point of congratulating the straight couples as they leave the marriage license office, the same-sex couples signing up for domestic partnership were studiously ignored. Sylvia didn't take this passively, however. "The guard was saying congratulations to all the straight people and nothing to us. So I said to the guard, 'Hey! We paid our money, too. You say congratulations to us, too.'"

Both women went back to work after they registered, but later in the day Sylvia began to feel that something was missing and realized that she really didn't want to let the day pass without acknowledging its specialness. She ended up alerting a favorite gay-owned restaurant about what they had done, asking them, with virtually no advance notice, to put together some sort of celebration. When she and Cathy arrived later that night, they found their table and chairs decorated with balloons and garlands normally used on New Year's Eve. Tiaras had been placed on the table for them to wear, and they were presented with a complimentary bottle of champagne. The staff cheered, applauded, and threw confetti, with even the chefs and dishwashers filing out of the kitchen to offer congratulations. The two women felt, at last, that they were being recognized for having done something worthwhile. So as the date of their twentieth anniversary approached a few months later, they realized that they wanted to mark its significance. Sylvia explained:

> I mean, we live together years and years and years and I guess that was part of the thing with the domestic partnership that got me. The domestic partnership was something that was given to us that doesn't mean very much and it's told to us that it doesn't mean very much. And our relationships, and for us, it's almost all our adult lives, and our relationships somehow, even for us, in certain subtle ways, don't mean what a married couple does.

Their friends, Ruth and Molly, who had been together almost as long as they had, were enthusiastic about collaborating on a wedding ceremony. But since Ruth and Molly live in two separate and small apartments, Sylvia and Cathy's relatively spacious high-rise apartment seemed like the obvious place to hold the event. In the end, they devised a plan for the ceremony in which each couple recited personal vows, but both (along with any other couples who decided to join in, as two others eventually did) ended by reading a "marriage contract" Cathy and Sylvia had written for the occasion. Each couple received a "Certificate of Marriage," with the same wording as the contract which read:

> *On this, the sixth day of November, 1993, in the* [ordinal number inserted here] *year of our relationship, we,* [names inserted here], *by the power of our love and our commitment to each other, declare ourselves married.*
>
> *Witnessed by:* [signatures inserted here at ceremony]

Sylvia and Cathy's statements at the ceremony focused on what it meant to them to claim the word *marriage* as their own. As the guests crowded into every available bit of space, craning their necks to see the proceedings, Sylvia read her comments, pausing as necessary when the jubilant crowd started laughing and applauding.

> *Marriage, to me, is a way two people not related by blood become family. In the modern marriage, the bond is affection, fidelity, and a commitment to support each other.*
>
> *For twenty years, in good times and bad, in sickness and health, Cathy and I have had this bond and this commitment. Our marriage resembles other marriages in all ways but one. The state does not recognize it. But this doesn't change who I wake up with in the morning and who I go to sleep with at night, who I have had breakfast and dinner with, for the past twenty years, the happiest twenty years of my life. And I can't think of anything better, anything more blissful than to spend the rest of my life having breakfast and dinner, going to bed and waking up with you, Cathy, my love, my spouse.*

Cathy spoke immediately afterward:

> *For the past ten years or so, friends have sometimes asked us, "What is the secret of your relationship?" We've only been able to figure out some parts of the answer: "Respect." "The same politics." "The way she touches me." "She's fun." "She doesn't run away when I practice my music."* [sustained laughter after this]
>
> *I tried today, but I can't put my deepest feelings into words. Sylvia, I thank you for our wonderful life together, and the circle of friends and family who are sharing it with us. Every day when I wake up next to you I am full of joy. Every day we spend together is the wedding day.* [cries of delight from the crowd at this]

Both Sylvia's and Cathy's statements focus on the ordinariness of their lives together, underscoring the fact of their long mutual commitment. The ineffability of their emotions, the fact that they resist articulation in a medium as crude as language, speaks to their intensity and truth. But equally important in the couple's presentation is their description of the repeating rhythm of daily life, the circle of breakfasts and dinners, waking up and going to sleep, that punctuate domestic routine. Cathy's reference to Sylvia's "not running away when I practice my music" reminds us that the kinds of family bonds the two women are claiming to have instituted through marriage are reliable and unequivocal, not ephemeral as friendship bonds supposedly are. Their relationship has already proven itself; rather than vowing to begin something anew, they are clearly reiterating the existence of a long-established reality. But in making sure to reference the political foundation of their bond as well, they clearly underscore their view of same-sex marriage as a confrontation to bias and a step toward liberation.

By keeping the proceedings secular, having the celebration in their home, and, except for the few minutes devoted to the couples' statements, generally adhering to the form of a party rather than a "wedding," Cathy and Sylvia avoid overlapping into the territory of heterosexual marriage. At the same time, however, they demand inclusion and equity, and insist through this ritual that their relationship merits the same respect as any other marriage.

Making Headlines

The reading of gay and lesbian weddings as subversive assumes a very different shape for those whose unions become the subject of legal or political controversy. Lest any of us be lulled by the trappings of propriety that seem to accompany weddings and the gestures of acceptance evidenced in some families and communities, these couples' experiences remind us that lesbian and gay marriages, and the rituals used to solemnize them, are still viewed as offensive and confrontational by a significant segment of the nongay population.

The couples whose petition to marry formed the basis of the Hawaii case, for example, were not fully prepared for the strain of public scrutiny that being litigants in a historic civil rights case has brought them. Joseph Melillo and Patrick Lagon, who joined two other couples in launching the case that demanded the legalization of same-sex marriage, were surprised that their desire to wed turned into an epic national controversy. They were so convinced of the rightness of their bond, that their meeting was "kismet," that when they decided to get married in 1990, it didn't occur to them that there would be any obstacles to their applying for a marriage license and receiving it. In a 1996 *New York Times* article, Melillo comments that they "were just two guys in love who wanted to get married," and both men profess amazement that their simple desire became "so political." Despite the intense controversy that has surrounded the case, Melillo and Lagon do little public speaking or fund-raising and fill their time instead with a range of domestic activities comparable to those of many other married couples: working in their jointly-owned T-shirt business, dealing with the termite problem in their house, and pursuing their interests in catering and flower arranging. But they still wonder at the fury that has raged around their modest desire, marveling that Congress and the various state legislatures attempting to enact laws that would invalidate such marriages if they become legal in Hawaii "have nothing better to do than decide if two guys or two girls can get married."[19]

The impact of wedding ceremonies on couples' lives can extend far beyond the personal issues involved in deciding to marry. How the wider community reacts, in fact, may have little to do with the ceremonies themselves. When hostile responses to same-sex ceremonies unfold, their effects may be felt in various areas of couples' lives, but have particularly painful repercussions when they threaten employment.

Atlanta residents Robin and Fran Shahar never expected the years of litigation and invasive publicity that followed upon their 1991 wedding just after Robin's graduation from law school. Robin and Fran's objectives in planning what they self-consciously called a "commitment ceremony," were hardly intentionally subversive. Robin detailed the process that led to their decision to have a Jewish *kiddushin* (sanctification) ceremony as having to do with their strong feeling that one must move through one's life in an intentional manner.

> We had been together for a while, probably about three, three and a half years. And the issue came up, did we want to spend our lives together? I think Fran and I are both committed to living consciously, to not just sort of drifting through life together without consciously deciding, yeah, you're who I want to spend my life with.

Fran explained that once they decided they should make a conscious commitment to one another, it was virtually automatic that they would decide to do so in a way that would be "Jewish."

> I think that the initial decision is . . . are we going to consciously choose each other as our spouse? And once we made that decision, the idea of doing it in community came very naturally. And doing it in a Jewish way came very naturally. . . . But the thing is, it wasn't enough for me to just say to Robin, "Okay, you're who I pick." I wanted to *publicly* say it, that this is who I pick. "Publicly" meaning "to my community, to my friends, to my family." Not just to each other. To the important people in my life.

Since the couple is actively involved in a Reconstructionist synagogue serving Atlanta's lesbian and gay community, it was enormously important to them to stage the ceremony in a Jewish community context. As they described the process of planning to me, it was clear that they were thinking mainly in terms of what a ceremony would do for their relationship. Their accounts of the various steps leading up to the *kiddushin* focused on how each part of the process clarified and enhanced their relationship. Planning the text of the ceremony, negotiating the *ketubah*, performing the *mikvah* ritual the night before—each element of the sequence either helped them to better understand their motivations and intentions or brought them closer together with friends and family.[20] As Robin explained, "It was a transformation process. . . . It felt like a year of defining for myself what it meant to be married to a woman, and specifically to Fran. Part of what I had to do was do a lot of writing about what it meant to give up the idea of marrying a man. So it really helped me come to terms with living my life as a lesbian." After the event, community members who had attended the ceremony told Robin and Fran that their relationship offered a "role model" for a positive, healthy relationship and thereby enriched the community.

The two women also hoped to have children together and to create, as Fran explained, "a whole new family entity." In line with these expectations, they decided to change their former surnames to a new, shared name that would make them clearly recognizable as a family unit and would mark their change of status in a way that would intensify their sense of its intentionality. They chose the name Shahar, which means "the act of seeking God" in biblical Hebrew and "dawn" in modern Hebrew, completing the steps necessary for a legal change of name some weeks before the ceremony.

But the name change had ramifications far beyond anything they anticipated. During law school, Robin had worked for a summer at the state attorney general's office and had secured a regular position there scheduled to start some time after graduation. While she was working at the attorney general's office, she had shared the information about being a lesbian with only a few coworkers. But before beginning regular employment, she was required to fill out confidential personnel forms indicating possible conflicts of interest, and since Fran was then employed by the state, Robin listed her name as "future spouse" and designated her own marital status as "engaged." Shortly before the wedding, she called the office to notify them of her change of name, saying only that the reason for the change was that she was getting married. Since this was the same procedure that would have been followed by a heterosexual woman who decided to change her name after marrying, she didn't anticipate that anyone would pay much attention to it, and certainly never guessed that it would later be perceived to be a deliberate provocation.

The news that Robin was marrying a woman and not a man, however, did find its way into office gossip, gossip that was eventually relayed to Georgia's attorney general, Michael Bowers. Based on information he had received concerning "a purported marriage between [Robin] and another woman," Bowers summarily withdrew his offer of employment, news Robin received only days before the wedding. His rationale was that failure to dismiss her would amount to tacit approval of her marriage. Later he argued that the marriage was in violation both of the state's marriage laws and its sodomy statute.[21] In his deposition he argued that "the natural consequence of a marriage is some sort of sexual conduct, I would think to most people, and if it's homosexual, it would have to be sodomy."[22]

Shahar v. Bowers, Robin's lawsuit against the attorney general, was filed in October 1991 and has been slowly wending its way through the federal courts since then. Though a three-judge panel of the Eleventh Circuit Court of Appeals issued a ruling favorable to Robin and Fran in 1995, agreeing with their argument that their relationship was protected by constitutional guarantees of freedom of association, in May 1997 the full court set aside that ruling on Bowers's appeal.[23] The attorney general's argument has been that Robin and Fran's relationship is not protected as freedom of association. He further argued, and the court agreed in its latest ruling, that even if the relationship were constitutionally protected, the presence of an employee who is known to have married a person of the same sex would disrupt the smooth operation of his office, and that the need to prevent such disruption supersedes Shahar's constitutional right to freedom of association. Robin's ACLU legal team has challenged Bowers to demonstrate some way in which such disruption actually occurs, citing her uneventful ten-week tenure in the very same office and her current successful employment by the City of Atlanta as evidence of the speciousness of his claims. Although both women continue to fear the effect that filing the suit might pose to their personal safety, particularly in the South, they feel they made the right decision. As Robin said:

> It was so blatant. I mean, to his credit, he put it in writing. "I'm firing you because of your purported marriage to another woman." We just couldn't let him get away with that. I would have gone through my life furious. Which isn't to say that if I lose this case I won't still be sad, but it will be different. I will have said no. I'm not going to just let [him] get away with that.

As the two women struggle to come to terms with the effects the lawsuit has had on their lives, their memories of their ceremony continue to serve as a source of strength and renewal. In this context, the argument that gay and lesbian couples ought not have commitment ceremonies, that as the remnants of patriarchy, such rituals are merely parodic, sounds hollow to Robin and Fran. "Why should gay people give up the positive traditions that straight people have just because straight people have screwed them up?" Robin inquired toward the end of our conversation.

> There is something different about making that conscious choice to live your lives together, and then to work for a year on defining what that relationship is going to look like. Or what we ideally want it to look like. I have a feeling that most heterosexuals when they get married don't go through the painstaking efforts that we did to work out a *ketubah* and work out what we want in our ceremony to reflect who we are. . . . I just think it makes a big difference in living your life consciously.

Robin and Fran never intended to generate publicity or to become the focus of a legal controversy. They decided to have a commitment ceremony for reasons that were explicitly personal—their desire to intensify the degree of intentionality that characterized their relationship and, by adopting a new, shared surname, to implement symbolism that would make them recognizable as a family. But because of the local political situation that surrounded them, particularly in the wake of the Supreme Court's decision on a Georgia case in *Bowers v. Hardwick*, they were catapulted into the position of having to put up a public fight for Robin to keep her job.[24] Their defiance of the assault by the Georgia attorney general, however reluctant, has shaped their lives since then, forcing them to contemplate levels of visibility that they ordinarily would not have sought. That their wedding was transformed by others into a symbol of resistance should remind us that opposition need not be either intentional or premeditated to transform the actors involved and powerfully affect the conditions of public life.

"Family Values"

But others who choose to assert their relationships ritually are well aware that in doing so they may become combatants in a complex cultural war which they may never see resolved. These men and women choose to defy heterosexism, moving into the public eye and purposefully using their unions to dramatize issues of social justice. But at the same time that they challenge opponents of same-sex unions, they also sometimes find themselves skirmishing with their own communities. By staging public commitment ceremonies, and thereby claiming equal rights to the potent symbolic capital associated with marriage, these couples must confront those lesbians and gay men who continue to define marriage as capitulation to the heterosexual domination imposed by patriarchy.

Pat and Karen Norman's journey into controversy exemplifies these complicated dynamics. Pat is a well-known activist in San Francisco's gay and lesbian community, a longtime health agency administrator, and a periodic candidate for local public office. An African-American mother and grandmother, fifty-four years old when I met with the couple in 1994, she began her relationship with Karen, who is Caucasian, in the early 1980s. Since their wedding in 1984, Karen, thirty-seven, an attorney and activist, has given birth to their two children, both conceived through donor insemination. The two women have forged a highly public identity as a biracial lesbian family. Probably their most visible moment in the wider community over the past few years involved their appearance on a billboard captioned "Family Values," in which a very pregnant Karen was pictured standing beside Pat, whose arm was around her shoulder. The billboard was prominently displayed in San Francisco, Los Angeles, and Atlanta for several months.

But despite their awareness of themselves as public symbols of a number of controversial social issues, both women explained their decision to have a ceremony in personal terms. Around the time that they met, Karen had decided that she wanted to find a woman to whom she could make a lifelong commitment; in the context of ongoing community discussion of monogamy and nonmonogamy, she felt that "trust" had become the key issue for her in evaluating relationships, and that she wanted some assurance that her relationship would involve "no betrayal." Ironically, although she didn't see her parents' marriage as a model relationship, she admired its longevity as an example of a firm and committed partnership. "My parents always said, 'Murder yes, divorce never.' And they're still together. They just had their thirty-ninth anniversary. So I was raised with that attitude, I guess."

After meeting at San Francisco's Gay and Lesbian Film Festival, Pat and Karen's relationship took off quickly, and by the time they had been together for four or five months, they agreed that they should have a ceremony.

> KAREN: It was pretty much mutual. Basically, I said, "Well, I want to have a ceremony." And Pat said, "I don't want to have a relationship unless this is it." It was like I got the feeling that [Pat was] saying, "Let's cement it. Let's seal it now. Don't mess around. If we're going to be together, let's be together."
>
> ELLEN: What about a ceremony felt that it was cemented?
>
> KAREN: Well, when you get married, you get married. You say, " 'till death do us part." It's a promise. And you're making that promise not just to yourself and the other person, but you're making it, in the context of the ceremony, you're making it to God and to your family and community. And I don't take that lightly. To me, it was a way of saying, "Yes, I want to be with you the rest of my life." . . . They say there are no guarantees. Well, getting married was my guarantee.

Striking a slightly different note, Pat's account of the planning process focused on her desire to feel that she was making progress toward achieving a personal emotional goal. She explained that she had had enough of the view that relationships are simply disposable when partners begin to experience problems, an approach that in the past had led her through a series of relationships that didn't last very long.

I had been looking for a person who would take seriously being in a long-term marriage, in a real marriage. . . . I remember going through couples counseling *after* I had broken up with somebody longer than we had been in a relationship. And so, you know, the reality for me was that either I could continue to be in ongoing monogamous relationships, and continue to make the same kinds of mistakes over and over again. . . . And just go from one relationship to another relationship, just doing this over and over and over and over. . . . [But] when we got together, I wanted to have that kind of security where we could actually put time and energy into developing a relationship. And I don't think that you can unless there's some kind of a commitment to say, okay, if it doesn't feel good, we'll look at it and go back and see how we can work this out kind of thing. Instead of, "I don't like that, I'll see you."

Pat felt strongly that the issue of commitment is no different for same-sex couples than for heterosexuals. "Commitment to me doesn't have anything to do with whether it has something to do with heterosexuals, or whether it has to do with lesbians. It has something to do with being able to make a commitment to a life that is productive and good."

Despite framing the issue of marriage in terms of personal emotional growth and the maintenance of tradition, Pat and Karen's commitment to one another assumed different proportions as they crafted their identities as a public couple. They had their ceremony before such occasions had become common occurrences in the gay and lesbian community. This meant that far from being able to assume acceptance from their close friends, they were conveying a message both to the heterosexual world and to other lesbians and gay men. Concepts of personal emotional development overlapped with constructions of nature, tradition, and history to take shape as an act of conscious political action. In the years since their wedding, the number of such ceremonies has grown dramatically, a trend they attribute to gay men and lesbians being increasingly able to define themselves as complete human beings, rather than solely in terms of their membership in an oppressed group. Pat summed up her observations:

I think that it's about people getting comfortable with filling their own needs, and I think that as people get older, too, that they also feel like, "I don't want to live by your rules," somebody else's needs and rules. And so I really do think that it has a lot to do with that. And most of the people who have gotten married are older. They're over that "I need to be so radical that I can't enjoy my life" period.

Pat and Karen's account of their own ceremony and their analysis of how their experience fit into the developing shape of lesbian and gay history, emphasized a fundamental opposition between personal and political goals. Political motivations, in their view, whether oriented toward the heterosexual mainstream, or toward the gay and lesbian community, generate behavior not necessarily reflective of an individual's authentic interests. Meeting personal emotional needs requires a level of accountability to the self, a commitment to psychic authenticity, that can only be distorted by attention to political exigencies. When a couple believes that formally solemnizing and honoring their union is right for them, then opposition from any quarter must be resisted. Pat and Karen saw themselves both as refusing to accept prohibitions against same-sex marriage, but also rebelled against the notion, widely accepted by lesbians and gay men they knew, that such couples could not enjoy the same pleasures and privileges claimed by heterosexuals. Their resistance was double-edged, directed both toward heterosexism and toward a construction of gay rights that depends on radical separation between heterosexuality and homosexuality as moral systems. Not only their ceremony but their "family values" billboard and their entire public presentation as a couple and family confronted all who would question the simple humanness of lesbians and gay men as well as all who seek to enshrine queerness as uncompromising difference.

Ambiguous Resistance

Locating symbolic references to resistance in the language of lesbian and gay commitment rituals cannot be achieved without reconfiguring what it is we mean by "resistance." Even as conventions are overturned in these ceremonial occasions, they are reinscribed and reinvented; by arguing that they don't need the trappings of legal marriage, couples simultaneously demand access to analogous symbolic resources.

At the same time that some gay and lesbian couples stage ceremonies that explicitly seize the terminology of weddings and seek to redefine the boundaries of marriage, others organize rituals that reject familiar images and thus attempt to repudiate the significance of marriage. These celebrants demand public affirmation of their relationships, all the while disavowing connections with marriage as we know it for heterosexual couples. Both strategies constitute resistance to heterosexist assumptions even though we would be hard-pressed to claim that they attempt a radical challenge to the institution of marriage. Their resistance is contained in their demand for inclusion, in their insistence that the mechanisms that validate heterosexual marriages be extended, at least affectively, to include their relationships. In putting forth these demands, the couples also implicitly demand that the very definitions of what homosexuality *is* be redrawn.

These actors demand what the conservative gay writer Bruce Bawer has called "a place at the table," and therefore assume that the table is a good place to be. But the broader impact of these demands cannot be dismissed as nothing more than an effort to assimilate, a repudiation of the subversive potential of being queer. Paradoxically, perhaps, participation in commitment rituals seems to foster openness in celebrants, an intensification of lesbian and gay identity that makes that identity more visible even as it argues it is not very different. Bruce Bawer, I noted earlier, is unwilling to retreat politely into whatever closet he may once have occupied; while he insists that gay people are not the outrageous creatures queer imagery portrays, neither is he willing to disappear or to yield what he views as his right to assert his identity, symbolized by the visibility of his gay relationship. And perhaps also paradoxical is the tendency of gay and lesbian rituals that emphasize resistance to bring couples to a sense of normality they had not previously experienced.

Lesbian and gay couples and their friends are not the only participants in the questioning of hallowed assumptions that takes place in same-sex commitment rituals. Perhaps most haunted by the debates are those clergy who believe they must take a stand in support of same-sex unions even as this stand distances them from their coreligionists. In order to make possible the full inclusion of gay men and lesbians in the life of American religion, the clergy must question authority and risk expulsion and separation. But they see the issue of gay marriage as diagnostic of the moral position of their denominations, and thus collaborate with couples to create new definitions of marriage and commitment.

Participants in lesbian and gay commitment ceremonies can invoke notions of resistance to construe the rituals they enact as political acts. But in so doing, they avoid unraveling the tangle of intentions that underlie their decisions. Events that have public significance may spring from intensely personal motivations at the same time that the self-conscious construction of alternative social forms may emerge from deeply held convictions about nature and heritage. Lesbian and gay commitment ceremonies offer symbolic resistance to heterosexist domination, but they often do so by exalting the very values they might claim to challenge. Moreover, and seemingly paradoxically, these rituals defy queer movement toward radical difference; celebrants not only demand a place at a mainstream table but also insist upon the right to collaborate in the definition of lesbian and gay culture.

8

MIXED MESSAGES

O n March 25, 1996, San Francisco's Herbst Auditorium was the scene of a new kind of civic ritual. One hundred seventy-four lesbian and gay couples (and one heterosexual couple) participated in a "mass wedding" that solemnized their domestic partner registrations. Presided over by recently sworn-in Mayor Willie Brown, along with both gay and straight members of the city's Board of Supervisors, the ceremony was described in the local press as "an important milestone in the fight to give gay and lesbian unions the same official recognition as straight marriages."[1]

Domestic partner registration itself had been available in San Francisco since 1991. Same-sex and other couples who registered through this mechanism lined up alongside heterosexual couples applying for mar-

San Francisco's "Mass Wedding," March 25, 1996
(Photo by Paul Sakuma courtesy the Associated Press)

riage licenses at the Office of the County Clerk, and though the process was superficially the same, the straight couples receiving their licenses could, for an additional fee, choose to be married by a judge only a few yards away in the City Hall rotunda. But those applying for domestic partnership status had no such ceremonial option available to them, and persistent grumbling over this inequity gradually became audible in official circles. The civil wedding ceremonies offered to straight couples occurred within the line of vision of everyone in the County Clerk's Office, or indeed, on the first floor of City Hall, becoming an irritant not only to same-sex couples but ultimately attracting the attention of city employees who had become sensitized to issues of equal rights.[2] In response to these concerns, in early 1996 the Board of Supervisors approved a plan to add a ceremonial option to the standard domestic partnership procedure, announcing that the first such ceremony would be a gala occasion held in the ornate city-owned auditorium.

The announcement that the city would offer a civil ceremony for same-sex couples came in the midst of heated national debate about whether gay men and lesbians should have access to the rights associated with legal marriage. Developments in the Hawaii case were making frequent headlines and the Defense of Marriage Act (DOMA) had leapt to national attention as both Democrats and Republicans around the country began to ponder the significance of the issue in an election year. In California, conservative lawmakers were contemplating proposed legislation withholding recognition from same-sex marriages performed in other states, while gay rights proponents and their allies were orchestrating opposition to such efforts.

But in San Francisco, the question of providing domestic partner ceremonies generated little debate. In an interview with a local newspaper, Assistant County Clerk Nancy Alfaro took a matter-of-fact tone in stating that "a large number of taxpayers have asked for this service from our department. Implementing ceremonies would resolve any access and fairness issues." With the city charging thirty dollars for the ceremonies in addition to the regular thirty-five-dollar registration fee, considerable income might be generated by the plan, she also noted. Along the same lines, lesbian San Francisco Supervisor Carole Migden, a key sponsor of the measure, described the plan as "non-controversial," adding that, "The City wholeheartedly embraced domestic partners, and here's a way to make a little money and provide some humanity."[3]

The Herbst Auditorium ceremony began with a fanfare by the city's Lesbian/Gay Freedom Band, followed by a musical number described in the program as a "medley in celebration of love and commitment." Performed by two men and two women soloists, it featured excerpts from popular songs by Cole Porter ("Night and Day") and from *West Side Story* and the animated film *Aladdin*. In his opening remarks, Mayor Brown took pains to acclaim the ceremony as an "only in San Francisco" event, an occasion that affirmed the city's role as a trailblazer in matters of social and cultural change, respect for diversity, and sense of style. This theme was reiterated by other city officials who helped to perform the ceremony, each one taking time to proclaim his/her support for the city's gay and lesbian citizens and to mark her/his resistance to homophobia. City supervisors Angela Alioto and Kevin Shelley, for example, neither of whom is homosexual, took a few minutes to remind the crowd that they are both lifelong and devout Catholics, but that they repudiate recent comments by San Francisco's Archbishop Quinn that attacked the morality of the plan to conduct domestic partner ceremonies. Later in the proceedings, when one couple appeared on the stage dressed in exaggerated nun's habits, bridal veils, and carnavalesque white makeup that identified them as members of the Sisters of Perpetual Indulgence, the two supervisors rushed up on stage and insisted on having their pictures taken with them. "For the Archbishop," they quipped.

Following opening remarks by the mayor and Supervisor Migden, celebrants were introduced by leading figures of San Francisco's lesbian and gay community, who read short personal statements about each couple as they headed down one of the aisles to the stage. Some dressed in wedding finery, others in more ordinary daytime clothing, though most of the couples wore sober business suits or other professional attire.[4] Nearly all the brief introductory remarks each couple provided specified the longevity of the relationship; while the majority had relationships of long standing (mention of the longest drew sustained applause from the audience), some others had only recently decided to make a formal commitment. Most statements also added some personal details about the couple, mentioning their businesses, children, pets, homes, ethnic or community affiliations. Not a few of the couples took pains to identify themselves with classic San Francisco icons, alluding to Victorian houses they were renovating, to their involvement in food-related occupations, or declaring their involvement with particular political causes.

The mayor and the members of the Board of Supervisors who officiated gathered groups of couples on the stage and read the following statement:

> We are gathered here in the presence of witnesses for the purpose of acknowledging the lifetime commitment you share for one another. By entering into this partnership together, you have chosen to share each other's lives in an intimate and committed relationship of mutual caring. May you flourish in your life together and draw strength from your love and devotion during times of both hardship and joy in the years ahead.

After being asked to face one another and join hands, the couples repeated these vows:

> I, [name], do willingly take [partner's name] to be my lifetime partner to love and to cherish forever. We pledge, while in this union, to be responsible for each other and to be committed to a relationship of loyalty and mutual caring.

The presiding official then intoned:

> Now that you have joined together through this agreement, may your love be enduring and may all your days together bring you boundless happiness. By the virtue of the authority vested in me by the people of the city and county of San Francisco, I hereby pronounce you to be lawfully recognized domestic partners.

The ceremony ended with the playing of the "Wedding March" from Mendelsohn's *A Midsummer Night's Dream*. Outside the auditorium, champagne and cake were distributed, friends and relatives gathered with celebrants for photographs, and one group of celebrants cavorted on a motorized cable car while waiting to be taken to another location for a more elaborate celebration.

Couples interviewed later in local media described a range of motivations for participating in the event. Mike Meischke and Tom Maravilla, proprietors of a local grocery store who were featured in an article in the *Noe Valley Voice*, a neighborhood monthly, explained that they first decided to be involved in the ceremony "as a political statement." But, they went on, "As we were doing it, it took on a much more significant emotional status. We both felt . . . different . . . afterwards. . . . It was pretty powerful."[5] A lesbian couple, Denise Ratliff and Deborah Oakley-Melvin, interviewed for the same article, also cited the political importance of the event as a chance to be "part of history." The two women, who had previously solemnized their commitment in a small ritual with a group of friends, saw the public celebration as different, "a real emotional apex." Perhaps most significant to them was the kind of recognition they received after the ceremony when they went to the Palace Hotel for a celebratory lunch.[6] After the maître d' spied their wedding corsages, he offered them free champagne and cake. "We were touched by that," said one of the women. "Here we were in the Palace Hotel, the bastion of conservative San Francisco, and we were treated to free cake and champagne in celebration of our wedding."[7]

Making Sense of Lesbian and Gay Commitment Ceremonies

San Francisco's first civil wedding ceremony for domestic partner registrants dramatizes many of the themes that have animated the commitment rituals discussed in this book. These events derive much of their momentum from the highly politicized conflict now raging over access to the material and symbolic rights associated with marriage that until now have been monopolized by heterosexual couples.

Like those who joined in the celebration at Herbst Auditorium, lesbian and gay couples I interviewed and whose ceremonies I attended spoke movingly of their desire to contribute to efforts to legalize same-sex marriage in Hawaii and, eventually, elsewhere. Many of them have been inspired by the spread of domestic partner registration to municipalities around the country and by the extension of benefits to same-sex partners by growing numbers of major employers. Many also have been enraged and offended by the blatantly unequal treatment they experience when a partner is hospitalized or dies, when they make a major purchase, and when they have children, whether this treatment is delivered by the state or by individuals who are family, friends, employers, or neighbors. Commitment ceremonies allow these couples to speak their discontent, and to demand recognition for the realities of their lives. From this perspective they can be considered rituals of resistance.

Furthermore, while many lesbian and gay couples conceive of their weddings as events that symbolize the legitimacy of their difference from heterosexuals, other couples are far more concerned with using their ceremonies to deliver a broader message of inclusion. In these scenarios, the subversive goal of demanding access to rights and entitlements that have been restricted to straight people is subsumed within a set of ideas about the nature of love, family, and community that, in a sense, make subversion superfluous. These commitment narratives argue that gay men and lesbians are *already* part of the wider society, already part of communities defined by class, ethnicity, or race, and already members of families because their love is authentic, their domestic routines unremarkable, and their participation in the culture at large already an established fact. In these versions, the ceremonies acknowledge and celebrate existing realities. They are desirable because they are seen to reinforce relationships, to confirm commitment to the common goals the celebrants share with the wider society, to garner the support of friends and family, and to provide a basis for increasing involvement in whatever the business of the society may be. They are, in this sense, rituals of accommodation or conformity.

But, as we have seen, lesbian and gay weddings are much more than rituals of resistance or rituals of accommodation, much more than performances that encode actors' refusal to accept marginalization and mistreatment or that symbolize their acceptance of the world they live in. The Herbst Auditorium celebration, like many other ceremonies I have detailed in these pages, also represents multilayered systems of expression that reveal the relationships gay men and lesbians have forged with the wider cultural landscape that makes up American life. Lesbians and gay men use weddings to reiterate values and beliefs, to offer interpretations of their place in society, and to project notions about the way life ought to be. They pursue these symbolic goals through rituals that act to intensify personal feelings of commitment, to heighten a sense that the bonds of love couples declare for one another are in fact sacred and special. In vocalizing these complicated and sometimes contradictory messages, these celebrants act as gay men and lesbians but also as *people* with diverse backgrounds and concerns.

Questioning Resistance and Accommodation

Scholarship on resistance grew out of concerns with the inequality of communication between dominants and subordinates and the fact that asymmetrical relationships tend to involve dissembling to one degree or another. Both parties to such relationships are loath to reveal their true feelings, though in the case of the subordinate the consequences of an inadvertent revelation of one's true feelings are apt to be more severe than they would be for the dominant person. Political theorist James Scott cites cases of slaves who maintained impassive demeanors—what he calls the "public transcript"—when they were treated abusively, even as they privately yearned for redress. Discourse that represents the subordinate's true feelings, which takes place "offstage" or out of sight, Scott describes as the "hidden transcript."[8]

But resistance has also been ascribed to the diverse cultural maneuvers of people who may not recognize fully the political implications of their actions. Scholars of youth culture, for example, have focused on the ways in which particular clothing or music signifies repudiation of mainstream values, though the resistance may not be easily decoded by those who perform it. To mention one such effort, Dick Hebdige's analysis of style depends on an examination of the relationship between the clothing, hairstyles, and other sartorial strategies of punks, mods, rockers, and other variants of 1960s and 1970s youth culture in Britain. All these styles incorporate some elements of mainstream culture, though often in ways that drastically transform them; while those who affect these styles are conscious about seeking disapproval, their management of the symbolic features of rebellion is rarely explicit.[9]

Like other actors operating on the level of the "pre-political," lesbians and gay men who stage commitment rituals may be said to be engaging in a kind of unconscious resistance, actors "who have not found, or [who have] only begun to find, a specific language in which to express their aspirations about the world."[10] Our understanding of these rituals as forms of resistance comes, at this level, more from our observations of their outcomes than on the claims explicitly made by actors. Resistance in these instances may only emerge as a consequence long after the "rebellion" is over, or may be significant chiefly in terms of how it later facilitates changes in consciousness.

The tendency in anthropological approaches to ritual and in political analyses of gay and lesbian struggles for liberation has been to dichotomize resistance and accommodation as symbolic processes.[11] This has meant that as the debate over whether the gay/lesbian civil rights struggle should move toward demanding the right to marry has unfolded, disputes have raged over whether same-sex marriage constitutes a callow effort to fit into the mainstream or a bold rebellion against the limitations of a rigid gender hierarchy. While, as we have seen, some proponents of gay marriage argue that it will convincingly demonstrate the underlying equality (and therefore equal value) of gay and straight relationships, other proponents favor it as a move that will aggressively challenge the assumptions at the heart of heterosexual marriage. Opponents bring similar concerns to the debate. Conservative adversaries of same-sex marriage claim that it will undermine the very foundation on which "family values" are built; radical foes of pursuing marriage believe that it will compromise the outsider status of gay men and lesbians, disrupting their ability to be "queer."

Some anthropological perspectives on resistance speak to these complexities. While ritual may serve the interests of the status quo, it may also undermine the authority of those in power and thereby constitute resistance. But Lila Abu-Lughod has characterized the relationship of many anthropologists to resistance as a "romance," and has suggested that this may be behind the tendency to see resistance in the smallest thoughts and actions of the disadvantaged. In some ways, then, anthropologists' view of resistance has become circular, a kind of wishful thinking: we assume it to be there because were it not, we would have to at least consider the possibility that people collaborate in their own oppression, that they are passive in the face of forces arrayed against them. Abu-Lughod reminds us that our attraction for resistance and subversion may sometimes be a last-ditch effort to inject hope into our studies of subjugated peoples, as well as a wish to locate nobility in seemingly undistinguished behavior.[12]

Looking at lesbian and gay weddings further undermines these dichotomous understandings of resistance and accommodation and opens the way for a reconsideration of the entire framework on which these concepts depend. To the extent that resistance facilitates accommodation and conformity depends upon subversion, these complex rituals suggest that a highly dichotomized view of these tendencies does violence to the real subtlety of cultural process.

Instead, I would submit that lesbian and gay commitment ceremonies dramatize key issues both in gay and lesbian cultures and in the wider panorama of American cultures. They may thus be seen to constitute a kind of "deep play" that enacts central contradictions as well as harmonies and inner logic.[13] In particular, same-sex weddings richly illustrate the *polyvocality* of ritual, the ability of the symbols arrayed in rituals to evoke different meanings to different audiences or under different conditions, or even to stand simultaneously for different things. They provide an instance in which the explicit aims of a ritual may be confounded not only by multiple subtexts that are also deployed, but by the varying interpretive stances taken by different participants and by the changing perspectives on the event that unfold over time. The symbolic direction of these ceremonies, then, is likely neither to be unitary nor stable, as one's point of view moves from subject to observer, and as immediate perceptions become colored by memory and reinterpretation. These rituals have the potential, in other words, to be simultaneously conservative and subversive, to enshrine presumed traditional values as they also satirize and undermine them, to protest convention and to insist upon inclusion within its boundaries.

From one perspective, the rituals seem symbolically to express adherence to values of monogamy, fidelity, domesticity, and love that don't differ significantly from those that characterize heterosexual ("ordinary") weddings. If one focuses on gay weddings (or the desire of gay people to be able to marry legally) from this point of view, they seem eminently conservative as symbolic statements. In this reading, a gay/lesbian wedding offers an opportunity for the couple to represent themselves within the larger tradition of marriage, to intensify their mutual commitment; nevertheless, it implicates the audience in the redefinition of a gay relationship as consonant with mainstream cultural values.

Andrew Sullivan's argument in favor of gay marriage rests on precisely these assumptions. "In fact," he says, "it's perfectly possible to combine a celebration of the traditional family with the celebration of a stable homosexual relationship. The one, after all, is modeled on the other. If constructed carefully as a conservative social ideology, the notion of stable gay relationships might even serve to buttress the ethic of heterosexual marriage, by showing how even those excluded from it can wish to model themselves on its shape and structure."[14]

But given that gay people are not ordinarily offered access to this particular ritual pathway, putting on a wedding also constitutes a demand, one that might be seen as having insurrectionary implications. By *insisting* upon the right to marry, even in the absence of the legal aspects of marriage, gay men and lesbians seem to resist the very conventions that may be said to bolster marriage in the first place—principally the assumption of heterosexuality and gender stratification that obtain in our male-dominated culture. Respectability is turned on its head in this reading, as what is conventional for heterosexuals becomes rebellion when staged by homosexuals.

My drive to investigate the ambiguities and discontinuities of forms of conformity and resistance grew directly from my long-term research on lesbian mothers and from the issues I confronted as I turned my interviews with both lesbian and heterosexual single mothers into my earlier book, *Lesbian Mothers: Accounts of Gender in American Culture*.[15] In that project, I focused on the meaning of motherhood both to lesbians who had had their children in marriages and to those who had sought out pregnancy or adoption after having defined themselves as lesbians, a group associated with the "lesbian baby boom" often discussed in the popular gay community press. Most striking was my finding that lesbians of both groups, in common with heterosexual mothers in comparable economic situations and household configurations, elevated "mother" to a central dimension of their identities, using it to stake their claim to the complex of personal virtues associated with the status of woman.

At first glance, this finding seemed commonsensical: lesbian mothers shared many of the same social and economic challenges faced by other mothers who didn't have husbands. But when considered in the context of the overlapping meanings assigned in our culture to "woman" and "mother," and the way in which lesbianism commonly signifies separation from or even opposition to femaleness, the cultural strategies mounted by lesbian mothers gained more complex meanings.[16] Lesbian mothers claimed the goodness—basically defined as altruism and spiritual abnegation—associated with motherhood. Moreover, by reinforcing these seemingly accommodationist values, lesbians demanded access to the status of woman, thus subverting their conventional exclusion from femaleness as a gender category.

Lesbian mothers, then, confront the traditional notion that only heterosexual women can be mothers while they also reinscribe and strengthen the long-standing conflation of womanhood and motherhood. The existence of lesbian mothers challenges the assumption that procreation and sexuality are necessarily connected, but lesbian mothers' constructions of their identities additionally point to a belief that mothers and nonmothers are different from each other in fundamental, natural ways.

This insight poses a potential challenge to the foundation of much recent "queer theory" as well as to conservative opponents of gay rights.[17] Both of these seemingly diametrically opposed groups claim that homosexuality (along with other sorts of sexual diversity) is intrinsically disruptive of the sex/gender system. The positions of social conservatives and religious fundamentalists with respect to the subversive potential of homosexuality are perhaps best known. Right-wing groups have opposed gay rights legislation on the grounds that there is a "gay agenda" or conspiracy afoot that threatens to undermine mainstream morality and to recruit young people into unhealthy lifestyles. While this view has found political expression most recently in efforts to short-circuit the possible legalization of same-sex marriage in Hawaii, it has been at the heart of a variety of measures over the years that have sought if not to obliterate homosexuality then at least to contain its visibility. One of the anxieties frequently articulated by antigay activists surrounds an apprehension that seemingly benign representations of homosexuality will cause impressionable young people to see being gay as a viable alternative sexuality.

While certainly not espousing the sort of conspiracy fantasized by conservative homophobes, queer theorists and political activists have, ironically, made some related assumptions. The "in-your-face" stance of Queer Nation links gay visibility to a frontal assault on conventional sensibilities, and while the "loudness" these activists advocate is undoubtedly more intentionally outrageous than the objectives of most gays and lesbians who seek a more open existence, they share with antigay conservatives a notion that a public and highly visible queer presence and the outing of closeted gay celebrities may transform the average person's perception of homosexuality by challenging people's unreflective dismissal of homosexuality as being remote from their own experience.[18] Articles with titles such as Cindy Patton's "Tremble, Hetero Swine!" revel in their ability to generate a "gay revenge fantasy" that "reverse[s] the roles of oppressor and oppressed rather than arguing for the ordinariness of homosexuality." These fantasies speak directly to conspiracy theorists on the right (who sometimes take these parodic creations literally) but also reveal the foundation of a strategy for staking out queer identity. Patton understands the project of refiguring queer identity as critical to "the hope of enabling more articulate strategies of 'resistance,'" arguing that "the crucial battle now for 'minorities' and resistant subalterns is not achieving democratic representation but wresting control over the discourses concerning identity construction."[19] The vision of queer activists is to destabilize conventionality by promoting homosexuality in its most intimidating guise. This strategy could hardly be more at odds with civil rights–oriented tactics intended to defuse images of gay existence as alien or threatening to mainstream values. That queer readings of culture can produce the same outcomes as those generated by more conservative, even accommodationist commentators— gay/lesbian public figures who position themselves far from the "queer" end of the political spectrum[20]—is perhaps the most fascinating piece of the puzzle gay and lesbian commitment ceremonies make.

Just as the explicit messages conveyed in these rituals often are about acceptance and conformity to wider community values—seemingly the opposite of anything we could easily recognize as "queer"—such rituals also incorporate messages of "queerness" at vital points. First, each event focuses on the couple and their (presumptively sexual) bond, calling attention to the very thing that sets the lesbian and gay couple apart from heterosexual norms. Second, many ceremonies, by foregrounding the incongruities between the same-gender couple and the deployment of powerful symbols of conventional heterosexuality (the white bridal dress and veil, tuxedos, white multitiered cakes, diamond rings, elaborate floral decorations, and, most notably, the use of wedding liturgies from various religious traditions), highlight contradiction and irony even as they shun parody. And third, some couples deliberately bring elements they consider to be "queer" into the construction of their ceremonies, explaining their wish to mark the occasion as gay or lesbian or to highlight the difference between these occasions and ordinary weddings.

How Do Lesbian and Gay Commitment Ceremonies Make Their Meanings?

Anthropologist Laurel Kendall has written in a similar vein on the changing shape of Korean weddings.[21] Her analysis of changing wedding customs focuses on how cultural conflicts and rapid change in Korean society get played out using the symbolic resources of weddings. Wedding customs associated with "tradition," for example, regardless of how faithfully they recreate ancient rituals, allow participants to define their position vis-à-vis the pervasive Westernization that has come to characterize Korean life. In like fashion, as Korea has urbanized and non-Korean influences expanded, framing weddings in Western style, with white wedding dresses and other such insignia, assumes meanings beyond those they had a generation or two earlier.

Lesbian and gay weddings are also multidimensional symbolic events, capable of invoking complex and even seemingly contradictory messages as they achieve their more explicit objectives. These ceremonies can stand simply for love and commitment, demonstrating to those who witness them the intensity and sincerity of the sentiments that a couple shares. That is, on one level, lesbian and gay commitment rituals simply do what they claim: to proclaim publicly the existence and significance of a particular union. What communicating that information means, how the

message is ramified and reconfigured by those who make it and those who
hear it, depends on circumstances that may vary along a number of axes.
Different participants have different readings of meanings. Interpretations may change as time and circumstances shape couples' lives.

On another level, lesbian and gay commitment rituals can help to
fashion complicated intersections of identity and affiliation. In particular, they elaborate notions of resistance and accommodation, sometimes
as contrasting poles of meaning, but often as perplexing conjunctions of
seemingly contradictory concepts. That these meanings not only confront one another but can also be mutually reinforcing, strongly suggests
that the understandings of resistance and accommodation that animate
much recent anthropological and queer theory depend on overly polarized contrasts. These contrasts may constitute symbolic oppositions, but
examination of lesbian and gay weddings points to their irrelevance to
the business of daily life. Real gay men and lesbians only sometimes have
carefully crafted messages of subversion to convey to the wider world;
more commonly, as we have seen, they want the world to know that they
are real people, with real feelings at the heart of their relationships.

These concerns with authenticity, though, despite their appearance,
are about more than simple conformity. They can simultaneously speak
to oppression and acceptance, invoke satire and sincerity, address exclusion and belonging. Often the symbolic mechanism that allows conformity to be communicated is outrageous or even parodic, as an examination of Nancy and Rachel's wedding (see chapter 6) reveals. In that
ceremony, the couple's claim to having "an ordinary Jewish wedding" was
embodied in their choice of a white bridal dress for Nancy and a tuxedo
for Rachel and comparably gendered clothing for the rest of the all-fe-
male wedding party. The rabbi's comments, which emphasized his view
of the ceremony as resisting the hypocrisies of mainstream Judaism, revealed embarrassment and confusion with the one dimension of the ceremony that we might say was the most subversive—its use of drag to invoke "tradition."

Similarly, Mike and Duane's country-western wedding, which used
the classic gay idiom of the theme party to make clear the two men's
commitment to being queer, also expressed sentiments that seem to con-
tradict their explicit desire to resist heterosexual images. Their use of
Jewish ritual material such as the *chuppah*, the tallith, and the Seven
Blessings stemmed both from Duane's appreciation of the theatrical potential of these elements and from Mike's desire to invoke his past, bring-

ing history, community, and gay identity together. The ceremony included friends and family, men and women, gays and straights in a way that emphasized their common humanity. At the same time, the couple's decision to incorporate the Jewish mourning prayer, the kaddish, into the ritual to mark the impact of the AIDS epidemic on their lives similarly played with conventional and resistant meanings, reconfiguring them to meet the two men's personal needs. While the kaddish is a traditional Jewish prayer, its insertion in a wedding drastically departs from accepted usage and was, in fact, the only element of the rather outrageous ritual that Mike's otherwise supportive mother found scandalous. The contrast between the ancient Hebrew words and their "inappropriate" placement in the commitment ceremony created a sort of symbolic tension that expressed the gravity of the epidemic's impact on Mike and Duane's lives probably more effectively than "correctly" deployed symbols of loss.

My concern here is to put both these notions of subversion aside and instead to focus on the more complicated, contradictory relationships between the ways gays and lesbians organize their lives and their views of their place in the wider society, as well as to confront the notion that homosexuals and heterosexuals automatically operate in inherently divergent, nonoverlapping, social arenas. Drawing a contrast that recalls Raymond Firth's classic distinction between *social structure* and *social organization*,[22] my inquiry into gay weddings opposes the *ideology* of queerness against an exploration of how lesbians and gay men *actually* play out specific aspects of their lives.

This approach also confronts the shape of the evolving field of lesbian and gay studies in anthropology in that it focuses attention away from a more typical preoccupation with sexual behavior and its cross-cultural variations. In contrast with what Kath Weston has aptly called the "ethnocartography" of homosexuality, my analysis is only marginally concerned with the distribution or expression of homosexuality or of same-sex marriage, however these phenomena may be defined in particular cultural contexts.[23] Rather, the focus on weddings, like my earlier attention to lesbian motherhood, squarely confronts the intersection between a particular sexual label and the construction of both identity and community based on that designation. From this perspective, then, my concern is with the formation of a sense of personhood and peoplehood, and with the ways that people conceptualize their histories and traditions in order to validate and explain their ongoing behavior and actions.

This emphasis recalls the process of cultural construction Benedict Anderson has evoked in *Imagined Communities*. Anderson's analysis of nationalism and nationality defines both phenomena as "cultural artefacts." "All communities larger than primordial villages of face-to-face contact (and perhaps even these) are imagined," yet he makes clear that this understanding of nations casts no doubt on their authenticity or reality. Nations tend to be described either in a language of *kinship* (e.g., "the motherland") or that of *home*; both constructions, Anderson points out, evoke "something to which one is naturally tied . . . something unchosen. In this way, nation-ness is assimilated to skin-colour, gender, parentage and birth-era—all those things one can not help. . . . Precisely because such ties are not chosen, they have about them a halo of disinterestedness."[24]

Such traditions serve especially to establish or symbolize the social cohesion of groups, creating a sense of identification with a "community" or "nation."[25] Putting these practices in Anderson's idiom, they might be viewed as the mechanisms that make the imagining of community possible; because they are construed as deeply entwined in "tradition" (i.e., the past), invented traditions facilitate naturalizing identity, whether it be articulated in terms of nation or community, or whether it serves to solidify the identities of majority or minority populations.

In examining gay and lesbian commitment ceremonies, I have argued that these rituals symbolically elaborate the imagining of community. But "community" for gay and lesbian Americans is neither unitary nor uncontested. Rather, the "invented traditions" that appear in same-sex commitment rituals often enshrine complex identity politics. Thus, they are less about the coalescence of a coherent gay/lesbian (or queer) "nation" than they are about the often paradoxical interrelationships between ideas and behaviors that constitute the changing shape of gay/lesbian identity in U.S. cultures as they fluctuate between attempts to represent resistance to the established sex/gender system and those that appear to express a yearning for conformity and acceptance. Motherhood (or parenthood) presents one such instance; the ritual marking of committed relationships suggests another and one that appears to be more self-consciously crafted. Both motherhood and commitment help to constitute identities, but while in both cases these identities are construed as "natural," they also tend to be multivalent and fragmented.

Similarly, lesbian and gay weddings invoke understandings about "family" and the place of celebrants in the constellations they identify as their families. Despite the fact that lesbian and gay marriage remains outside the realm of legal possibility, despite the fact that lesbian and gay couples who make their relationships public never receive benefits and rewards equivalent to those showered on their heterosexual siblings, couples who have commitment ceremonies understand these occasions to be about their relationship to their families. Even as friends (what many, along with Kath Weston, call "chosen families") may take center stage at the rituals, relatives (either in person or represented symbolically) join with coworkers, neighbors, and children as members of a varied cast of not necessarily gay witnesses. The absence of relatives may be as marked and emotionally intense as their presence; in either case, both are taken note of and interpreted at length after the fact.

Further, the very illegitimacy and illegality of same-sex wedding ceremonies constitutes a vital element of their ability to subvert as well as to solidify conventional understandings of love and commitment. Celebrants struggle to overcome the limitations that accompany the statutory invisibility of their unions, but it is that lack of status that also makes the rituals as emotionally compelling as they are. Most notably, the enactment of gay and lesbian weddings outside the context of convention endows them with an aura of sincerity and authenticity that often eludes heterosexual couples.

The controversy over same-sex marriage has joined with women's rights, abortion, school prayer, immigration, multiculturalism, and a host of other elements of the late twentieth century's "culture wars" to ignite passions that have moved to the center of recent political maneuvering. In the battle to define what it will mean to be American in the years to come—a battle that increasingly has depended on grounding particular views of the culture in varying versions of eternal truth—the struggle over access to the ritual embodiment of kinship has assumed enormous symbolic significance.

I would submit that there is no single, seamless interpretation that can be made of these vital and evolving rituals. Symbols have no reality apart from those who enact them, and the shifting meanings that attach to symbols of tradition, community, family, authenticity, and resistance should serve to remind us of their flexibility and of the levels of choice actors make in interpreting and manipulating symbols. Gay and lesbian weddings make many levels of symbolic statements, enacting key conflicts from both lesbian/gay and majority culture, at least partly because the couples who create them are, in fact, members of both cultures.

There really ought not be a paradox here: the seemingly accommodationist and the seemingly subversive readily merge because they are only
intermittently at odds. Is there really any significant difference between
accommodation and resistance, between conformity and subversion?
Lesbian and gay rituals of commitment enshrine these differences at the
same time that they undermine them. They offer us a perspective on the
fragile nature of symbolic processes, on the unstable ground on which
ritual expression rests. They remind us that, in recognizing ourselves,
lesbians and gay men who marry also recognize our bonds with a broader constituency, staking a claim to a right to exist that is neither queer
nor compliant.

NOTES

Prologue

1. The days of riots that took place after a police raid at Greenwich Village's Stonewall Inn on June 27, 1969, are generally credited as having signaled the start of the gay and lesbian liberation movement in the United States. See D'Emilio 1983; Duberman 1993; Kennedy and Davis 1993.

2. Hole and Levine 1971.

3. Rich 1980.

4. Echols 1989; Herman 1996; Polikoff 1993.

5. Diamant 1985.

6. According to Anita Diamant, the *chuppah*, a canopy supported by four poles under which the couple stands during the wedding ritual, symbolizes the home and the tents of the Jewish people's nomadic ancestors (among other things). This temporary structure is open on four sides to invoke the tent of Abraham, whose legendary hospitality was symbolized by the doors on all four sides of his home. Many couples use a tallith, a prayer shawl, the ritual fringes of which are regarded as talismans against evil spirits. The *chuppah* is thus also understood as a sign of God's presence at the wedding and in the home to be established (Diamant 1985:91–93).

The *ketubah* (pl., *ketubot*) was originally a legal contract, written in Aramaic (the legal language of Talmudic law) and signed by two witnesses, that attested to the fact that the groom had "acquired" the bride and agreed to support her. It was given to the bride and provided her with written proof of her rights and her husband's obligations to her, and thus protected her from capricious divorce. More modern *ketubot* may be written to express the couple's desire to establish a Jewish home or to emphasize their intention to have a marriage based on equality and mutuality. Although a wide range of boilerplate *ketubot*, in which individual names and dates are inserted, can be purchased (including some for same-sex unions), many couples have them made to order by artists, sometimes at considerable expense (Diamant 1985:71–81).

7. When, just the week before the ceremony, I was called to the Federal Building for jury duty, I refused to use the upcoming event as a way to avoid service, despite

my friends' urging me to do so. Only after I was excused for other reasons from the first jury on which I was seated did I very tentatively ask for a delay in my service because I was about to get married. To my complete mortification, the clerk to whom I had quietly confided this information started shrieking with delight, removing my name from the list completely and enlisting the other potential jurors to congratulate me.

8. Kertzer 1988:8–11.

9. But see my caveat about assuming that lesbians and gays studying other lesbians and gays are automatically "insiders" (Lewin 1995).

10. Sullivan 1995; Geertz 1973b:93.

1. Equal Rites

1. Rev. Troy Perry founded the Universal Fellowship of Metropolitan Community Churches in 1968, after having been defrocked by his Pentacostal church for being gay. MCC congregations can be found throughout the United States and in a number of overseas locations, ministering primarily to gay and lesbian Protestants of all stripes as well as to persons who come from other religious traditions.

2. We were part of a tiny contingent representing the Society of Lesbian and Gay Anthropologists (SOLGA).

3. See Seligson (1973:282–87) for a report on early 1970s MCC weddings marked by a "what-will-they-think-of-next" tone of astonishment.

4. See, for example, Adam 1987; Cruikshank 1992; D'Emilio 1983; Duberman 1993.

5. See especially Duberman's (1993) description of Franklin Kameny.

6. Hooker 1957.

7. A number of scholars have described same-sex unions cross-culturally, although a host of questions about comparability accompany efforts to employ these customs as justifications for contemporary demands to legitimate homosexual marriages. See, for example, B. Butler 1990; Eskridge 1993.

8. Boswell 1994.

9. Katz 1976.

10. B. Butler 1990:20. Controversy now surrounds the Tipton story and similar instances of "passing" in terms of whether such individuals should be considered lesbian, gay, or transgendered (Feinberg 1996).

11. Chauncey 1994:87 and 290–91. Esther Newton, author of *Mother Camp* (1972), reports that these usages were also standard among 1960s drag queens (personal communication, July 12, 1996).

12. Faderman 1991:73. On Gladys Bentley, see Albertson 1972; Chauncey 1994:251; Garber 1988.

13. While I am aware that same-sex commitment ceremonies occur in other countries, both Western and "Third World," I have focused my attention in this book on their emergence in the context of contemporary America. For more on the marriage issue in other countries, see, for example, Gevisser and Cameron 1995; Miller 1992; Reinfelder 1996.

14. Miller 1989:28, 96, and 104.

15. Ibid., 159, 160–62.

16. Ibid., 163.

17. Barrett 1990:79.

18. Clunis and Green 1988:110; Uhrig 1984.

19. Ayers and Brown 1994:14–15; B. Butler 1990:35; Martin and Lyon 1972: 99–100.

20. *Baker v. Nelson*, 291 Minn. 310, 315, 191 N.W. 2d 185, 187 (1971), cited in Hunter (1995), emphasis added.

21. *Jones v. Hallahan*, 501 S.W. 2d 589 (Ky. Ct. App. 1973), cited in Hunter 1995. See also Wolfson (1994–95:568n2) for more examples of early cases challenging the prohibition against lesbian and gay marriage, undertaken prior to decisions regarding equal protection and the right to marry that now make such litigation more viable.

22. Ayers and Brown 1994:15–16; Brown 1995.

23. Eskridge 1996:90; Eskridge 1996 and Eskridge 1993.

24. Greene, quoted in Rochman 1995; Nichols quoted in Dunlap 1995.

25. See *New York Times* 1995.

26. Hunter 1995:117.

27. Ibid.

28. Characteristically, San Francisco launched its new policy with a mass "wedding" on March 25, 1996, that united some 160 couples. The event, held in the same ornate concert hall that hosted the inaugural session of the United Nations some fifty years earlier, was presided over by Mayor Willie Brown and most members of the city's Board of Supervisors. Leading figures from the gay community introduced the couples as they walked down the aisle, and the event was featured in both local and national media (see chapter 8). More recently, San Francisco enacted legislation that requires companies contracting with the city to provide domestic partner benefits to employees registered in San Francisco or in other municipalities offering this option. This legislation prompted acrimonious battles with large companies like United Airlines and with the Archdiocese of San Francisco's social service agencies. See, for example, Golden 1997; King 1996; Ness 1996.

29. Hunter 1995:117–18.

30. Jefferson 1994.

31. Verhovek 1993b; Verhovek 1993a.

32. Eskridge 1996:5.

33. Eskridge 1996; Hunter 1995:111.

34. Wolfson 1994–95.

35. Capps 1996; Dunlap 1996; Kirkpatrick 1996.

36. See, for example, Gallagher 1997.

37. Purdum 1996; Schmitt 1996.

38. See Sullivan (1997) for a useful collection of arguments on both sides of the issue by a variety of commentators, gay and straight. See also Baird and Rosenbaum 1997; Strasser 1997.

39. Teal 1971.

40. Bawer 1993; Sullivan 1995; Vaid 1995.

41. Duggan 1995; Stein 1993; Walters 1996; Warner 1993.

42. Bawer 1993:254 (emphasis in original).

43. Ibid., 261, 262–63 (emphasis in original).

44. Stoddard 1992:13. Stoddard's own wedding to Walter Rieman was the lead "Talk of the Town" item in *The New Yorker*, December 20, 1993.

45. Ettelbrick 1992:14, 16. Since this essay was written, Ettelbrick's work with the Empire State Pride Agenda seems to have led her to modify her position on same-sex marriage. As the Hawaii case has become a prominent dimension of gay rights activism around the country, Ettelbrick has become a persuasive advocate for the legalization of same-sex marriage. See also Browning 1996.

46. Polikoff 1993:1546 (on Eskridge 1993). See also Pollitt 1996 for a similar argument by a well-known feminist political commentator.

47. Hunter 1995:109–10, 119.

48. Hawkeswood 1996.

49. Kaplan 1997:235.

50. Wolfson 1994–95:607.

51. Sullivan 1995:178, 183–84, 185.

52. Hirsch and Keller 1990; Mitchell and Oakley 1986; Vaid 1995.

53. Wolfson 1994–95:599; see also Dunlap 1995.

54. Thomas 1996.

55. Ayers and Brown 1994.

56. Pfaff 1996:22.

57. Jackson-Paris 1994. The couple's later breakup also received considerable attention in the gay media (see Frutkin 1996).

58. Perry 1995:106–109.

2. Heroes in Our Own Dramas

1. Turner 1967:30.

2. Kertzer 1988:9.

3. Turner 1969:41–42.

4. As David Kertzer puts it, "The complexity and uncertainty of meaning of symbols are sources of their strength" (1988:11).

5. Geertz 1973b:112, 93; Singer 1959.

6. Turner 1987:42.

7. Myerhoff 1992a:234; Turner 1987:124–26.

8. Gluckman 1963:112; Gluckman 1965:299.

9. See Marriott 1966:211; see also Scribner 1978. Along the same lines, in a study of what she calls "ceremonies of confrontation and submission," Eva Hunt also offers an analysis of how rituals of reversal can keep "potential conflict" under control while allowing frustrations to be ventilated (1977:144–45).

10. Christel Lane's (1981) study of ritual in Soviet society, for example, argues that rituals of rebellion, "rituals which mock or question the social order," were too dangerous to be tolerated. And historian Le Roy Ladurie's (1979) *Carnival in Romans* gives an account of the circumstances under which a rite of inversion can explode

into violence, as does the work of another historian, Natalie Zemon Davis, who has put forward a number of compelling readings of rituals of rebellion in early Modern Europe (1971:41).

11. Kertzer 1988.

12. Comaroff 1985:213; see also Lanternari 1963.

13. As Bruce Kapferer has noted, rituals can promote *reflexivity* not only for the ritual's subjects and performers but for spectators, including those whose relationship to the ritual is relatively distant. According to Kapferer, "First, rituals promote reflexivity by enabling individuals to objectify their action and experience in the context of the rite, and to stand back or distance themselves from their action within the rite so they can reflect upon their own and others' actions and understanding. Second, rites promote reflexivity to the degree that they reflect back on other contexts of meaning in the performance setting or in the social and cultural world out of which ritual emerges" (1984:180–81).

14. Sarris 1993:85; Rosaldo 1989:129.

15. Lewin 1993:10–11; Leap 1996:138–39 (see also Kleinman 1988).

16. Weston 1991; see also Zimmerman 1984 on coming out as a bildungsroman and Lewin 1991.

17. For example, historian Carolyn Steedman's (1987) portrayal of her mother's life as a working-class woman in England shifts as her point of view moves from her mother's to her own, and as Steedman, the daughter-narrator, wrestles with her simultaneous role as historian-analyst. Similarly, Louise Krasniewicz's (1992) innovative ethnographic study of the Women's Peace Encampment draws its energy from the interplay between the stories of peace activists and town residents, both constituting themselves as "women" and as "community."

18. Ginsburg 1989; Abu-Lughod 1993; Wolf 1992. See also *Translated Woman* (1993) in which Ruth Behar plays the voice of her Mexican Indian informant, Esperanza, off against her own sense of self, suggesting parallels between their lives that are perhaps rendered more dramatic by the fundamental oppositions that geopolitical forces exact between them.

19. Rabinow 1977.

20. Marcus and Fischer 1986.

21. See Altorki and El-Solh 1988; Limón 1991; Ohnuki-Tierney 1984.

22. See Jacobs, Thomas, and Lang 1997; Lewin 1995; Lewin and Leap 1996.

23. Williams 1996.

24. Sabine Lang (1996), for example, has described a field situation among North American Indians in which her race and nationality loomed larger than her lesbianism, and Elizabeth Kennedy and Madeline Davis (1993, 1996) have spoken of the problems they experienced trying to balance community membership with generational and class differences.

25. Murray 1996b.

26. Narayan 1993; Abu-Lughod 1991; see also Sarris 1993. Many of the more influential commentaries on these reflexive tendencies have focused on their relevance for artistic forms and the evolution of aesthetic sensibilities, drawing the notion of the postmodern into the study of changing social and cultural forms. For anthropologists, these perspectives have been most pronounced, perhaps, in an assault on

structural functionalism driven by fundamental skepticism about notions of continuity and symmetry, once staples of the discipline. Paying close attention to sources of irony and disharmony as these are played out in social and cultural process, the authors who have chosen this stance are particularly concerned to highlight the struggle of individuals to understand and define their identities (Abu-Lughod 1991:143).

27. See, for example, Rabinow 1977.

28. Clifford and Marcus 1986.

29. Behar and Gordon 1995.

30. The reflexive turn in anthropology, then, has intersected with the postmodern sensibility to produce an influential body of experimental ethnographic writing that both engages the question of how the investigator's stance or identity shapes the emergence of "data" and that pays as much attention to discontinuity and paradox as it does to system and structure. Some of the more outstanding examples of this genre promote experimental use of narratives, and sometimes multiply positioned narratives, to destabilize the object of inquiry. Works such as Anna Tsing's *In the Realm of the Diamond Queen* (1993) and other ethnographic reflections of postmodern feminism aim at making the reader suspicious of consistency, uncomfortable with regularity, and alert to contradiction. Other examples of this impulse may be found in the recent works of Abu-Lughod (1993), Kondo (1990), and Krasniewicz (1992) to mention only a few contributors to this genre.

31. Lewin 1995.

32. On the problems of locating representative samples of lesbian and gay populations, see Carrington n.d.; Stein 1997; Weston 1991.

33. See, for example, Ayers and Brown 1994; B. Butler 1990; Miller 1989; Sherman 1992.

34. Myerhoff 1992b.

35. Schneider 1968.

3. Old Symbols, New Traditions

1. Associate artistic director Doug Holsclaw told me that San Francisco's mainstream newspapers, the *Chronicle* and the *Examiner*, virtually always sent reviewers to Theatre Rhino's shows. He didn't know why this particular offering was ignored.

2. The lighting of "unity" candles is a common feature of mainstream heterosexual wedding ceremonies as well as of same-sex rituals and can take a number of specific forms. In some rituals the two candles lighted by the couple are used to light a third candle and are then extinguished, symbolizing the new importance of the couple and the fading significance of their separate lives. In others, the two candles remain burning after the lighting of the third, presumably representing the couple's commitment to preserve their personal identities. The custom appears to have secular roots, though it is frequently a key element of religious ceremonies.

3. Jameson 1991:96.

4. Stacey 1990; Johnson 1988. *Plus ça change, plus c'est la même chose* may be a tired aphorism, but it is oddly applicable to the evolution of these "new" family forms. See Lewin (1993) for a discussion of "new" family types that reads recent developments rather differently.

5. Warner 1993:xxvi; J. Butler 1990:25 (see also Becker 1963; Goffman 1963; Mac-Intosh 1968). The sensibility described by Butler is played out evocatively in the cinematic study of Harlem drag queens, *Paris Is Burning* (Livingston 1991). The subjects of the film, who have elaborated a kind of drag that manipulates not only gender but class and race, effectively proclaim that all an individual needs to do to assume a desired identity is to don the costume associated with it. This means, for example, that if one can look like a stockbroker or a Yale undergraduate by wearing a conservative suit and tie or a letter sweater, one can "be" either of these identities. The same is true, in this logic, of "being" a man or a woman. Some of the most effective moments in the film come when the camera randomly scans "normal" people (i.e., non-drag queens, presumed to be "straight") on the street. After watching the drag performers relentlessly reconfiguring their identities, the "ordinary" people begin to look like drag performers as well, wearing their drabness and conventionality in a manner at least as performative as the hyperartificial style of the drag queens.

6. Newton 1972.

7. Kessler and McKenna 1978; see also Garfinkel 1967.

8. Bérubé and Escoffier 1991; Walters 1996; Warner 1993.

9. Feinberg 1996.

10. See Newton's (1972) classic discussion of camp.

11. Schechner (1988) argues that ritual and theater are overlapping domains.

12. Cohen 1974:39, 38, 104–105, and 13.

13. According to marketing research conducted by *Modern Bride Magazine* in 1995, the average cost of a formal wedding in the United States is $17,634. These figures (taking 174 as the average number of wedding guests) are broken down to indicate the average amount spent on the reception, music, flowers, photographers, clothing, rings, and other necessary and discretionary items. The costs incurred by couples in my research were, on average, somewhat lower than these, a difference probably accounted for mainly by the smaller numbers of guests invited and the rarity of engagement rings in this population. (*Modern Bride*'s average cost for an engagement ring was $2,909, the most expensive item apart from the costs for receptions—$6,503—which included catering, food, and liquor.)

14. Since the publication of John Boswell's (1994) study of same-sex unions in premodern Europe, many have cited that work as confirmation that gay and lesbian marriage has deep roots in Christian tradition. The ritual texts he presented in that work have found their way into more than a few same-sex ceremonies in recent years.

15. Every time I mention my work to others, they supply some new example of a lesbian or gay wedding they heard about or witnessed. In most cases, they are eager to report whatever facet of the ceremony they perceived to be most original or surprising.

16. According to a note on the program distributed at this service, the Unitarian Church voted to recognize and approve ceremonies celebrating the union of gay and lesbian couples on June 30, 1984.

17. Eric's vows, in Spanish, read: *Allen, mi amor, este es mi compromiso a tí: en felicidad y cariño, para lo bueno y lo mejor; para siempre escuchar y comprender tus pensamientos y sentimentos, aunque diferencien de los míos; para ser siempre honesto contigo, aunque mi honestidad te cause dolor; para siempre respetarte como mi amigo*

mejor, mi único amor, y mi compañero del alma en esta vida y en el más allá; yo nunca permiterá a alguién o algo convirtirse más importante para mí que esto, nuestro compromiso mutúo.

18. On the feminist spirituality movement, see Adler 1986; Eller 1993.

19. For an extended discussion of self-help organizations that originate with Alcoholics Anonymous, see Rapping 1996.

20. Both elements are common features of weddings in many Protestant denominations.

21. Alisa and Cynthia explained that sage is more commonly used for purification in these rituals, but because of Alisa's environmental-illness-induced allergy to many scents, they used the alternative of purification with salt water.

22. *Tikkun olam* refers to the need to repair the "broken world." This key concept in Judaism holds that Jews have a particular responsibility to contribute to the well-being of the world and to do what they can to make it a better place (Einstein and Kukoff 1989).

23. Aside from their number, the seven blessings did not parallel the content of the *Sheva B'rachot*, which in traditional Jewish weddings serve to put marriage in the context of the seven days of biblical creation (Diamant 1985).

24. "One day at a time" is an Alcoholics Anonymous saying, commonly quoted in twelve-step materials. See Robertson 1988.

25. The program explained the custom of smashing the wine glass as a "Jewish wedding tradition, here reinterpreted to represent smashing homophobia and affirming love."

26. Another complicated rationale for the name they finally selected was based on theories Mark had studied in classes he took for his college psychology minor. He felt that they should pick a name starting with a letter from the first half of the alphabet. That would make it more likely that their child would be seated on the left side of the classroom, a prime location because most teachers are right-handed.

27. As they explained the process, applicants for new names must publish an announcement in a newspaper for four weeks and then appear in Superior Court to finalize the change. They are asked at that time whether they are changing their names to avoid financial or legal obligations, but otherwise the court appearance is pro forma. Mark immediately changed his name at work and on his softball team; Bob implemented the change gradually at work, completing the process when he was promoted and began to work in a different facility.

28. See Rubin (1994) for a more detailed discussion of leather. Lesbians also partake of some leather-related activities, though more recently and overall on a more limited scale than do men. Whereas for men, the images of masculinity that leather highlights make feminine (or drag) images somewhat problematic (though some men do both leather and drag), women's leather styles center not only on "masculine" butch representations but allow for a femme expression as well (Gayle Rubin, personal communication, April 27, 1997).

29. Rubin 1994:273.

30. The rainbow-design Gay Pride flag was designed by Gilbert Baker for the 1978 San Francisco Gay Freedom Day parade and soon became an international symbol of lesbian and gay pride, appearing not only in flags but in decals, jewelry, and cloth-

ing displayed by lesbians and gay men. The original version of the flag had eight stripes, but that was later reduced to six to facilitate manufacturing (Stryker and Van Buskirk 1996:70).

The Leather Pride flag, introduced in 1989 by Tony DeBlase, a national leather community leader and businessman, is composed of nine horizontal stripes. Eight of these alternate black and royal blue, with a white stripe running across the middle, and a red heart in the upper left-hand corner (Rubin 1994:303–304). While not an exact replica, the flag suggests the general motif of an American flag. Like the rainbow flag, the Leather Pride design has been reproduced in many other formats including pins, decals, and clothing.

31. Bob told me that he doesn't find it easy to put his feelings into words. He found the text he used in a card shop, and since it perfectly conveyed his emotions, appropriated it for the occasion.

32. This is a pseudonym for Bob's full name before the wedding.

33. Bob explains that he never liked his original given name. The legal name change opened up a perfect opportunity to give himself a name he would feel better about. Since Robert was a family name on his maternal side, adopting this as his new first name allowed him to even more clearly break his ties with his father and his father's family.

34. While Bob and Mark assured me that they would be happy with either a boy or a girl, they shared the view that it would be more satisfying to have a girl. Girls can be expected, they explained, to be more loyal and devoted to their fathers and to have sweeter dispositions. Although their surrogate had not yet become pregnant, they had a girl's name picked out and had clearly done a fair amount of fantasizing about what their future life as parents would be like.

35. Perhaps the most amusing example of such interest came from their next-door neighbor, who asked if they'd like him to play his calliope for the wedding. The instrument, a relic of the long-defunct amusement park, Playland-at-the-Beach, has particularly cachet as a piece of historic San Francisciana.

36. Schneider 1968.

37. Anderson 1983; Hobsbawm and Ranger 1983; Williams 1977.

38. Hobsbawm 1983:1.

39. Anderson 1983:4; Williams 1977:112–13.

40. Myerhoff 1977:199; Myerhoff 1992a:161.

4. *This Circle of Family*

1. Chauncey 1994; Kennedy and Davis 1993; Krieger 1983; Newton 1972; Newton 1993.

2. Goffman 1963.

3. Murray 1996.

4. See, for example, Chauncey (1994); Kennedy and Davis (1993); Newton (1993).

5. Weston 1991.

6. Carrington 1998.

7. Leap 1996.

8. Actually, these concerns are not so recent. See, for example, Barth (1969); Leach

(1954). But they have become more central to anthropological scholarship with the advent of postcolonial and transnational perspectives in the discipline (Appadurai 1990; Clifford 1997).

9. David commented, "My father's got big problems," when he described this conversation. Whether his father assumed that only a black (i.e., undesirable in his eyes) baby would be available for adoption by gay men, or whether his comment reflected an unconscious amalgamation of stigmatizing identities, is hard to determine.

10. Literally, "[God] who has kept us alive." This is a blessing for beginnings and other happy occasions such as birth and marriage. It is also said at the candle lighting and other specific times during festival observances (Einstein and Kukoff 1989).

11. *Namaste* (lit., "I bow to you" or "Salutation to you"), from a Sanskrit root that means to salute or make an obeisance, is a standard greeting used by Hindus in situations that call for great politeness and formality.

12. This is most likely a reference to John Boswell's research on early Christianity, later published as *Same-Sex Unions in Premodern Europe*, though this book had not yet appeared at the time of this ceremony (Boswell 1994).

13. Weston 1991.

5. *Communities Interwoven*

1. Omi and Winant 1994.

2. Leonardo 1984:133–34 (emphasis in original).

3. Waters 1990:147; see also Gans 1979.

4. Takezawa 1995; on gay and lesbian identity, see D'Emilio 1983.

5. Herrell 1992:239.

6. See, for example, Epstein (1987); Phelan (1989). Much as 1970s feminism sought to establish origins for the status of women that would make the category "woman" meaningful across national and historical boundaries, so some gay activists have turned to the construction of tradition as a way of legitimizing gay/lesbian claims to peoplehood. Similar efforts have also been launched by those who speak for other sexual minorities, including bisexuals and transgendered persons. See, for example, Feinberg (1996) and others.

7. See Lewin (1996). Similar debates are taking place about women and feminism in general. See, for example, Collins (1991); hooks (1984, 1989); Mohanty, Russo, and Torres (1991); Spelman (1988); and Walker (1984).

8. Phelan 1994:64–65, 67.

9. Murray 1996a:182ff; Bellah et al. 1985.

10. Murray 1996a:191, 198–208.

11. Anderson 1983:4.

12. Shulamith identifies her class background as "working class," but since her father worked in one of the semiprofessions, a more objective categorization would seem to be the one I have used.

13. Blum 1982.

14. In traditional Jewish weddings, the bride circles the groom either three or seven times, sometimes led by her mother and the groom's mother, either before entering the *chuppah* or at some other time in the ceremony, although the practice is

not required. Interpretations of the practice vary. Circling may be seen as a way for the bride to protect the groom from evil spirits or from the temptations of other women; it also may signify the bride's shifting allegiance from her family to the groom and the creation of a new family circle (Diamant 1985:104).

15. *Tanakh* 1985.

16. A typical element of most *ketubot* is some sort of wording in which the couple vow to establish a "Jewish home" together. The traditional *ketubah* is a legal contract that testifies to the groom's "acquisition" of the bride and that specifies her rights and her husband's obligations. The custom originated at the end of the first century, c.e., and was considered a great advance for women at the time because it provided them with legal status and protected them in case of divorce. Modern *ketubot*, especially among Reform Jews, sometimes address the concerns of late-twentieth-century couples; they may contain language that more explicitly specifies an egalitarian view of marriage, for example, and they may also add sections that refer to emotional aspects of marital commitment. *Ketubot* are often very beautifully decorated and calligraphed, and custom-made versions can be quite expensive. See Diamant (1985:71–91) for a more extended discussion and for examples of traditional and updated *ketubot*.

17. A comparison of the ritual with a traditional Jewish wedding ceremony indicates, however, that while specifically Jewish elements were prominent features of the ceremony, little of the liturgy reflected Jewish tradition.

18. Blue and white are the colors of the Israeli flag. Green, black, and red represent African nationalism and are derived from the colors of the flag originally created by Marcus Garvey and later revived by Dr. Ron Karenga when he devised a flag (*bendera* in Swahili) to be displayed during Kwanzaa, the African-American holiday he invented. Green represents the African land and the future hopes and dreams of African-Americans; black stands for unity of all black people; red stands for the struggle of the past and present or for the blood of the African people. See Karenga (1989).

19. "Dodi Li," as mentioned above, draws its lyrics ("My beloved is mine, and I am my beloved's") from the Song of Songs. These verses are often used in Jewish weddings and are also frequently engraved on wedding rings. "Eli, Eli" ("Oh Lord, My God"), in contrast, is based on a nature poem by Hannah Senesch, a Zionist martyr, and is a staple of Jewish summer camps; this association and the simple fact that its lyrics are in Hebrew probably account for its sentimental appeal to many Jews (Yoel Kahn, personal communication, May 15, 1997).

20. Another omen Shulamith mentioned was the fact that her nails, which she keeps impeccably manicured and polished, were perfect on the day of the ceremony.

21. Tagore 1985:49.

22. Ayers and Brown 1994:118.

23. I am indebted to Gayle Rubin's detailed explanation of these images (personal communication).

24. Although technically only men can be bears, some women participate in bear functions such as the bear tip, often going shirtless at well.

25. I have transcribed these vows and the other texts used in Travis and Manuel's ceremony from the script they provided me. Like many of the other narrators,

Manuel and Travis have the script for their vows stored in their computer and were able to print out fresh copies at a moment's notice. Besides inserting pseudonyms, I have altered punctuation and spelling to enhance clarity.

26. In Manuel's translation, the poem reads:

> *Put your hand in my hand,*
> *And at your side the whole world I'll run.*
> *Come with me, close your eyes,*
> *And in silence, without words,*
> *I will tell you a thousand things . . .*
> *Accompany me!*

27. "Basic" and "c4" refer to levels of achievement in square dancing; "work-shop" is the process square dance club members go through to figure out difficult calls and patterns.

28. After a more permissive period, the Catholic Church banned Dignity from using its facilities. Dignity chapters hold their meetings and religious services in a variety of spaces, often facilities loaned by or rented from Protestant churches with sympathetic congregations and clergy.

29. Weston 1991.

6. The Real Thing

1. Orvell 1989:198ff; Lears 1994.

2. Bellah et al. 1985.

3. Certainly the bildungsroman or novel of personal development offers particularly dramatic instances of this, as do "novels of awakening" (Zimmerman 1990:35–37). Studies of stigmatized populations often reveal that the theme of authenticity figures centrally in narratives of identity. See, for example, Liebow (1993).

4. Zimmerman 1984; see Kennedy (1996) for another view of the closet. But also consider the popular reaction to the "coming out" episode of the TV sit-com *Ellen* in the spring of 1997. Letters to the editor from gay and lesbian viewers around the country emphasized the role the episode had in helping them to experience their identities as legitimate. Many commentators saw the increasingly public expression of gay/lesbian identity as a matter of inevitability.

5. Herman 1995.

6. See Jones (1993) on the authority of experience; see Personal Narratives Group (1989) on feminist uses of narratives.

7. Schneider 1968:27, 37; see Weston's revision and extension of this argument in her consideration of how gay men and lesbians create "families we choose" (Weston 1991).

8. Schneider 1968:39.

9. Giddens 1992.

10. Seidman 1991:47.

11. Cancian 1987:4–6.

12. In preparation for this first fieldwork outing, we had discovered that there was nothing in our closets dressy enough for the occasion and so just days before had

hurriedly made our way through several San Francisco stores in search of suitable attire. I was given to making wry jokes at this time about the likelihood that I was the only anthropologist in recent memory who could write off formal wear as a professional expense.

13. See Diamant (1985) for details on these ritual elements.

14. The parishioners are reputed to be at least three-quarters gay, and though the priest has steadfastly refused to acknowledge the unions of gay and lesbian couples within the congregation, he has taken a leadership role in establishing AIDS services in the community.

15. Excerpted from the Book of Ruth.

16. Norris 1985.

17 Attendance at three heterosexual Protestant weddings in 1995 confirmed this.

18. See, for example, Murray (1996a), ch. 1.

7. *Making a Statement*

1. Hobsbawm 1959, quoted in Kennedy and Davis 1993; Scott 1985:36.

2. Kennedy and Davis 1993.

3. Chauncey 1994.

4. D'Emilio 1983.

5. Bérubé and Escoffier 1991:12 (emphasis in original); Duggan 1995:165.

6. The overlap with attributes of the postmodern sensibility is clearly not fortuitous.

7. Berlant and Freeman 1993.

8. Newton 1993:77, 80, 81, 180. Although women sometimes joined in these parties, most lesbians tended to be less enthusiastic about costumes, preferring to avoid "female" attire so as neither to compete with the extravagant presentations of the drag queens nor to have to wear clothing associated with conventional femininity, but also being wary of cross-dressing, since that would have implications of a commitment to butch/femme imagery. Instead, most Grove "girls" wore casual masculine clothing such as polo shirts, shorts, and slacks as everyday wear, not as costumes, and maintained the same look for parties (Newton 1993:212).

9. Odets 1995.

10. See, for instance, Boswell (1994) and other works discussed in chapter 1.

11. See Levine (1992) for an especially affecting instance.

12. Although there are, of course, lesbians who are infected with HIV and/or diagnosed with AIDS, I focus here on the consequences of the epidemic among men because they are the population upon whom it has had the greatest impact. See Schneider and Stoller (1995) on the experience of women with AIDS.

13. Butler and Rosenblum 1991:95–96.

14. Butler and Rosenblum 1991:96.

15. Ibid., 97, 98 (emphasis in original), 99, 100.

16. Phenix 1994.

17. The Sisters of Perpetual Indulgence are a group of gay men who have been performing a particularly outrageous form of political street theater in San Francisco for many years. The Sisters dress as nuns, but in the exaggeratedly incongruous

style of "gender fuck," they typically wear their nuns' habits with such accessories as full beards, motorcycle boots, and chains. The Sisters adopt pseudonyms such as Sister Missionary Position and often focus their performances around themes that are both political and sexually charged.

18. *Brinkin v. Southern Pac. Transp. Co.*, 572 F.Supp. 236 (N.D. Cal. 1983).

19. Goldberg 1996:6.

20. Traditional Jewish practice, particularly for Orthodox Jews, calls for the bride and usually also the groom to be immersed in a *mikvah*, a ritual bath, in preparation for the wedding. The Torah prescribes such immersion under a number of circumstances, including conversion to Judaism, that involve human encounters with the holy and that require purification, though the best-known use of the bath is for a married woman each month after her menses in preparation for renewed sexual contact with her husband.

As explained by Anita Diamant in *The New Jewish Wedding*, the Talmud says that "the ultimate source of all water is the river that emerged from Eden. By immersing themselves in the *mikvah*, people participate in the wholeness of Eden and are reborn as pure as Adam and Eve. *Mikvah* also represents the physical source of life—the womb—from which humans enter the world untouched by sin" (Diamant 1985:151). Diamant goes on to explain that the *mikvah* may be considered the private counterpart to the public change of status symbolized by the *chuppah*. No religious "expert" is needed for the *mikvah* ritual. In many Jewish traditions, the prenuptial visit to the *mikvah* may be the occasion for a women's party or for other festivities.

21. Robin pointed out that at the time she was fired by Bowers the Georgia marriage statute did not mention same-sex or gay-lesbian marriage at all, and certainly did not specify it as an illegal act. In 1996, however, the marriage law was rewritten to prohibit civil same-sex marriages. The Georgia sodomy statute applies to heterosexuals as well as homosexuals, proscribing oral and anal sex, though the Supreme Court's decision in *Bowers v. Hardwick* seemingly legitimated selective prosecution of homosexuals for acts performed by consenting adults in a private setting. See Halley (1993) on *Hardwick*, Cain (1993) on *Shahar v. Bowers* and other lesbian and gay rights cases.

22. Quoted in Cain 1993:1637.

23. *Shahar v. Bowers*, 836 F.Supp. 839 (N.D. Ga. 1993), affirmed in part, vacated in part by 70 F.ed 1218 (11th Cir. 1995), reh'g en banc granted, opinion vacated by 78 F.3d 499 (11th Cir. 1996).

24. See Halley (1993).

8. Mixed Messages

1. Lynch 1996:A1.

2. Author interview with San Francisco Supervisor Tom Ammiano, March 21, 1996.

3. Ness 1996:A12. Migden's sponsorship of the domestic partner ceremonial option came in the midst of her (successful) campaign to represent much of San Francisco in the California Assembly, replacing Willie Brown who had just become mayor.

4. The two members of the Sisters of Perpetual Indulgence provided a noteworthy exception to this pattern.

5. Minor 1996:1.

6. The historic Palace Hotel, part of the Sheraton chain at this time, is an elegant site for dining, particularly in the famous Garden Court, a huge restaurant inside a restored stained-glass atrium.

7. Minor 1996:5.

8. Scott 1990:4.

9. Hebdige 1979.

10. Hobsbawm 1959:2.

11. A focus on resistance has been particularly fruitful in studying the experience of women and other subordinated people insofar as it offers an alternative to viewing such people as hapless victims of false consciousness. Besides the applications of these ideas to studies of ritual, feminist anthropology has used the study of work and the body, in particular, to explore strategies of resistance. Louise Lamphere, Karen Sacks, and Aihwa Ong's studies of women workers, for example, stand out as exemplars of this genre; their ethnographies examine how women in factory and service occupations develop solidarity as they manipulate gender expectations (Lamphere 1987; Ong 1987; Sacks 1988). Along similar lines, Emily Martin argues that women, particularly those who are neither white nor middle-class, do not necessarily share the disparaging views of the female body and its functioning that are implicit in Western medical practice and education, and that they often resist efforts of medical experts to define their experience (Martin 1987).

12. Abu-Lughod 1990. I might add to her assessment by pointing out that many of those who most actively seek these approaches are those scholars who have definitively come to terms with the powers that be—academics whose self-images as "radicals" seem unaffected by their having climbed the tenure ladder at major academic institutions and having shifted their intellectual activity from a critique of the established order to a way of generating professional prestige.

13. Geertz 1973a.

14. Sullivan 1995:112.

15. Lewin 1993.

16. Newton 1984.

17. Warner 1993.

18. See, for example, Berlant and Freeman (1993).

19. Patton 1993:143, 175, 173.

20. See, for example, Bawer (1993); Sullivan (1995); Vaid (1995).

21. Kendall 1996; see also Edwards 1989.

22. Firth 1951.

23. Weston 1993. My purposes here also diverge from those who seek to justify same-sex marriage by demonstrating that it has historical precedents or that it can be found in non-Western cultures. See, for example, Boswell (1994) and Eskridge (1993, 1996) for examples of such arguments.

24. Anderson 1983:4, 6, 143.

25. Hobsbawm 1983:9.

REFERENCES

Abu-Lughod, Lila. 1990. "The Romance of Resistance: Tracing Transformations of Power Through Bedouin Women." *American Ethnologist* 17(1): 41–55.

———. 1991. "Writing Against Culture." In Fox, ed., *Recapturing Anthropology*, 137–62. Santa Fe, N.Mex.: School of American Research Press.

———. 1993. *Writing Women's Worlds: Bedouin Stories*. Berkeley: University of California Press.

Adam, Barry D. 1987. *The Rise of a Gay and Lesbian Movement*. Boston: Twayne.

Adler, Margot. 1986. *Drawing Down the Moon: Witches, Druids, Goddess-Worshippers, and Other Pagans in America Today*. Boston: Beacon Press.

Albertson, Chris. 1972. *Bessie*. New York: Stein and Day.

Altorki, Soraya and Camillia Fawzi El-Solh, eds. 1988. *Arab Women in the Field: Studying Your Own Society*. Syracuse, N.Y.: Syracuse University Press.

Anderson, Benedict. 1983. *Imagined Communities: Reflections on the Origin and Spread of Nationalism*. London: Verso.

Appadurai, Arjun. 1990. "Disjuncture and Difference in the Global Cultural Economy." *Public Culture* 2(2): 1–24.

Ayers, Tess and Paul Brown. 1994. *The Essential Guide to Lesbian and Gay Weddings*. San Francisco: HarperCollins.

Baird, Robert M. and Stuart E. Rosenbaum, eds. 1997. *Same-Sex Marriage: The Moral and Legal Debate*. Amherst, N.Y.: Prometheus Books.

Barrett, Martha Barron. 1990. *Invisible Lives: The Truth About Millions of Women-Loving Women*. New York: Harper and Row.

Barth, Fredrik, ed. 1969. *Ethnic Groups and Boundaries: The Social Organization of Cultural Difference*. Boston: Little, Brown.

Bawer, Bruce. 1993. *A Place at the Table: The Gay Individual in American Society*. New York: Poseidon.

Becker, Howard. 1963. *Outsiders*. New York: Free Press.

Behar, Ruth. 1993. *Translated Woman: Crossing the Border with Esperanza's Story*. Boston: Beacon Press.

Behar, Ruth and Deborah Gordon, eds. 1995. *Women Writing Culture*. Berkeley: University of California Press.

Bellah, Robert N., Richard Madsen, William M. Sullivan, Ann Swidler, and Steven M. Tipton. 1985. *Habits of the Heart: Individualism and Commitment in American Life*. Berkeley: University of California Press.

Berlant, Lauren and Elizabeth Freeman. 1993. "Queer Nationality." In Warner, ed., *Fear of a Queer Planet*, 193–229. Minneapolis: University of Minnesota Press.

Bérubé, Allan and Jeffrey Escoffier. 1991. "Queer/Nation." *Out/Look*, no. 11: 14–16.

Blum, Ralph. 1982. *The New Book of Runes*. 3d ed. New York: Oracle Books/St. Martin's Press.

Boswell, John. 1994. *Same-Sex Unions in Premodern Europe*. New York: Villard.

Brown, Jennifer Gerarda. 1995. "Competitive Federalism and the Legislative Incentives to Recognize Same-Sex Marriages." *Southern California Law Review* 68: 745–839.

Browning, Frank. 1996. "Why Marry?" *New York Times*, April 17, A17.

Butler, Becky, ed. 1990. *Ceremonies of the Heart: Celebrating Lesbian Unions*. Seattle: Seal Press.

Butler, Judith. 1990. *Gender Trouble: Feminism and the Subversion of Identity*. New York: Routledge.

Butler, Sandra and Barbara Rosenblum. 1991. *Cancer in Two Voices*. San Francisco: Spinsters Book Company.

Cain, Patricia A. 1993. "Litigating for Lesbian and Gay Rights: A Legal History." *Virginia Law Review* 79(7): 1551–1641.

Cancian, Francesca M. 1987. *Love in America: Gender and Self-Development*. Cambridge: Cambridge University Press.

Capps, Steven A. 1996. "Gay Marriage Ban Gets an OK, But Senate Demos Add Provisions Likely to Draw Governor's Veto." *San Francisco Chronicle*, July 10, A1, A10.

Carrington, Christopher. 1998. "Constructing Lesbigay Families: The Social Organization of Domestic Labor(s) in Lesbian and Gay Families." Ph.D. diss. (sociology), University of Massachusetts, Amherst.

Chauncey, George. 1994. *Gay New York: Gender, Urban Culture, and the Making of the Gay Male World*. New York: Basic Books.

Clifford, James. 1997. *Routes: Travel and Translation in the Late Twentieth Century*. Cambridge: Harvard University Press.

Clifford, James M. and George E. Marcus, eds. 1986. *Writing Culture: The Poetics and Politics of Ethnography*. Berkeley: University of California Press.

Clunis, D. Merilee and G. Dorsey Green. 1988. *Lesbian Couples: Creating Healthy Relationships for the '90s*. Seattle: Seal Press.

Cohen, Abner. 1974. *Two Dimensional Man: An Essay on the Anthropology of Power and Symbolism in Complex Society*. Berkeley: University of California Press.

Collins, Patricia Hill. 1991. *Black Feminist Thought: Knowledge, Consciousness, and the Politics of Empowerment*. New York: Routledge.

Comaroff, Jean. 1985. *Body of Power, Spirit of Resistance: The Culture and History of a South African People*. Chicago: University of Chicago Press.

Cruikshank, Margaret. 1992. *The Gay and Lesbian Liberation Movement*. New York: Routledge.

Davis, Natalie Zemon. 1971. "The Reasons of Misrule: Youth Groups and Charivaris in Sixteenth-Century France." *Past and Present* 50: 41–75.

D'Emilio, John. 1983. *Sexual Politics, Sexual Communities: The Making of a Homosexual Minority in the United States, 1940–1970*. Chicago: University of Chicago Press.

Diamant, Anita. 1985. *The New Jewish Wedding*. New York: Summit Books.

Duberman, Martin. 1993. *Stonewall*. New York: Dutton.

Duggan, Lisa. 1995. "Making It Perfectly Queer." In Lisa Duggan and Nan D. Hunter, *Sex Wars: Sexual Dissent and Political Culture*, 155–72. New York: Routledge.

Dunlap, David W. 1995. "For Better or Worse, a Marital Milestone." *New York Times*, July 27, B1, B4.

——. 1996. "Fearing a Toehold for Gay Marriages, Conservatives Rush to Bar the Door." *New York Times*, March 6, A7.

Echols, Alice. 1989. *Daring to be Bad: Radical Feminism in America, 1967–1975*. Minneapolis: University of Minnesota Press.

Edwards, Walter. 1989. *Modern Japan Through Its Weddings*. Stanford, Calif.: Stanford University Press.

Einstein, Stephen J. and Lydia Kukoff. 1989. *Every Person's Guide to Judaism*. New York: UAHC Press.

Eller, Cynthia. 1993. *Living in the Lap of the Goddess: The Feminist Spirituality Movement in America*. Boston: Beacon Press.

Epstein, Steven. 1987. "Gay Politics, Ethnic Identity: The Limits of Social Construction." *Socialist Review* 17 (3–4): 9–50.

Eskridge, William N., Jr. 1993. "A History of Same-Sex Marriage." *Virginia Law Review* 79(7): 1419–1513.

——. 1996. *The Case for Same-Sex Marriage*. New York: Free Press.

Ettelbrick, Paula L. 1992. "Since When Is Marriage a Path to Liberation?" In Sherman, ed., *Lesbian and Gay Marriage*, 20–26. Philadelphia: Temple University Press.

Faderman, Lillian. 1991. *Odd Girls and Twilight Lovers: A History of Lesbian Life in Twentieth-Century America*. New York: Columbia University Press.

Feinberg, Leslie. 1996. *Transgender Warriors*. Boston: Beacon Press.

Firth, Raymond. 1951. *Elements of Social Organization*. London: Watts.

Fox, R. G., ed. *Recapturing Anthropology: Working in the Present*. Santa Fe, N.Mex.: School of American Research Press.

Frutkin, Alan. 1996. "Wedding Bell Blues." *The Advocate* (December 10): 22–28.

Gallagher, John. 1997. "The Marriage-Go-Round." *The Advocate* (January 21): 63–64.

Gans, Herbert J. 1979. "Symbolic Ethnicity: The Future of Ethnic Groups and Cultures in America." *Ethnic and Racial Studies* 2: 1–20.

Garber, Eric. 1988. "Gladys Bentley: The Bulldagger Who Sang the Blues." *Out/Look* (Spring): 52–61.

Garfinkel, Howard. 1967. *Studies in Ethnomethodology*. Englewood Cliffs, N.J.: Prentice-Hall.

Geertz, Clifford. 1973a. "Deep Play: Notes on the Balinese Cockfight." In Geertz, *The Interpretation of Cultures*, 412–53. New York: Basic Books.

——. 1973b. "Religion as a Cultural System." In Geertz, *The Interpretation of Cultures*, 87–125. New York: Basic Books.

Gevisser, Mark and Edwin Cameron, eds. 1995. *Defiant Desire: Gay and Lesbian Lives in South Africa*. New York: Routledge.

Giddens, Anthony. 1992. *The Transformation of Intimacy: Sexuality, Love, and Eroticism in Modern Societies*. Stanford, Calif.: Stanford University Press.

Ginsburg, Faye D. 1989. *Contested Lives: The Abortion Debate in an American Community*. Berkeley: University of California Press.

Gluckman, Max. 1963. *Order and Rebellion in Tribal Africa*. Glencoe, Ill.: Free Press.

——. 1965. *Politics, Law, and Ritual in Tribal Society*. Chicago: Aldine.

Goffman, Erving. 1963. *Stigma: Notes on the Management of Spoiled Identity*. New York: Simon and Schuster.

Goldberg, Carey. 1996. "For Couple who Stirred Issue of Same-Sex Marriage, Surprise Mixes with Dismay." *New York Times*, July 28, 6.

Golden, Tim. 1997. "San Francisco Makes 2 Deals to Close Rift." *New York Times*, February 8, 8.

Halley, Janet E. 1993. "Reasoning About Sodomy: Act and Identity in and After *Bowers v. Hardwick*." *Virginia Law Review* 79(7): 1721–80.

Hawkeswood, William G. 1996. *One of the Children: Gay Black Men in Harlem*. Berkeley: University of California Press.

Hebdige, Dick. 1979. *Subculture: The Meaning of Style*. London: Methuen.

Herman, Ellen. 1995. *The Romance of American Psychology: Political Culture in the Age of Experts*. Berkeley: University of California Press.

——. 1996. "All in the Family: Lesbian Motherhood Meets Popular Psychology in a Dysfunctional Era." In Lewin, ed., *Inventing Lesbian Cultures in America*, 83–104. Boston: Beacon Press.

Herrell, Richard K. 1992. "The Symbolic Strategies of Chicago's Gay and Lesbian Pride Day Parade." In G. Herdt, ed., *Gay Culture in America: Essays from the Field*, 225–52. Boston: Beacon Press.

Hirsch, Marianne and Evelyn Fox Keller, eds. 1990. *Conflicts in Feminism*. New York: Routledge.

Hobsbawm, E. J. 1959. *Primitive Rebels: Studies in Archaic Forms of Social Movement in the Nineteenth and Twentieth Centuries*. Manchester: Manchester University Press.

——. 1983. "Introduction: Inventing Traditions." In Hobsbawm and Ranger, eds., *The Invention of Tradition*, 1–14. Cambridge: Cambridge University Press.

Hobsbawm, Eric and Terence Ranger, eds. 1983. *The Invention of Tradition*. Cambridge: Cambridge University Press.

Hole, Judith and Ellen Levine. 1971. *Rebirth of Feminism*. New York: Quadrangle Books.

Hooker, Evelyn. 1957. "Adjustment of the Male Overt Homosexual." *Journal of Projective Techniques* 21(23): 17–31.

hooks, bell. 1984. *Feminist Theory: From Margin to Center*. Boston: South End Press.

——. 1989. *Talking Back: Thinking Feminist, Thinking Black*. Boston: South End Press.

Hunt, Eva. 1977. "Ceremonies of Confrontation and Submission: The Symbolic Dimension of Indian-Mexican Political Interaction." In S. F. Moore and B. G. Myerhoff, eds., *Secular Ritual*, 124–47. Assen: Van Gorcum.

Hunter, Nan D. 1995. "Marriage, Law, and Gender: A Feminist Inquiry." In Lisa Duggan and Nan Hunter, *Sex Wars: Sexual Politics and Political Culture*. New York: Routledge.

Jackson-Paris, Rod and Bob. 1994. *Straight from the Heart: A Love Story*. New York: Warner Books.

Jacobs, Sue-Ellen, Wesley Thomas, and Sabine Lang, eds. 1997. *Two-Spirit People: Native American Gender Identity, Sexuality, and Spirituality*. Urbana: University of Illinois Press.

Jameson, Fredric. 1991. *Postmodernism: Or, the Cultural Logic of Late Capitalism*. Durham, N.C.: Duke University Press.

Jefferson, David J. 1994. "Gay Employees Win Benefits for Partners at More Corporations." *Wall Street Journal*, March 18, A1, A6.

Johnson, Colleen Leahy. 1988. *Ex Familia: Grandparents, Parents, and Children Adjust to Divorce*. New Brunswick, N.J.: Rutgers University Press.

Jones, Kathleen B. 1993. *Compassionate Authority: Democracy and the Representation of Women*. New York: Routledge.

Kapferer, Bruce. 1984. "The Ritual Process and the Problem of Reflexivity in Sinhalese Demon Exorcisms." In J. J. MacAloon, ed., *Rite, Drama, Festival, Spectacle: Rehearsals Toward a Theory of Cultural Performance*, 179–207. Philadelphia: Institute for the Study of Human Issues.

Kaplan, Morris B. 1997. *Sexual Justice: Democratic Citizenship and the Politics of Desire*. New York: Routledge.

Karenga, Maulana. 1989. *The African-American Holiday of Kwanzaa: A Celebration of Family, Community, and Culture*. Los Angeles: University of Sankore Press.

Katz, Jonathan Ned. 1976. *Gay American History: Lesbians and Gay Men in the USA*. New York: Avon.

Kendall, Laurel. 1996. *Getting Married in Korea: Of Gender, Morality, and Modernity*. Berkeley: University of California Press.

Kennedy, Elizabeth Lapovsky. 1996. "'But We Would Never Talk About It': The Structures of Lesbian Discretion in South Dakota, 1928–1933." In Lewin, ed., *Inventing Lesbian Cultures in America*, 15–39. Boston: Beacon Press.

Kennedy, Elizabeth Lapovsky and Madeline D. Davis. 1993. *Boots of Leather, Slippers of Gold: The History of a Lesbian Community*. New York: Routledge.

——. 1996. "Constructing an Ethnohistory of the Buffalo Lesbian Community: Reflexivity, Dialogue, and Politics." In Lewin and Leap, eds., *Out in the Field*, 171–99. Urbana: University of Illinois Press.

Kertzer, David I. 1988. *Ritual, Politics, and Power*. New Haven: Yale University Press.

Kessler, Suzanne J. and Wendy McKenna. 1978: *Gender: An Ethnomethodological Approach*. New York: Wiley.

King, John. 1996. "A Move to Expand S.F. Domestic Partner Benefits." *San Francisco Chronicle*, May 21, A15.

Kirkpatrick, Melanie. 1996. "Gay Marriage: Who Should Decide?" *Wall Street Journal*, March 13, A15.

Kleinman, Arthur. 1988. *The Illness Narratives: Suffering, Healing, and the Human Condition*. New York: Basic Books.

Kondo, Dorinne K. 1990. *Crafting Selves: Power, Gender, and Discourses of Identity in a Japanese Workplace*. Chicago: University of Chicago Press.

Krasniewicz, Louise. 1992. *Nuclear Summer: The Clash of Communities at the Seneca Women's Peace Encampment*. Ithaca, N.Y.: Cornell University Press.

Krieger, Susan. 1983. *The Mirror Dance: Identity in a Women's Community*. Philadelphia: Temple University Press.

Ladurie, Le Roy. 1979. *Carnival in Romans*. New York: George Braziller.

Lamphere, Louise. 1987. *From Working Daughters to Working Mothers: Immigrant Women in a New England Industrial Community*. Ithaca, N.Y.: Cornell University Press.

Lane, Christel. 1981. *The Rites of Rulers: Ritual in Industrial Society—the Soviet Case*. Cambridge: Cambridge University Press.

Lang, Sabine. 1996. "Traveling Woman: Conducting a Fieldwork Project on Gender Variance and Homosexuality Among North American Indians." In Lewin and Leap, eds., *Out in the Field*, 86–107. Urbana: University of Illinois Press.

Lanternari, Vittorio. 1963. *The Religions of the Oppressed: A Study of Modern Messianic Cults*. New York: New American Library.

Leach, Edmund R. 1954. *Political Systems of Highland Burma: A Study of Kachin Social Structure*. Boston: Beacon Press.

Leap, William L. 1996. *Word's Out: Gay Men's English*. Minneapolis: University of Minnesota Press.

Lears, Jackson. 1994. *Fables of Abundance: A Cultural History of Advertising in America*. New York: Basic Books.

Leonardo, Micaela di. 1984. *The Varieties of Ethnic Experience: Kinship, Class, and Gender Among California Italian-Americans*. Ithaca, N.Y.: Cornell University Press.

Levine, Martin P. 1992. "The Life and Death of Gay Clones." In G. Herdt, ed., *Gay Culture in America*, 68–86. Boston: Beacon Press.

Lewin, Ellen. 1991. "Writing Lesbian and Gay Culture: What the Natives Have to Say for Themselves." *American Ethnologist* 18(4): 786–92.

——. 1993. *Lesbian Mothers: Accounts of Gender in American Culture*. Ithaca, N.Y.: Cornell University Press.

——. 1995. "Writing Lesbian Ethnography." In Behar and Gordon, eds., *Women Writing Culture*, 322–35. Berkeley: University of California Press.

—-, ed. 1996. *Inventing Lesbian Cultures in America*. Boston: Beacon Press.

Lewin, Ellen and William L. Leap, eds. 1996. *Out in the Field: Reflections of Lesbian and Gay Anthropologists*. Urbana: University of Illinois Press.

Liebow, Elliot. 1993. *Tell Them Who I Am: The Lives of Homeless Women*. New York: Penguin Books.

Limón, José. 1991. "Representation, Ethnicity, and the Precursory Ethnography: Notes of a Native Anthropologist." In Fox, ed., *Recapturing Anthropology*, 115–35. Santa Fe, N.Mex.: School of American Research Press.

Livingston, Jennie. 1991. *Paris Is Burning* (Miramax, 78 min.).

Lynch, April. 1996. "Gay Couples Joyously Exchange Vows in S.F." *San Francisco Chronicle*, March 26, A1, A11.

MacIntosh, Mary. 1968. "The Homosexual Role." *Social Problems* 16(2): 182–92.

Marcus, George E. and Michael M. J. Fischer. 1986. *Anthropology as Cultural Critique: An Experimimental Moment in the Human Sciences*. Chicago: University of Chicago Press.

Marriott, McKim. 1966. "The Feast of Love." In M. Singer, ed., *Krishna: Myths, Rites, and Attitudes*, 200–12. Honolulu: East-West Center Press.

Martin, Del and Phyllis Lyon. 1972. *Lesbian/Woman*. San Francisco: Glide.

Martin, Emily. 1987. *The Woman in the Body: A Cultural Analysis of Reproduction*. Boston: Beacon Press.

Miller, Neil. 1989. *In Search of Gay America: Women and Men in a Time of Change*. New York: Harper and Row.

——. 1992. *Out in the World: Gay and Lesbian Life from Buenos Aires to Bangkok*. New York: Vintage.

Minor, Denise. 1996. "Noe Valley Couples Celebrate Gay Rites." *Noe Valley Voice*, May, 1, 4–5.

Mitchell, Juliet and Ann Oakley, eds. 1986. *What Is Feminism?* New York: Pantheon.

Mohanty, Chandra Talpade, Ann Russo, and Lourdes Torres, eds. 1991. *Third World Women and the Politics of Feminism*. Bloomington: Indiana University Press.

Murray, Stephen O. 1996a. *American Gay*. Chicago: University of Chicago Press.

——. 1996b. "Male Homosexuality in Guatemala: Possible Insights and Certain Confusions from Sleeping with the Natives." In Lewin and Leap, eds., *Out in the Field*, 236–60. Urbana: University of Illinois Press.

Myerhoff, Barbara. 1977. "We Don't Wrap Herring in a Printed Page: Fusion, Fictions, and Continuity in Secular Ritual." In S. F. Moore and B. Myerhoff, eds., *Secular Ritual*, 199–226. Assen: Van Gorcum.

——. 1992a. "A Death in Due Time: Conviction, Order, and Continuity in Ritual Drama." In M. Kaminsky, ed., *Remembered Lives: The Work of Ritual, Storytelling, and Growing Older*, 159–90. Ann Arbor: University of Michigan Press.

——. 1992b. "Surviving Stories: Reflections on *Number Our Days*." In M. Kaminsky, ed., *Remembered Lives: The Work of Ritual, Storytelling, and Growing Older*, 277–304. Ann Arbor: University of Michigan Press.

Narayan, Kirin. 1993. "How Native Is a 'Native' Anthropologist?" *American Anthropologist* 95: 671–86.

Ness, Carol. 1996. "S.F. Tunes 'Wedding' Bells for Gays." *San Francisco Examiner*, January 24, A1, A12.

Newton, Esther. 1972. *Mother Camp: Female Impersonators in America*. Chicago: University of Chicago Press.

——. 1984. "The Mythic Mannish Lesbian: Radclyffe Hall and the New Woman." *Signs* 9(4): 557–75.

——. 1993. *Cherry Grove, Fire Island: Sixty Years in America's First Gay and Lesbian Town*. Boston: Beacon Press.

New York Times. 1995. "Marriage License Is Denied to Gay Male Couple in Ithaca." *New York Times*, December 4, B12.

Norris, Gunilla. 1985. *Learning from the Angel: Poems*. Detroit: Lotus Press.

Odets, Walt. 1995. *In the Shadow of the Epidemic: Being HIV-Negative in the Age of AIDS*. Durham, N.C.: Duke University Press.

Ohnuki-Tierney, Emiko. 1984. " 'Native' Anthropologists." *American Ethnologist* 11(3): 584–86.

Omi, Michael and Howard Winant. 1994. *Racial Formation in the United States from the 1960s to the 1990s*. 2d ed. New York: Routledge.

Ong, Aihwa. 1987. *Spirits of Resistance and Capitalist Discipline: Factory Women in Malaysia*. Albany: State University of New York Press.

Orvell, Miles. 1989. *The Real Thing: Imitation and Authenticity in American Culture, 1880–1940*. Chapel Hill: University of North Carolina Press.

Patton, Cindy. 1993. "Tremble, Hetero Swine!" In Warner, ed., *Fear of a Queer Planet*, 143–77. Minneapolis: University of Minnesota Press.

Perry, Troy D. 1995. "The Wedding: A Demonstration for the Rights of Lesbian, Gay, and Bi Couples." In K. Cherry and Z. Sherwood, eds., *Equal Rites: Lesbian and Gay Worship, Ceremonies, and Celebrations*, 106–109. Louisville, Ky.: Westminster John Knox Press.

Personal Narratives Group. 1989. *Interpreting Women's Lives: Feminist Theory and Personal Narratives*. Bloomington: Indiana University Press.

Pfaff, Tim. 1996. "Love That Lasts: Six Couples, with More Than 130 Years of Togetherness, Talk about Life, Love, and the Long Haul." *San Francisco Frontiers* (February 1): 22–24.

Phelan, Shane. 1989. *Identity Politics: Lesbian Feminism and the Limits of Community*. Philadelphia: Temple University Press.

——. 1994. *Getting Specific: Postmodern Lesbian Politics*. Minneapolis: University of Minnesota Press.

Phenix, Lucy Massie. 1994. *Cancer in Two Voices* (Women Make Movies, 43 min.).

Polikoff, Nancy D. 1993. "We Will Get What We Ask For: Why Legalizing Gay and Lesbian Marriage Will Not 'Dismantle the Legal Structure of Gender in Every Marriage.'" *Virginia Law Review* 79(7): 1535–50.

Pollitt, Katha. 1996. "Gay Marriage: Don't Say I Didn't Warn You." *The Nation* (April 29): 9.

Purdum, Todd S. 1996. "Gay Rights Groups Attack Clinton on Midnight Signing." *New York Times*, September 22, A12.

Rabinow, Paul. 1977. *Reflections on Fieldwork in Morocco*. Berkeley: University of California Press.

Rapping, Elayne. 1996. *The Culture of Recovery: Making Sense of the Self-Help Movement in Women's Lives*. Boston: Beacon Press.

Reinfelder, Monika, ed. 1996. *Amazon to Zami: Toward a Global Lesbian Feminism*. London: Cassell.

Rich, Adrienne. 1980. "Compulsory Heterosexuality and Lesbian Existence." *Signs* 5(4): 631–60.

Robertson, Nan. 1988. *Getting Better: Inside Alcoholics Anonymous*. New York: Fawcett.

Rochman, Sue. 1995. "The Tie That Binds: Ithaca Gay Couple Seeks Recognition of Their Wedding Vows." *Ithaca Times*, June 8–14, 6, 8.

Rosaldo, Renato. 1989. *Culture and Truth: The Remaking of Social Analysis*. Boston: Beacon Press.

Rubin, Gayle. 1994. "The Valley of the Kings: Leathermen in San Francisco, 1960–1990." Ph.D. diss. (anthropology), University of Michigan, Ann Arbor.

Sacks, Karen Brodkin. 1988. *Caring by the Hour: Women, Work, and Organizing at Duke Medical Center*. Urbana: University of Illinois Press.

Sarris, Greg. 1993. *Keeping Slug Woman Alive: A Holistic Approach to American Indian Texts*. Berkeley: University of California Press.

Schechner, Richard. 1988. *Performance Theory.* New York: Routledge.

Schmitt, Eric. 1996. "Senators Reject Gay Marriage Bill and Job-Bias Ban." *New York Times,* September 11, A1, A11.

Schneider, Beth E. and Nancy E. Stoller, eds. 1995. *Women Resisting AIDS: Feminist Strategies of Empowerment.* Philadelphia: Temple University Press.

Schneider, David N. 1968. *American Kinship: A Cultural Account.* Englewood Cliffs, N.J.: Prentice-Hall.

Scott, James C. 1985. *Weapons of the Weak: Everyday Forms of Peasant Resistance.* New Haven: Yale University Press.

——. 1990. *Domination and the Arts of Resistance: Hidden Transcripts.* New Haven: Yale University Press.

Scribner, Bob. 1978. "Reformation, Carnival, and the World Turned Upside Down." *Social History* 3: 303–29.

Seidman, Steven. 1991. *Romantic Longings: Love in America, 1830–1980.* New York: Routledge.

Seligson, Marcia. 1973. *The Eternal Bliss Machine: America's Way of Wedding.* New York: William Morrow.

Sherman, Suzanne, ed. 1992. *Lesbian and Gay Marriage: Private Commitments, Public Ceremonies.* Philadelphia: Temple University Press.

Singer, Milton, ed. 1959. *Traditional India: Structure and Change.* Philadelphia: American Folklore Society.

Spelman, Elizabeth V. 1988. *Inessential Woman: Problems of Exclusion in Feminist Thought.* Boston: Beacon Press.

Stacey, Judith. 1990. *Brave New Families: Stories of Domestic Upheaval in Late Twentieth-Century America.* New York: Basic Books.

Steedman, Carolyn Kay. 1987. *Landscape for a Good Woman: A Story of Two Lives.* New Brunswick, N.J.: Rutgers University Press.

Stein, Arlene. 1997. *Sex and Sensibility: Stories of a Lesbian Generation.* Berkeley: University of California Press.

—, ed. 1993. *Sisters, Sexperts, Queers: Beyond the Lesbian Nation.* New York: Plume.

Stoddard, Thomas B. 1992. "Why Gay People Should Seek the Right to Marry." In Sherman, ed., *Lesbian and Gay Marriage,* 13–19. Philadelphia: Temple University Press.

Strasser, Mark. 1997. *Legally Wed: Same-Sex Marriage and the Constitution.* Ithaca, N.Y.: Cornell University Press.

Stryker, Susan and Jim Van Buskirk. 1996. *Gay by the Bay: A History of Queer Culture in the San Francisco Bay Area.* San Francisco: Chronicle Books.

Sullivan, Andrew. 1995. *Virtually Normal: An Argument About Homosexuality.* New York: Knopf.

—, ed. 1997. *Same-Sex Marriage: Pro and Con, A Reader.* New York: Vintage.

Takezawa, Yasuko I. 1995. *Breaking the Silence: Redress and Japanese American Ethnicity.* Ithaca, N.Y.: Cornell University Press.

Tanakh, a New Translation of the Holy Scriptures According to the Traditional Hebrew Text. 1985. Philadelphia: The Jewish Publication Society.

Teal, Donn. 1971. *The Gay Militants: How Gay Liberation Began in America, 1968–1971.* New York: Stein and Day.

Thomas, Leroy. 1996. "First Person: Romance." *San Francisco Examiner*, February 11, A10.

Tsing, Anna. 1993. *In the Realm of the Diamond Queen*. Princeton: Princeton University Press.

Turner, Victor. 1967. *The Forest of Symbols*. Ithaca, N.Y.: Cornell University Press.

———. 1969. *The Ritual Process: Structure and Anti-Structure*. Ithaca. N.Y.: Cornell University Press.

———. 1987. *The Anthropology of Performance*. New York: PAJ Publications.

Uhrig, Larry J. 1984. *The Two of Us: Affirming, Celebrating, and Symbolizing Gay and Lesbian Relationships*. Boston: Alyson.

Vaid, Urvashi. 1995. *Virtual Equality: The Mainstreaming of Gay and Lesbian Liberation*. New York: Anchor.

Verhovek, Sam Howe. 1993a. "Texas County Retreats Over Apple's Gay Policy." *New York Times*, December 8, A10.

———. 1993b. "A Texas County Snubs Apple Over Unwed-Partner Policy." *New York Times*, December 2, A1, A10.

Walker, Alice. 1984. *In Search of Our Mothers' Gardens*. San Diego: Harcourt Brace Jovanovich.

Walters, Suzanna Danuta. 1996. "From Here to Queer: Radical Feminism, Postmodernism, and the Lesbian Menace (Or, Why Can't a Woman Be More Like a Fag?)." *Signs* 21(4): 830–69.

Warner, Michael, ed. 1993. *Fear of a Queer Planet: Queer Politics and Social Theory*. Minneapolis: University of Minnesota Press.

Waters, Mary C. 1990. *Ethnic Options: Choosing Identities in America*. Berkeley: University of California Press.

Weston, Kath. 1991. *Families We Choose: Lesbians, Gays, Kinship*. New York: Columbia University Press.

Williams, Raymond. 1977. *Marxism and Literature*. Oxford: Oxford University Press.

Williams, Walter L. 1996. "Being Gay and Doing Fieldwork." In Lewin and Leap, eds., *Out in the Field*, 70–85. Urbana: University of Illinois Press.

Wolf, Margery. 1992. *A Thrice-Told Tale: Feminism, Postmodernism, and Ethnographic Responsibility*. Stanford: Stanford University Press.

Wolfson, Evan. 1994–95. "Crossing the Threshold: Equal Marriage Rights for Lesbians and Gay Men and the Intra-Community Critique." *New York Review of Law and Social Change* 21(3): 567–615.

Zimmerman, Bonnie. 1984. "The Politics of Transliteration: Lesbian First-Person Narratives." *Signs* 9(4): 663–82.

———. 1990. *The Safe Sea of Women: Lesbian Fiction, 1969–1989*. Boston: Beacon Press.

INDEX

BETWEEN MEN ~ BETWEEN WOMEN

Lesbian and Gay Studies
Lillian Faderman and Larry Gross, Editors

Timothy F. Murphy and Suzanne Poirier, editors, *Writing AIDS: Gay Literature, Language, and Analysis*

Noreen O'Connor and Joanna Ryan, *Wild Desires and Mistaken Identities: Lesbianism and Psychoanalysis*

Don Paulson with Roger Simpson, *An Evening in the Garden of Allah: A Gay Cabaret in Seattle*

Judith Roof, *Come As You Are: Sexuality and Narrative*

Judith Roof, *A Lure of Knowledge: Lesbian Sexuality and Theory*

Claudia Schoppmann, *Days of Masquerade: Life Stories of Lesbians During the Third Reich*

Alan Sinfield, *The Wilde Century: Effeminacy, Oscar Wilde, and the Queer Moment*

Jane McIntosh Snyder, *Lesbian Desire in the Lyrics of Sappho*

Chris Straayer, *Deviant Eyes, Deviant Bodies: Sexual Re-Orientations in Film and Video*

Dwayne C. Turner, *Risky Sex: Gay Men and HIV Prevention*

Ruth Vanita, *Sappho and the Virgin Mary: Same-Sex Love and the English Literary Imagination*

Thomas Waugh, *Hard to Imagine: Gay Male Eroticism in Photography and Film from Their Beginnings to Stonewall*

Kath Weston, *Families We Choose: Lesbians, Gays, Kinship*

Kath Weston, *Render Me, Gender Me: Lesbians Talk Sex, Class, Color, Nation, Studmuffins . . .*

Carter Wilson, *Hidden in the Blood: A Personal Investigation of AIDS in the Yucatán*

Jacquelyn Zita, *Body Talk: Philosophical Reflections on Sex and Gender*